D0847960

The
ROARING GAME

The ROARING GAME

A SWEEPING SAGA OF CURLING

DOUG CLARK

KEY PORTER  BOOKS

Library and Archives Canada Cataloguing in Publication

Clark, Doug, 1952–
   The roaring game : a sweeping saga of curling / Doug Clark.

ISBN 978-1-55263-944-3

   1. Curling. I. Title.

GV845.C53 2007   796.964   C2007-903969-3

ONTARIO ARTS COUNCIL
CONSEIL DES ARTS DE L'ONTARIO

The publisher gratefully acknowledges the support of the Canada Council for the Arts and
the Ontario Arts Council for its publishing program. We acknowledge the support of the
Government of Ontario through the Ontario Media Development Corporation's Ontario
Book Initiative.

We acknowledge the financial support of the Government of Canada through the Book
Publishing Industry Development Program (BPIDP) for our publishing activities.

Key Porter Books Limited
Six Adelaide Street East, Tenth Floor
Toronto, Ontario
Canada M5C 1H6

www.keyporter.com

Text design: Marijke Friesen
Electronic formatting: Jean Lightfoot Peters

Printed and bound in Canada

07 08 09 10 11 5 4 3 2

This book is gratefully dedicated to John (J.L.) Clark who inspired me, to Dr. Tom Russell who encouraged me, to Paul Knox and Hec Mackenzie who taught me, and to George Thomas who made curling fun and made me a better curler.

TABLE OF CONTENTS

FOREWORD

I still remember the day Doug Clark shared his manuscript with me. After a voracious marathon read, I felt dizzy. The scope of Clark's vision, the sheer size of the curling landscape he painted, was one of a kind. The book wasn't about a famous athlete or a specific championship, nor a how-to guide, and not a purely historical tome. It was all that and so much more, delightfully bobbing and weaving among virtually every nuance of curling. This had never been done before.

It must be said that the loving care this man has taken with our sport in prose means as much as the commitment shown by thousands of curling fans, players, administrators, and volunteers on a daily basis.

Clark seems the epitome of a curler. He's been writing this book for years (curlers are a notoriously stubborn breed); he's embraced and then broken up with two previous publishers (curlers are wont to change their team lineups as much as any freewheeling pro-sport GM); and he tells simply wonderful stories (just park yourself at a table after a curling game and listen to the tales).

To the average curler, this year of 2007—or, specifically, this curling season of 2007–08—is somewhat unexceptional. The glow of the Turin Olympics is beginning to fade and Vancouver's turn is still almost three years away. But 2007 marks the fiftieth anniversary of *The Curling News*, the two-hundredth birthday of the Royal Montreal Curling Club, and the 467th anniversary of the first reputed grudge match on ice in Scotland. And, of course, the appearance of this singularly remarkable work.

Never before has the entire story of curling been told with such a sweeping arc through history and hyperbole, pop culture and personality, and competition and catastrophe. Names are alternately well known and unheralded, places are legendary and obscure. And the stories—oh, the stories!

But most tantalizing is *The Roaring Game*'s potential for smashing through the wall between devoted curler/curling fan—an important distinction—and anyone else.

This wall has been crumbling over the last decade, thanks mostly to curling's Olympic status. But Clark's ability to intrigue readers might make this book more than just an essential read for the savvy; it could become the premiere guide for the uninitiated.

Many curlers I know have struggled with their own place in the sporting and social world for a long time. Whereas the pastime was deeply respected at its Scottish roots, the modern era first saw the sport dismissed as a mere game, not for real athletes and definitely not sexy.

I remember discussing the sport in a bar in the early 1990s; my teammates were horrified, and pretended not to know me.

"Don't tell them you curl," one hissed.

"Why?" I asked.

"It's embarrassing."

Imagine. And this from an otherwise proud competitor, at least when on the ice and hidden from general viewing.

Times have certainly changed. And for any Neanderthals who continue to snicker at the concept of men with brooms (and women, and children, and people with disabilities), the book makes a hefty weapon to bonk them on the head.

In sum, *The Roaring Game* is something special, providing something these eyes haven't seen in any previous curling book. And we've seen more than a few!

—George Karrys, silver medallist at the 1998 Nagano Olympics, and publisher, *The Curling News*
May 25, 2007

PREFACE

"*W*e are curlers, hear us roar!"

What better anthem to trumpet the roaring success of the roaring game? More people curl or are watching others curl than ever before across Canada and around the world. The sport is played on five of the seven continents—and may well have been played on all seven. Africa may seem unfertile ground for curling to take root, but there is, or at least was, an arena for both hockey and curling in Abidjan, in Ivory Coast, that was set up back in the early 1980s. Two teams from Cameroon competed in an exhibition series at the 2007 World University Games, and, while no one really expects an African team to join the World Curling Federation anytime soon, it all counts. Antarctica is a no-brainer. Someone almost certainly has thrown a block of something somewhere, sometime, in the land of ice. And if no one has, someone will. Curling has become just that universally popular, prompting the World Curling Federation to promote the sport from Asia to America. Such undeniable success begs the simple question: Why? That is the focus of this book.

I'm not the first to ask the question. In fact, the *Regina Province* asked the question so well early in the twentieth century that the *Sudbury Journal* reran its examination of the sport in 1914, and then it was asked again in *A Social Draw*, Paul Mandziuk's history of one hundred years of curling in that Nickel

City: "Will some philosopher please step up and explain the psychology of curling? Will someone tell us what it is that sends men—men of affairs and responsibilities, for such it is makes up our curling clubs—stark raving mad, roaring mad over a game which seems to possess no more elements of excitement than the horseshoe pitching of our boyhood days!"

This, of course, was before the modern era of expansive television coverage, curling's inclusion in the Olympic Games as a full-medal sport, and, most recently, a fundraising calendar of naked women curlers—all linked to a sport once described as "chess with attitude."

But even these don't fully answer the question.

The early curling literature, written by historians, journalists, and curlers themselves, focused on how to play the sport and its history at the club, provincial, regional, national, and international levels. Later works chronicled curling icons and elite bonspiels, dramatic blends of sport history, team profiles, and biography. There were even guides written for the "Idiots" and "Dummies" among us and training videos for the less literate.

Building on that rich documented history and evolution, *The Roaring Game* is my shot at exploring how curling culture has morphed into pop culture to have a surprisingly broad impact on our lives and lifestyles. Certainly television and the Olympics have spread the gospel of the rings to disciples anxious to cast their first stone, with the former lining up every late-night talk show host and faux news anchor to take their own shots at the sport. Innovations like plastic Little Rocks, which are light enough for children to throw, and the throwing stick, which allows curlers to deliver stones from an upright position, are luring people onto the ice at an earlier age and keeping them there longer. Improved ice has added science to art to allow shots once thought impossible. All of that has contributed to the sport's popularity, but I believe it is primarily because the house has become a home to anyone who enters.

Curling is the great emancipator. The sport embraces everyone, regardless of sex, age, or physical, mental, and athletic ability. All can compete equally. For every curler who strolls or rolls onto the world stage because he or she is good, legions more cast their first stone because they could, whether five or ninety-five, whether blind, deaf, or with physical or intellectual disabilities.

So cue the pipers and join us in the house that has been a home to millions over the years. Why is curling so popular? Because virtually anyone with a pulse can play and enjoy it.

INTRODUCTION

CASTING THE
FIRST STONE

Curlingito, ergo sum—"I curl, therefore I am."

For the Latin purists among you who may feel compelled to argue that seventeenth-century French philosopher René Descartes actually said "I think, therefore I am," I would suggest that the Gaelic translation varies slightly. Besides, I strongly doubt that Descartes ever curled. His loss. But in keeping with the more established translation, I donned my thinking tam to muse on the roaring success of the roaring game. And I found that there are those who are defined, at least in part, by the fact that they can curl. They may not be good, but they cast their first stone because they could. I know. I'm one of them.

I was born with a hole in my heart in 1952. That was a death sentence back then. I'm still here, the result of loving parents (alternately advised to enjoy me while they had me or not to get too attached or to just have another kid). Our small-town doctor kept me alive with endless doses of penicillin until medical advances allowed the cardiac specialists to put me, at age five, under the knife. The deal was simple: Have the operation and be able to run with the other kids. Or die. If that seemed a simple choice, bear in mind that no child before me had survived the surgery (VSD, for you doctor curlers in the crowd). Sadly, none of the ones who followed immediately behind me lived either. But, in 1957, I pulled through; it was a defining year for me, but my story was lost among the headlines of the day—Sputnik soared, the Edsel tanked, and the Arkansas National Guard brought racial integration to Little Rock High School. Dr. Seuss published *The Cat in the Hat*, and Moose Jaw native Art Linkletter moved *Kids Say the Darndest Things* from radio to TV alongside *Leave It to Beaver*. Humphrey Bogart died, Jackie Robinson retired, Bobby Fisher became a chess master at the age of thirteen...and Russ Howard turned one, presumably with a hearty roar.

That year was also a benchmark for curling. Matt Baldwin's Edmonton Granite Club team won the thirtieth Brier (the Canadian men's championship), the first back-to-back Tankard victories prior to Clan Richardson sweeping out of Regina and swooping up the hardware in four of the following five years. Bernie Sparkes won the Alberta schoolboys' title en route to winning four consecutive provincial men's championships, three Briers (voted all-star second at four), and three world championships with Ron Northcott's team a decade later. Moving to British Columbia in 1970, "Sparkie" added eight more men's provincial titles and a mixed championship. Named to the Lethbridge, Alberta, Sports Hall of Fame for baseball, he has also been elected to curling halls of fame in Alberta and British Columbia. Half a century after winning schoolboy, he plies a brush of a different kind, painting memorable curling scenes that he posts on his website Curlingpaintings.com, and has been known to attend matches sporting a T-shirt that reads "Old age and treachery beats youthful enthusiasm every time."

That same year, 1957, saw the birth of the *Canadian Curling News*, while Saskatchewan became the first province to complete its stretch of the new Trans-Canada Highway, and its native son John Diefenbaker was elected prime minister of Canada. The hottest corner of Canada's curling nation had celebrated its provincial golden jubilee in Saskatoon two years earlier, cheering the Curling Campbells (Lloyd, Glenn, Don, and skip Arnold) of the Avonlea Curling Club to their first Brier title on home ice before what was then a jubilant record crowd of fifty-two thousand ecstatic fans.

South of the border, 1957 saw fledgling WGN-TV Channel 8 broadcast the highlights from the first U.S. men's curling championship tournament from Chicago Stadium, won by Harold Lauber and his squad from Hibbing, Minnesota.

I was oblivious to all that. We weren't a curling family. I had never heard of the Brier, although it must have been hard to miss on our five-channel universe. Besides, I was a tad preoccupied, usually outdoors testing my new heart.

The city doctors reneged on their part of the bargain. Unsure of what to do with their sole survivor, and apparently forgetting that the heart is a muscle that needs exercise, they banned me from minor sports. I was tossed out of minor hockey at age six but later allowed to play baseball (with the reasoning that I could stop at any base if I got tired; try explaining that to your coach!) and bowling (but only five-pin: smaller, lighter ball). My breakthrough came in Grade 9, when I argued successfully for permission to curl schoolboy. Even then, the doctors worried that lifting the rock too high or sweeping too hard could damage my heart. I scoffed. They scolded. My family physician, Dr. Tom Russell (whose frequent house calls had kept me alive all those years) suggested I ignore them. Thus I found a sport I could play without restrictions. To compensate, the specialists banned me from high school gym class.

My initial exposure to the roaring game had occurred years earlier, when I glanced down through the cracked plywood separating arena bleachers from the curling club in Fergus, Ontario, during a hockey intermission. I didn't know the club was historic and I had no clue what those guys on the painted ice were doing. It was a small town, so I knew most of them as someone's father or my parents' friend. The local pillars of the community seemed to stand alone in the "target," snorting occasionally from a flask, chomping their pipe or stogie, while the factory guys and volunteer firefighters ran up and down the ice, sweeping faster when their cigarette ashes dropped in front of the large rock rumbling down the ice. Brooms were raised and praises shouted even when they missed the "bull's eye" by several coloured rings. I was baffled, even after Rick, my friend who did hail from a curling family, tried to explain. When the hockey teams skated back onto the ice, I turned my back on curling. Literally. Until I hit high school.

My older brother John was my role model. He skipped. He was smarter, but I could yell louder. I also had a bum heart, which for once played in my favour. My coach knew I was banned from phys. ed., so, perhaps haunted by visions of me dropping in mid-sweep, soon elevated me to skip. In fairness, I could read ice fairly well, plot strategy, and occasionally hit the broom. With all that stewing in the background, I made my curling debut in the fall of 1966, on the eve of Canada's centennial, Expo 67 in Montreal, and the Leafs winning the final Stanley Cup of the six-team National Hockey League. I scraped my first high-cut curling boot in a cold rink long before curling was cool. Frost coated my bulky schoolboy sweater and blisters broke on my numb hands as I swept for screaming old men who still heard incoming shells from Flanders in their sleep. I honoured the rules and spirit of the game; my only conscious deception was to trim the working end of my straw broom to allow its inner leather strap to protrude ever so slightly so it would produce that reassuring *whap* on the ice, which lulled skips into thinking I was sweeping harder than I probably was. And that sole transgression was more hormonal rite of passage than disrespect for the rules and sanctity of the good and noble sport: *whap* was as macho as curling got.

About the time I was sliding down the ice for the first time, Ontario's Alf Phillips Jr. went 9–1 at the Ottawa Brier, supplanting defending champion Northcott's Calgary team, which finished fourth (7–3) in what was then a round-robin series with no playoff and modest media coverage. (The Westerners would rebound to win the next two Briers and be crowned back-to-back world champions—the first to win the Air Canada Silver Broom when it replaced the Scotch Cup in 1968.) Betty Duguid's Manitoba team won the Canadian Lassie crown.

On the world stage, Nancy Greene's final downhill dash made her the first woman champion in World Cup ski racing by seven hundredths of a second, en route to Olympic gold in the giant slalom in Grenoble a year later. Billie Jean King won her first Wimbledon title. And curling organizers were taking baby steps behind the scenes to rejoin the Olympic movement. At the final Scotch Cup, delegates from seven curling nations, including Canada, had created the International Curling Federation in their bid for approval from the International Olympic Committee for status as a full-medal sport for the roaring game—a dream unfulfilled for another three decades.

It was a heady time, and if I was oblivious to most of the national and international changes brewing, I was improving with each end we played. That does not mean that every end ended well. During all those years, my parents never saw John or me curl. Dad worked straight nights for the shift bonus and Mom was busy doing what moms did back when your role models were Lucy Ricardo or June Cleaver. Dad died young at age fifty-eight (my brother hit that same age in 2006 and I'm closing in, our gene pool adding a unique "Hurry! Hard!" urgency to finish this book). We'll never know if Dad would have been bitten by the curling bug, but there's no doubt it's chomped down hard on Mom. She's rarely been inside a curling club, has never thrown a rock, and has swept everywhere but on the ice. But when the big games are on TV, you can't pry her away. She's fascinated by those who stand at the far end of the ice and put the rock exactly where they said they would—usually.

So, in a way, my family is a microcosm of the state of the game in the twenty-first century. We've been part of history (the Fergus Curling Club), tradition (my brother joined and curled extensively in the military; our son John has curled in a police funspiel to raise money for the Special Olympics), and just plain family fun. Our daughter Jodi curled in high school gym class, and although my wife, Irene, joined me to curl mixed one season she was never quite convinced that a heated arena that housed ice was anything but cold. We've tasted competition, met challenges (or not!), and revelled in camaraderie on the ice and in the clubhouse.

The Fergus Curling Club is another microcosm, wearing its heart on its sheet and its heritage on its walls, including an original wooden "stone" dating to 1834. Its sheets are numbered 1, 8, 3, and 4 to commemorate its roots, tormenting visitors unaware of the significance of the numbering. Touring Scottish teams still stop by to play and to celebrate the town's ancestry. Bill Thompson still curls despite having gone blind over the years—ironically the only member of the club's 2007 Seniors championship team, skipped by Sam Harrop, who does not use the curling stick. Harrop estimates the average age of his squad, which also includes veteran curlers Paul Langdon and Jim Marsden, at "seventy-three or seventy-four" and chuckles his agreement that they're all reached the age where either the eyes or knees start to go. Club historian Emery Nelson continued to curl into his nineties until his retirement in 2006, passing his longevity title to Gord Byers, then a youthful ninety. A local physician, Dr. Bob English, has been known to add a novel twist to the club's storied history by dragging recent medical graduates onto the ice to persuade them that the town would be a good place to set up practice.

But there is no monopoly on pride or passion among Fergus curlers who may still settle family feuds and historic grudges on the ice. Across Canada and around the world, a few may dream of one day taking to the ice to trade shots with a truly elite, possibly an Olympic, curler. No other sport offers that or the chance to share a drink and swap a tale between icon and hack. But neither that nor the void created for winter-sport fanatics by the 2004–05 NHL lockout, can explain the curling's explosive popularity. The game has grown in complexity, marked by the introduction of stopwatches and state-of-the-art sweepers. Shorty Jenkins added science to art by learning, then teaching, how to make near-perfect ice. But the essence remains the same: read the ice, call the shot—then pray your sweepers and planets align.

Elite teams from across Canada—male and female, young and old—now vie for national titles and international prestige in front of capacity crowds, with legions more glued to their televisions. As a full-medal Olympic sport, curling offers a new dream to a new generation who add "older and wiser" to the "faster, higher, stronger" credo of the rings.

Curling is a winter sport that is no longer confined to winter play. Another indication of the roaring game's growing popularity is the increased number of summer leagues and bonspiels, as proven by recent introductions in Pittsburgh, Pennsylvania; Cape Cod, Massachusetts; and Guelph and Oakville, Ontario. In Nelson, British Columbia, they have been casting midsummer stones for more than sixty years.

Club curling allows families and sweethearts the chance to socialize while sharing in something they enjoy. Feelings can run high. Romance has blossomed on the ice—and died there too.

There are, quite simply, some loving couples who make ideal partners but horrific teammates. Adults can curl with their parents who can, in turn, share the ice with their grandchildren as they learn to throw the smaller, lighter Little Rocks. Similarly, the curling stick has added years to seniors' curling for those who can still shoot but not crouch or sweep—a rare athletic forum that can help youths mature and keep seniors young.

A game of steadfast friendships and infinite learning, curling is perhaps the only sport where opponents shake hands before and after their match, and etiquette requires the winners to stand the losers to a drink. Then the losers reciprocate. Pervasive and enduring, the game blends art with science within a venue where the players freely admit their sins. It is perhaps the sole sport to have no blatant official on the playing surface to ensure fair play, as none is needed—an amazing constant considering the eclectic horde who have felt at home in the house over the centuries.

The heart of the curling world is the curling club. No matter how many tens of thousands of men and women, juniors and seniors chase their dream to compete in a national championship that can give them a shot at the world (and the Olympic Games), the reality is that when the pipers lead the curlers in, only four players and possibly an alternate on each provincial team—less than five dozen in total—have made the cut. The club hacks provide solid footing for, and are homes to, more than a million worldwide—and 90 per cent of them are said to be curling in Canada.

Curling is competition defined by fair play among competitors who respect the game and each other, spurn separate dressing rooms (except at the highest elite level), and easily swap yarns, laughs, and a drink, regardless of the final score. Curlers chuckle along with Jay Leno as he tries to make sense of the game and determine, on national late-night TV, if it is truly a sport. They take pride in having David Letterman take the time to offer his top ten ways to improve the sport, laughing along as he mocks the rocks.

How perfectly Canadian. How typical of all who comprise the global curling nation.

Yet there is a darker side to the history of curling. Curlers and their rocks have fallen through the ice, been shipwrecked, and torpedoed at sea. Curling clubs served as morgues for the Lockerbie victims in Scotland and the *Titanic* dead brought to Halifax. Nine curlers perished, and scores more were injured, in April 1974, when a twister split off from a deadly series of tornadoes blasting through Michigan and neighbouring states to crush the Windsor Curling Club in that Ontario border city. The club relocated, but reportedly later succumbed to rising taxes.

Time passes, memories fade, but curling—the sport immortalized by Scottish bard Robbie Burns and *Ivanhoe*'s Walter Scott, satirized by W.O. Mitchell, popularized by television and the Olympics, and, yes, commercialized by the movie *Men with Brooms*—survives and thrives.

Och, aye, there's the rub.

Curling's universal appeal may rest in its emancipating qualities. Where else can men and women compete equally, bound by the same rules, using identical equipment? The greatest swing ice is still a level playing field. It's the same for those who cannot see the broom or hear the rocks, and it's just as true for those with physical and intellectual disabilities as it is for anyone else. None are challenged or disabled: they are curlers, savouring competition, challenge, and camaraderie just as surely as any sighted, hearing, or walking curler.

Big business continues to come on board. Although curling may be considered a poor relation among high-profile sports, with cashspiels only recently coming into vogue, and while there

have been times when men's and women's national championships have briefly been orphans, curling continues to spark a
gleam in the eyes of well-heeled corporate sponsors. If adoptions
have sometimes been brief, there has always been someone to step
up to the plate. In 1982 women's curling, once the longest-suffer-
ing unwanted child, found the ideal provider in Scott Paper, now
the longest continuous sponsor of an amateur sport. Only the
name of the national championship it sponsors has changed—
from Scott to Scotties—in all that time. By contrast, Tim Hortons
is the latest in a longer list to sponsor the men's Brier, having earlier produced a national ad that featured a coffee-mainlining
icemaker named Shorty "The King of Swing" Jenkins. That exposure catapulted him into a cameo appearance in *Men with
Brooms*, a 2002 Canadian film that happened to be about curling
and happened to make money—changing how movies are
financed in Canada.

Such evident serendipity cannot totally explain curling's
healthy broadcast ratings and live attendance figures in recent
years. Nor can the purists' claims that curling is so simple that a
child can learn to play in a day, yet so complex that few can master it in a lifetime. Curling is a game of tradition, etiquette, and
mystery, where anything can happen, where nothing is preor-
dained, and where, as the immortal Scottish bard might have
properly proclaimed, "the best-laid plans of ice and men go
awry." Then everyone shakes hands, laughs, and has a drink, be
it juice, a pop, or nectar of the gods. Curling's traditions seem to
have bloomed through three stages—evolving from Stone Age to
Ice Age and finally the World Stage, as the roaring game pro-
gressed from frozen lakes and wilderness tracts to heated clubs
and vast arenas.

The Stone Age marks the origins and growth of the sport as
irons replaced boulders and granite replaced steel. The Ice Age

rises through the scientific advances fostered by Shorty Jenkins, who taught himself, and then the world, how to make ice as perfect as it can be. His pioneering research led to doctoral theses and everyone from popular television science show hosts to Nobel laureate scientists mucking about to try to explain why rocks curl and exactly what sweeping does. The World Stage elevates traditional curling culture to international pop culture, from W.O. Mitchell's *The Black Bonspiel of Willie MacCrimmon* to Paul Gross's *Men with Brooms*, from hot rock videos to naked curlers calendars, all complemented by expanded television coverage and full-medal status at the Olympic Games.

All of this matters. Each element contributes something to the roaring success of the roaring game. But there is another, often overlooked, reason curling continues to gain popularity. Quite simply, seemingly anyone with a pulse can enjoy a sport where heart and desire count more than strength and agility. The curling world is learning the lesson I learned forty years ago: everyone wants to curl well, but for some, the true joy of curling is that they can do it at all. Curlers with physical or intellectual disabilities, blind curlers, and deaf curlers compete keenly and on their own terms; wheelchair curlers simply shoot from an elevated hack without the benefit of sweepers. Police and firefighters boast their own national championships. Ditto for the Royal Canadian Legion and service clubs. The house is a welcoming home for unions and associations to curl congenially with government executives and corporate CEOs. Some of these groups have curled for more than a century and some of the sport's biggest names curl to raise money for a variety of good causes. Any excuse to throw a stone is welcomed by them all.

That's my take. You can draw your own conclusions as we explore this sweeping saga.

IN THE HACK

IN-TURN, OUT-TURN, U-TURN

I squat in the hack, eyes on the broom. My loose grip gently slides the rock back and forth to prevent it from sticking to the frosted ice. In that instant, gauging distance, weight, and angle, I calculate the backswing height, throwing weight, and sliding distance I need to deliver the rock to where my high school coach taps the distant ice with his broom. I have been curling schoolboy just long enough to learn my in-turn from my out-turn and other basics of the game. I prefer the in-turn; I tend to push the out-turn. From that moment, all bets are off as to where it will go and how it will get there.

All seems well on this occasion. Coach calls for an in-turn draw. I vow to my sweepers to throw "hack weight" like I know what that actually means. Their blank stares suggest they are unconvinced. I don't persist. Inhaling sharply, I rear back, raising the rock upward and behind me, then push hard from the hack as I swing it down onto the ice and stretch my full body length. I release later than my sweepers would have liked and they're on the rock quickly.

Coach calls them off.

The rock does not curl.

I learn later that I "lost my handle." For now, I just stare. Fascinated.

The rock finally starts to curl, slowly—in the wrong direction.

27

My in-turn has become an out-turn. I have thrown my first U-turn.

I beam. My sweepers mock. Coach smirks.

I blame the ice.

THE FIRST END

HAGGIS, BREAKFAST OF CHAMPIONS

*T*he most common estimate for the number of curlers worldwide has generally been set at about 1.2 million participants, with 90 per cent of them in Canada. The Canadian Curling Association (CCA) estimated, prior to the 2006 Turin Olympics, that 872,000 people curl in Canada. More than half (487,000 or 56 per cent) are regulars who curl ten or more times annually. Another 128,000 (15 per cent) curl occasionally, and 257,000 (29 per cent) are social curlers who take to the ice a couple of times a season. When they're not curling, they're watching and cheering. The CCA website estimates that 3,573,000 Canadians watch curling on TV. Roughly half (1,507,000) tune in at least once a month and 886,000 average once a week. While some city clubs have closed, new ones have sprung up in small towns. Perhaps Brad Gushue's Newfoundland team's win of Canada's first Olympic gold medal in men's curling will cause those numbers to rise. Canada leads the Olympic pack with its total of six medals in men's and women's Olympic curling from Nagano, Salt Lake, and Turin—two gold, two silver, and two bronze. But that is recent history and not enough to explain the soaring popularity of the sport. It may help to explore the roaring game's lineage.

The hack has been a home to an astounding cast of characters, from royalty to rock stars and everyone in between. The Beatles curled. James Bond curled. Arnold Schwarzenegger, the son of an Austrian national champion, has testified before a U.S. Senate committee that the sport was character building in his youth. Sweden's King Gustav V curled and Britain's Queen Victoria tried (to explain her failure, it was deemed that her royal hand was "too small" for the sport).

Closer to home, the traditional Friars Brier plays out to test the faith of the devout behind the scenes of the national Brier with the same good humour that has transformed curling into pop culture on both the small and large screens. The hit Canadian television comedy *Corner Gas* featured champion curlers Randy Ferbey and Dave Nedohin in its "Hurry Hard" episode; the sitcom *An American in Canada* used curling as a backdrop to its romantic-comedy storyline. A televised game may have cured insomnia for the acerbic Dr. Greg House in a May 2007 episode of the Fox medical drama *House*, but hey, at least he *was* watching. Curling has provided fodder for late-night hosts Jay Leno, David Letterman, and Jon Stewart (Stephen Colbert has just discovered Junior hockey, so give him some time...) and TV advertisers have associated the sport with everything from improved sex drive to getting bankers out of your back pocket. On the big screen, iconic Canadian rock band the Tragically Hip, who are reputed to be such avid curlers that they plan their winter gigs around the curling season, wrote much of the soundtrack for *Men with Brooms* and had a cameo role

Moving from humour to history, we find that Sir Sandford Fleming curled at two Ottawa clubs and watched the Last Spike driven home amidst—you guessed it—other curlers. Fathers of Confederation, including John A. Macdonald, curled and Governors General played and lent their names to curling trophies: Lord Dufferin for men's competition and Lady Tweedsmuir (not a Governor General but the wife of one) for women's. While there is no evidence that Lord Tweedsmuir (who, as John Buchan, authored the espionage thriller *The Thirty-Nine Steps*, the basis for an early Alfred Hitchcock movie) was an avid curler, he was a passionate spokesman for the roaring game. At a dinner for touring Scottish curlers in 1938, the Governor General proclaimed, "My toast is—The Scottish Curlers. We ken them fine. They're a wheen decent bodies." After lamenting that Robert Burns never wrote the great curling poem he could have, aside from the short lines in his ode to his friend Tam Samson, Lord Tweedsmuir recalled his childhood pleasures of the gatherings at the local mill dam where curling created equality in the countryside:

> It was a wonderful example of true democracy, for there you had the minister, in moments of excitement, weeping on the shoulder of the local ne'er-do-weel, and the sheriff wringing the hand of the local poacher whom in a week or two he was to sentence to sixty days. Curling obliterated all restrictions of class, education and character in a common sporting interest. I do not suppose I shall ever again have such an appetite for a meal as I had for what we called curlers' fare—boiled beef and greens; to-day things are very different. Artificial ice is the rule, and the curlers do not congregate at the mill dam, but go in by the morning train to Edinburgh. No doubt in art and skill much has been gained, but something, too, has been lost.

Lord Tweedsmuir then treated the visiting Scots to a brief history of curling in Canada:

> Scotland may be the birthplace of curling, but I fancy Canada to-day is its chief home. You will see many strange and novel things in Canada. For one thing you

will see the proper kind of winter, where there is nothing half-hearted about the frost and snow.... In the Ottawa and St. Lawrence valleys we curl not with the familiar channel-stanes, but with mighty discs of iron, which personally I find hard to manage. I am told that this practice originated with the British regiments who in the old days garrisoned certain Canadian cities. Being far from Crawfordjohn they could not get the proper channel-stanes, so they seem to have followed the Scriptural injunction—not beating their swords into ploughshares, but beating their antiquated guns into the implements of curling!

That last observation seems to be an oblique reference to the Seventy-eighth Fraser Highlanders. Legend has it that they melted cannonballs into curling irons following the fall of Quebec to pass the winter of 1759–60 and await the spring to see whether a French or English fleet would be first up the St. Lawrence River to claim Canada for its king. Explorers, traders, Hudson Bay factors, and even the vaunted North West Mounted Police later carried the game on their Great March West. At least one may have ventured south, but found himself in no position to be melting cannonballs: Alamo defender John MacGregor.

MacGregor arrived in Texas from Perthshire via Prince Edward Island. A veteran of the British army, he was one of four Scots and nineteen British-born defenders—equal to the actual number of Texans on those adobe walls. During the thirteen-day siege by an overwhelming Mexican force, the piper "duelled" with Tennessee fiddler Davy Crockett (also reputed to have Scottish ancestry) to revive spirits among that doomed garrison. MacGregor won, playing louder and longer. Both fell in the final assault.

It is logical to assume that MacGregor curled, but it is likely unprovable. Even the legend of the curling Scots at Quebec has been debated by revisionist historians, but we'll soon prove their arguments to be specious. Others artfully cite Belgian Renaissance artist Pieter Bruegel's oil paintings *Winter Landscape with Skaters and a Bird Trap* and *Hunters in the Snow*. Those masterpieces suggest that his Flemish countrymen invented curling *and* hockey but may prove only that he travelled and incorporated what he saw elsewhere into his art. For example, his *Winter Landscape* actually seems to illustrate *eisschiessen* ("ice shooting"), a Bavarian game played with a long stick-like handle. That game is more closely associated with Hitler's 1936 Winter Olympics and with actor/politician Arnold Schwarzenegger, who played it long before he curled his first barbell, moved to America, and conquered Hollywood, the extended Democratic Kennedy clan, and California Republican voters. The game is reportedly still popular today, presumably in the Alps. Back in the Low Countries, some point to the R. de Baudous engraving *Hyems* ("Winter"), which portrays players apparently sliding large wooden discs along a frozen waterway. Other sketches from around the same time show a Dutch game called *kuting*, played with frozen lumps of earth, far less conducive to roaring.

It seems bizarre that so many people claim to distrust politicians and the media, yet will take a painting at face value, never questioning that an artist might have just made something up or inserted a rock or clump of clay as an afterthought. To their credit, the Scots make no claim to creating windmills or waffle irons, and it seems only just that if the Dutch or Belgians are to be credited with inventing curling, they must also lay claim to whipping up haggis out of gutted sheep and stuffed entrails. With everyone from the Egyptians to the Irish at some time or other laying claim to skirling the first bagpipes, can we not let the Scots

have curling? Yet while that debate raged, a solitary voice from
the west further muddied the ice by playfully claiming curling to
be a Norse invention: "Curling is an ancient Viking sport brought
to Newfoundland via Scotland during an unseasonably early
thaw that extended the traditional raiding season several hundred
years ago."

Thus quipped "Fast Eddie," Grand Chief of Clan Lukowich,
nearly a quarter-century ago in the introduction to *The Winning
Team Curling Book*, which he wrote with legendary skips Rick
Folk, who christened the first Labatt Brier Tankard by upchuck-
ing into it, and Paul Gowsell, known for his scraggly mane and
wild-eyed Viking impersonation—and for ordering pizza to the
ice during slow matches.

It would be convenient to think that the legendary Calgarian
(from North Battleford, Saskatchewan) merely confused "Norse
Saga" with the sweeping saga of the sport, but his curling creden-
tials give us pause. Nicknamed for the hard, fast shots of his
youth—and also known as "Cool Hand Luke" for his composure
under pressure—Lukowich is no slouch when it comes to curling.
Since pushing his first rock with both hands at age five, the
Canadian and Alberta Hall of Famer, two-time schoolboy champion, and three-peat provincial titlist won two of the five Briers
he contested in the 1980s, adding a Silver Broom world championship in 1986 and a bronze medal in the demonstration sport at
the 1988 Calgary Winter Olympics. The author of four curling
books has produced a sixty-minute training video, was co-
founder and an executive director of the World Curling Tour, and
provided colour commentary for Rogers Sportsnet's World
Curling Tour telecasts for nearly a decade. As further evidence of
the family's devotion to the sport, his wife, Judy, has curled in the
Canadian juniors and the Scott Tournament of Hearts. It was
while working with BBC Scotland in 2000 that Lukowich report-

edly noticed the raw talent of the American curlers. Seeing a chance to develop their elite athletes and promote the sport to an emerging, and potentially powerful, new market, he was named athlete development director by the United States Curling Association in 2001.

The American men missed the playoffs at the Salt Lake Olympics in 2002 and the women lost the bronze-medal game. At Turin in 2006, the women missed the cut but the men won bronze—the first U.S. medal for Olympic curling. It was a pretty picture for Lukowich, which brings us back to the debate over the origin of curling. And so, we take our cue from Fast Eddie's tongue-in-cheek Viking theory to consult the pre-eminent oracle of the twenty-first century—*The Da Vinci Code*.

Historically, to fathom art, which is the basis of the contrary claim, we had to study the artist and his times. But times have changed. Today, we have Dan Brown's fictional code to help decipher the genesis and pronounce the gospel of the holy grail of curling. There are important clues to resolve this long-standing argument over who invented the sport of curling. Let's start with the date of Bruegel's inconvenient painting, 1565. The first pencil was unveiled that year, raising the possibility that the artist drew handles on the rocks just to see what it could do. Sadly, the eraser apparently had not yet been invented, requiring that he add handles to the rest of the rocks to preserve symmetry. While such plausible artistic creativity was creating curling on canvas, the Knights Hospitaller were defending Europe, making their heroic stand at the island fortress of Malta. They defeated an overwhelming Turkish invasion force, marking a true turning point in history. The major difference between them and the Knights Templar, who appear prominently in the code, is that they wore white crosses on their tunics, while the latter wore red crosses. The trail to the Holy Grail concludes at Edinburgh's Rosslyn

Chapel, apparently skipping over Holland and Belgium, making their champions' claims seem as thin as spring-thaw ice. Alas, the code is also mum on Vikings. Such omissions could not be accidental in a quest for something as historically and culturally significant as who invented curling.

Ergo, the Scots invented curling and would invent another sport that involves hitting a ball, chasing it yourself, and hitting it again and again and again...until it falls into a hole. But don't take our word for it. Here's how more learned scholars tackled the dispute.

Those who argue that Continentals must have cast the first stone cite as their evidence the sixteenth-century paintings and words associated with the sport, like *bonspiel*, which, they insist, are not Scottish. How can anyone be certain of a word's origin with a race of people like the Scots, who initially urged sweepers to *"Soop, soop"*? The strongest historical question seems to be whether Flemish sportsmen imported the game when they immigrated to Scotland during the reign of James VI (James I of England). But records are scarce and conjecture is inconclusive, so debate naturally flourished.

The initial controversy over the origin of curling flared in Gladsmuir, where Reverend John Ramsay's book *An Account of the Game of Curling*, published in Edinburgh in 1811, argued the case for the Continental genesis. His research into the origins of curling words—"bonspiel," "brough," "colly," "curl," "kuting," "quoiting," "rink," and "wick"—led him to conclude that they were derived from Dutch or German. The Belgians were lumped in along the way. By this logic, if the words are foreign, so is the game. No one on the Continent seems to have stepped forward to claim curling as their own, yet this Continental theory apparently thrived unchallenged for nearly seventy years before Reverend John Kerr, a noted historian, disputed Ramsay's views. In his

1890 book, *A History of Curling*, Kerr asked why, if the Flemings had brought the game to Scotland in the 1500s, had Scottish poets and historians made no mention of its introduction before 1600? He also argued that for every apparent Continental term, there were as many, or more, that were Celtic or Teutonic in origin, such as "channel stone," "crampit," "draw," "hack," "hog," "skip," "tee," "toesee," "tramp," and "tricker." The documentary evidence—history's paper trail, dating to the first grudge match in 1540, apparently waged more than played—grows increasingly compelling, assuming a literary mantle of Scottish prose and poetry unmatched by any other nation's.

The lingering debate is not so surprising when you realize that nothing may be what it seems from the early days of curling. For example, if you think the sport's name is due to the curling of the rocks, there are those who would argue that you are wrong. Historian W.H. Murray insists the name comes from the low murmuring *curr* sound made by the early palm-sized "loofies" as they scudded across the ice. In fact, primitive curling involved little more than simply sliding rocks of varying sizes down the ice for distance. When the house was created and became a target, the bigger the rock the better. If your village strongman could get one close to the button, any attempt to budge it with smaller rocks was futile, as they'd just ricochet off. Size did matter. The rocks, or "stanes," evolved from notched hand grips on their sides to imbedded handles on their tops. The handles made it possible to twist the rocks on delivery to make them curl, but apparently that didn't come into vogue until the early nineteenth century.

Murray suggests that because curling was so universally popular in Scotland, certainly among the Lowlanders, it is safe to assume there were some prominent Scots in their ranks. One of the more notable was Robbie Burns. While no record seems to have been found of a match that actually involved the legendary

Scottish bard, the game is featured in his poetry, and one of his closest friends, Tam Samson, was a renowned curler. When Samson came close to shedding his mortal coil, Burns composed an elegy to his old friend, and Samson, reportedly perturbed upon hearing of this premature farewell, asked Burns to read it to him. Two stanzas stand out:

> When winter muffles up his cloak,
> And binds the mire like a rock;
> When to the loughs the curlers flock,
> Wi' gleesom speed,
> Wha' will they station at the cock? —
> Tam Samson's deid!

> He was the king o' a' the core
> To draw, or guard, or wick a bore,
> Or up the rink like Jehu roar,
> In time o' need;
> But now he lays on Death's "hog-score"—
> Tam Samson's deid!

Murray doesn't mention how Samson responded to the kind curling analogies, but he does note that the fifteen-stanza ode ended each verse with "Tam Samson's deid!" At the curler's apparent insistence, Burns added another stanza, ending the dirge with: "Tam Samson's leevin!"

Such thoughtfulness is a trademark of the sport. Everyone knows that curling is the friendliest, most gregarious game on the planet. The law of the rings is governed by an on-ice etiquette that borders on chivalry, requiring you to compliment your opponent who has just bludgeoned you with a hammer and to penalize yourself for inadvertently nudging your own rock. While the curling rule book condones rubbing and even biting, its enshrined codes of ethics for players and coaches frown gravely on poor sportsmanship. No one, then, should be surprised to learn that Sir Walter Scott, creator of the virtuous *Ivanhoe*, was an early fan, proclaiming the sport to be "the manly Scottish exercise"—a sentiment echoed verbatim by the legendary bard Burns. Among competitive undertakings, curling must surely stand alone for having its own code that requires participants from club to elite levels to pledge: "I resolve that whether I win or lose, I will win or lose graciously, for success is never final and failure never fatal."

How curious, then, that the first recorded curling game was a grudge match, played with all the warmth and endearment of a duel.

Many curling histories make at least passing reference to what is believed to be the first handwritten account of what could be called a curling game. In February 1540, John McQuhin of Scotland documented, in Latin, a challenge "to a game on ice" between a monk named John Sclater and his associate, Gavin Hamilton. Sounds pretty straightforward, but there's more. The account initially seemed to be a tale of good friends engaging in a bit of sport on a winter's day, but more recent evidence suggests the game had a more sinister purpose. In 1977, some old documents, including certain protocol books that had been unearthed the previous year, caught the attention of Sheriff David Smith, Scotland's principal curling historian at the time. Educated in the classics, Smith could interpret Latin and deduced that McQuhin, a notary, was actually documenting a grudge match. The monk's "associate" was in fact the recently appointed lay governor of the abbey. Smith, a reputed expert at deciphering ancient handwritten manuscripts, translated the description of the ensuing events this way:

February 6, 1540–41, Sclater went to the ice which was between the orchard and the late Abbot's room and there threw a stone along the ice three times, asserting that he was ready to carry out what had been promised on the first day of Gavin's arrival concerning a contest of throwing this sort of stone over the ice.... Hamilton, a short while later, responded by intimating to Sclater that he would go to the ice in the appointed place and that they would there have a contest with stones thrown over the ice.

Smith's interpretation, published in *The Scotsman*, caught the eye of John Durkan, back then a research fellow in the Department of Scottish History of the University of Glasgow, who was using the protocols to glean new information about the pre-Reformation Paisley Abbey and the lifestyle of the abbey's inhabitants in the sixteenth century. He now realized he was reading an account of a quarrel that could well have led to a duel if one of the antagonists had not been a monk. This first recorded curling match was not, he said, a friendly game but rather a "legally recorded" challenge that was a way to "settle some argument or dispute." He also found further evidence that Hamilton, the recent appointee, was not popular. Still, he added, with a hint of wry humour, a monk could hardly challenge his abbot's representative to a duel. And so it appears to have been curling stones at dawn. There is no record of the result. The cause of the conflict remains a mystery.

There is a better-known religious reference to an early curling incident that touched off a scandal: records from the Glasgow Assembly of Presbyterians accused a Bishop Graham of Orkney of a terrible act seemingly bordering on heresy—curling on the Sabbath—in 1638. The issue of Sunday curling would endure for centuries and span continents as the six-day workweek and lack of indoor rinks made it almost impossible for curlers to find the time to take to the ice except at ungodly hours or on sacrilegious days. Ice conditions appear to have been equally unfavourable back then. For example, a small item on Scotland's climate in the early sixteenth century claims it grew milder, which was no doubt more comfortable for living, but lousy for curling as frozen lochs turned to mush. Another source says that winters in Scotland at that time were so bitter that the era was referred to as "the Little Ice Age." In any event, there were said to be so few days of good ice some years that games often extended into the night to take advantage of ideal conditions whenever they occurred. On those occasions, skips are said to have waved white handkerchiefs to help their curlers see the target.

If the debut grudge match poses a conundrum for curlers and their fans who grew up believing in the sanctity of the friendly game, it is really just another strand in the web of the sport's murky past that continues to unravel after nearly five centuries. In the end, we must trace the history on the evidence available, and that is mostly literary in this instance. But the evolution of the sport from a test of strength to a contest of strategy meant curling also evolved from an apparent grudge match to become likely the only sport to include a section on fair play and codes of ethics for players and coaches in its rule book:

Curlers' Code of Ethics
I will play the game with a spirit of good sportsmanship.
I will conduct myself in an honourable manner both on
    and off the ice.
I will never knowingly break a rule, but if I do, I will
    divulge the breach.
I will take no action that could be interpreted as an

attempt to intimidate or demean my opponents,
teammates or officials.

I will interpret the rules in an impartial manner, always
keeping in mind that the purpose of the rules is to
ensure that the game is played in an orderly and fair
manner.

I will humbly accept any penalty that the governing
body at any level of curling deems appropriate, if I
am found in violation of the Code of Ethics or rules
of the game.

Coaching Code of Ethics

The coach shall act with integrity in performing all
duties owed to athletes, the sport, other members of
the coaching profession and the public.

The coach shall strive to be well prepared and current in
order that all duties in his/her discipline are fulfilled
with competence.

The coach shall act in the best interest of the athlete's
development as a whole person.

The coach shall accept both the letter and the spirit of
the rules that define and govern the sport.

The coach shall accept the role of officials in providing
judgment to ensure that competitions are conducted
fairly and in accordance with the established rules.

The coach's conduct toward other coaches shall be char-
acterized by courtesy, good faith and respect.

The coach shall maintain the highest standards of personal conduct and support the principles of Fair
Play.

Fair Play

Fair Play begins with the strict observance of the written
rule; however, in most cases, Fair Play involves something more than even unfailing observance of the
written rule.

The observance of the spirit of the rules, whether written
or unwritten, is important.

Fair Play results from measuring up to one's own moral
standards while engaged in competition.

Fair Play is consistent demonstration of respect for team
mates and opponents, whether they are winning or
losing.

Fair Play is consistent demonstration of respect for officials, an acceptance of their decisions and a steadfast
spirit of collaboration with them.

Sportsmanlike behaviour should be demonstrated both
on and off the ice. This includes modesty in victory
and composure in defeat.

So, there you have it. Aside from Ed Werenich's isolated
"wrenching" body slam performed long ago on Glenn Howard in
his zeal to sweep a rock in the house, there is no cross-checking
in curling. Heckling from the stands and high-fives on the ice
have admittedly crept into the sport, but only one curler has ever
tested positive for a banned substance. Old-timers joke that the
sport will remain uniquely pristine in the face of increasingly zeal-
ous and complex international drug testing as long as no one
wheels in a portable Breathalyzer. And even the tradition of alco-
hol associated with curling is waning, tempered by the new
generation of young curlers who treat diet and fitness as vital
components of the game that has soared to international promi-
nence. There, too, we may find guidance from the Scots, for

nothing says protein like haggis—that Gaelic breakfast of champions that stipulates grazing after praising. For while the bard spoke well of curling, Burns immortalized the ritual consumption of stuffed sheep intestines with his cherished and oft-recited ode *To a Haggis*. This "Great Chieftan o' the Puddin-race" is ceremoniously stabbed even as it is revered thusly:

> His knife see Rustic-labour dight,
> An' cut you up wi' ready slight,
> Trenching your gushing entrails bright
> Like onie ditch;
> And then, O what a glorious sight,
> Warm-reekin, rich!

Ah, the Scots. The wily warrior-poets reputed to have tossed uprooted trees to span chasms, then christened their bridge a caber and called it a sport. The thrifty sportsmen who devised a diversion requiring you to hit a ball into a hole, retrieve it, and go looking for another hole. The sole race to be walled out of the ancient Roman Empire and to have converted a musical instrument into a universally recognized weapon of war. How hard can it be to concede that the people who gave us cabers and golf and haggis also gave us curling? If you balk at "gushing entrails" and "warm-reekin" grub in your breakfast bowl, find solace in the Royal Caledonian Curling Club's genteel "Curler's Grace":

> O Lord wha's love surrounds us a'
> And brings us a' thegither;
> Wha' writes your laws upon oor hearts,
> And bids us help each ither.

We bless Thee for Thy bounties great,
For meat and hame and gear
We thank Thee, Lord, for snaw and ice—
But still we ask for mair.

Gi'e us a hert to dae whit's richt,
Like curlers true and keen;
To be guid friends along life's road,
And soop oor slide aye clean.

O Power abune whose bounty free,
Oor needs and wants suffices;
We render thanks for Barley Bree,
And meat that appetises.

Be Thou our Skip throughout life's game,
An' syne we're sure to win;
Tho' slow the shot and wide the aim,
We'll soop each ither in.

For the uninitiated, it may help you to learn that *soop* means "sweep," *abune* means "above," *syne* means "since," and Barley Bree, you may have guessed, is whiskey. But it is important to note that the Scots did not restrict their curling literature to pre-meal dirges. As the game evolved, it warranted its own anthem, and while the author's identity has been lost to posterity, his work has not.

Here's to the sport of fair renown,
Here's to the roarin' game;
Here's to the stones that go gliding down,
Here's to the icy lane:

Here's to the skip with shout so bold,
Here's to his players' fling,
Here's to the game that is never old,
Here's to the songs we sing.

O curlers, come, we're brithers a',
Come join the curling game;
Our eyes are keen, our arms are true,
Our courage is aflame;
In winter air, and sport so rare,
The stones our weapons be,
We'll make the fight with honest might,
To gain the victory:
A man who is a curling man,
No better man than he.

There seems to be no record of any other nation making prolific literary references to curling. That seems a pivotal argument
to support Scotland's claim that it originated the sport and did
not just guide its evolution. In the wake of the first recorded
grudge match between monk and lay governor—more a legal
than a literary account—curling became increasingly documented
in prose and poetry. Perhaps the first literary account appeared in
a seventeenth-century elegy published by Henry Adamson, following the death of his close friend, M. James Gall of Perth.
Terming the departed merchant "a gentleman of goodly stature
and pregnant wit," Adamson noted that Gall enjoyed "golf,
archerie, curling and jovial companie," despite the ravages of
tuberculosis. His homage, "The Muses Threnodie, or, Mirthful
Mournings on the Death of Master Gall," published in 1639,
evolved from a two-part poem he'd penned in 1620. "Curling
stones" are cited twice in the text and "curling" is highlighted as

one of Gall's accomplishments in Adamson's preface. That signif-icant reference was apparently overlooked for years by curling historians, whether because the original work was scarce or because historians, like most readers, skipped reading the preface. Assigned the role of "chief mourner" in the poetry, George Ruthven lists Gall's cupboard chattels as "His hats, his hoods, his bels, his bones, / His allay bowles, and curling stones."

The early curling doggerel was apparently poetry to the ears of the curlers. As the game spread and evolved, the chroniclers and poets kept pace, documenting its history in lore and legend. At the time of the American Revolution (or the War of Independence, for our American readers), James Graeme finally got around to describing the game itself in his poem "1773":

> The goals are marked out; the centre each
> Of a large random circle; distance scores
> Are drawn between, the dread of weakly arms
> Firm on his cramp-bits stands the steady youth
> Who leads the game: low o'er the weighty stone
> He bends incumbent, and with nicest eye
> Surveys the further goal, and in his mind
> Measures the distance; careful to bestow
> Just force enough; then, balanc'd in his hand
> he flings it on direct; it glides along
> Hoarse murmuring, while, plying hard before,
> Full many a besom sweeps away the snow
> Or icicle, that might obstruct its course....

If the Scots chronicled and immortalized curling, they also developed the tools needed to play the game. For 150 years, dat-ing to 1500, the Scots used kuting stones to curl. Varying in weight from four to twenty-five pounds, they were gripped using

a thumb hole bored into the top and finger grooves notched into
the bottom. They were essentially oblong bowling balls. The next
stage in the evolution involved larger boulders that were eventually equipped with handles of varying design and placement. And
the stone, or "stane" as it was known, like Tam Samson and haggis and the sport itself, rated its own elegy as Reverend George
Murray, minister to a small parish at Balmaclellan, praised his
hand-picked curling rock in seven stanzas and may have given the
sport its nickname in the process:

> Where lone Penkiln, mid foam and spray
> O'er many a linn leaps on his way,
> A thousand years and mair ye lay
> Far out of sight;
> My blessings on the blythesome day
> Brought thee to light.
>
> Though ye were slippery as an eel,
> Rab flashed ye frae the salmon wiel,
> And on his back the brawny chief
> Has ta'en ye hame,
> Destined to figure at the spiel
> And roaring game.
>
> Wi' mony a crack he cloured your crown,
> Wi' mony a chap he chipped ye down,
> Fu' aft he turned ye roun and roun,
> And aye he sang
> A 'ither stanes ye'll be aboon
> And that ere lang.

Guided by mony a mould and line
He laboured next with polish fine,
To make your mirrored su'face shine
With lustre rare—
Like lake, reflect the forms divine
Of nature fair.

A handle next did Rab prepare,
And fixed it with consummate care—
The wood of ebony so rare,
The screw of steel—
Ye were a channel-stane right fair,
Fit for a spiel.

Ye had nae name for icy war—
Nae strange device, nor crest, nor star—
Only a thread of silver spar
Ran through your blue;
Ilk curler kenned your flinty scar
And running true.

A time will come when I no more
May fling thee free from shore to shore;
With saddened heart I'll hand thee o'er
To some brave chiel,
That future times may hear they roar
At ilka spiel.

And so we learn the saga of selecting, finishing, shooting—
and evidently loving—your hand-picked curling stone. The Scots
taught us two more things about curling: that you need a broom

to clean the ice on an outdoor rink and that you can learn to curl in minutes but never master the sport in a lifetime.

Despite the accumulated evidence that the Scots invented curling, some insist that the origin remains a mystery. But everyone agrees the Scots did the most to enhance, promote, and export the game. By the eighteenth century, curling had become a common pastime in Scotland, its heritage documented in the poetry and prose of the era that recorded numerous bonspiels and curling societies and hailed curling as a great national game. The record seems clear. Once and for all, let's state the obvious and move on. The Scots invented curling; they did not invent *eisscheissen*! But no matter which side you take in this debate, on one point there is no disagreement—the Scots introduced curling to Canada. The Canadians would champion the sport to the world. The roaring game was set to soar.

IN THE HACK

COTTAGE COUNTRY'S ACE OF CLUBS

*B*ill Woods comes from good curling stock. His father, William, has been curling for fifty-three years at the Metcalfe Curling Club, which he helped found in the 1920s. His mom, Beryl, is entering her fifty-second year of curling there. Their grandchildren, Billy and Olivia, also curl in Metcalfe, marking four generations of Woods, most of them named Bill, who have helped show the staying power of small-town curling clubs.

We should also mention that Micheline, Bill's wife, a distant relation to the Bill who started it all, also curls at the Metcalfe club.

Billy skipped his St. Mark High School team to the Ottawa School Board championship in 2006 and went to provincials; Olivia played second for Osgoode Township High School at the provincial championships. But Bill Woods the younger (middle?), who has curled for thirty-two years, may lay claim to a unique honour in a much-honoured family: he has built his own club.

The Dalhousie Lake Curling Club, which he bills as "the oldest open-air curling club in the world," is located near his cottage on the upper stretch of eastern Ontario's Mississippi River. Woods's claim is sanctioned by both the Ontario Curling Association and the Ottawa Valley Curling Association—a powerful endorsement from two associations that sometimes don't seem to agree on much.

The quest began back in the late 1980s, when the federal government urged Canadians to devise novel ways to celebrate Canada's 125th birthday, in 1992, by connecting to our past. What better link than curling? Woods registered his club, then a mere glint in his eye, with the OCA and the OVCA. Both confirmed there were no other open-air clubs in operation. He shopped around, buying sheets of used rocks where he could find—and when he could afford—them. New rocks were just too expensive. He acquired two sheets (thirty-two rocks) and picked up extras here and there. Curling on lake ice did not really require finely honed edges. "Sharp or dull, it doesn't have a noticeable impact on your shot," he says, chuckling.

Even a modest rise in temperature can create surface water on the sheets, forcing curlers to throw harder and then savour the rooster tails that splash out as the rock lumbers down the ice. They have learned by experience what works and what does not.

Woods uses Jell-O and Kool-Aid powders to paint the rinks' lines, having discovered that fluorescent paint weakened the button, dropping it a couple of inches, causing a rock to just plunk into the hole and sit there, despite all efforts to move it. Open-air curlers begin and end all games in daylight, having learned that "darkness and whiskey" are a bad combination and that lighting the rink with snowmobile and truck lights just doesn't do the trick. Woods also learned to leave a wide snow berm of fifteen to twenty feet between his two sheets to help preserve them longer. It complicates scraping but deters top-water flooding.

The club boasts scoreboards, pebbling cans, scrapers, and a measuring device. The season is dictated by the weather more than by the calendar, normally starting between Boxing Day and New Year's. The wrap-up championship tournament is held on the second weekend in February. If that conflicts with Valentine's Day, the bonspiel moves up a week—a concession to the wives and girlfriends who have been excluded from the men-only club. (That gender restriction has cracked under pressure—one female curler has been admitted to what remains an overwhelmingly male-dominated club.)

Membership hovers around thirty and has been as high as forty-five. Several live hours away but sign up just to play in the championship. About four junior players represent the club in local bonspiels and the Governor General's Prize, the historic two-team total-point competition instituted by Lord Dufferin in 1874. Sanctioned by the Canadian Branch of the Royal Caledonian Curling Club, that competition was initially open to all curling clubs in Canada, but now draws teams primarily from the Ottawa Valley of eastern Ontario and western Quebec to about Montreal. While the club, even with the gender barrier broken, has yet to contest the similarly formatted and sanctioned Lady Tweedsmuir Prize, instituted in 1938, a mixed team has competed in the Lady Gilmour. The boys have played in the Doug Washer Branch Event—the single-team junior competition of the Canadian Branch of the Royal Caledonian Curling Club—and the men in the Jubilee single events.

Fun is the primary goal, and while safety is a factor, it is not really a concern. If someone actually fell through the ice, he would land, at worst, in chest-deep water. In that unlikely event, he would be rescued and bundled off to a roaring fire and a shot of whiskey.

"There is no downside here," Woods quips. "We're not going to the Brier, but I figure if they have an award for most sociable club, we're in the running. No one can touch us."

THE SECOND END

FROM TEE TO
SHINING TEE LINE

*T*he most historic rock in Canada has never touched a sheet of ice. In fact, at first glance, it seems to have precious little to do with curling. But, with all due respect to Fergus, with its carefully preserved and enshrined 1834 wooden stane, and to those curling clubs in Quebec and eastern Canada that have kept their early irons on display, the Mackenzie Rock in British Columbia marks the Scottish expansion to the Pacific Coast. And where the Scots went, curling followed.

For Canadians who may have forgotten their history, Alexander Mackenzie was dispatched by his employer, the North West Company, to find a land route to the Pacific Coast that could expand the fur trade farther west. His arduous seventy-two-day trek from Lake Athabaska covered more than 2,000 kilometres (1,240 miles) of unmapped wilderness. Hailed as Canada's one-man equivalent to America's better publicized Lewis and Clark, Mackenzie preceded that government-sanctioned expedition by a dozen years, becoming, in 1793, the first European to cross the Rocky Mountains and reach the west coast. Or at least very, very close to the coast. In one of those ironies of history, Mackenzie hooked up with the native Nuxalk clan, who guided him down the Bella Coola River to what is today known as Dean Channel. And that was apparently just an example of the hospitality of these inhabitants of what the white strangers dubbed the "Friendly

Village." Unfortunately for Mackenzie, his hosts seemed to be decidedly unfriendly with their coastal neighbours, the Heiltsuk, preventing the intrepid Scot from actually reaching the Pacific Ocean. Still, he was close enough to see the sea, and that was good enough for Mackenzie to declare his mission complete.

To commemorate the event, perhaps inspired by the nearby native petroglyphs that record early indigenous history, the adventurer crafted perhaps the first, and what must certainly be the most famous, graffiti in Canadian history. Mixing vermilion with bear grease to create a crude red paint, Mackenzie daubed a large rock at end of his trail with the commemorative words "Alex Mackenzie from Canada by land 22nd July 1793." Immortalized as "Mackenzie's Rock," that inscription was permanently carved into the stone by later surveyors. A prominent forty-foot memorial cairn stands above the rock, and a plaque, erected in 1926 by the Historic Sites and Monuments Board of Canada, also acknowledges the friendly natives. The Scots had reached the Pacific coast. Curling would follow.

Curling historians and writers, after debating at length the European Lowlands' role in the genesis of curling—a claim that seems never to have been made by the Lowlanders—predictably recount the rise of the roaring game in Canada, usually offering little more than a chronology of curling club histories and the creation of the provincial governing associations. That is normal and proper, yet may be missing a larger, vital context. The rise and spread of curling in Canada is directly linked to the country's history and westward expansion. Hidden behind the larger topics of study—from the Hudson's Bay Company to the railways, the North West Mounted Police, and Canadian immigration policy—is the fact that while each played its vital, well documented role in the creation of Canada, there was a less visible aspect that involved the social aspects of daily life.

While it may seem the epitome of human nature to seek warmth and shelter from the cold, settlers also required a social outlet to survive and stay sane amid the savage isolation of a Canadian winter. "Cabin fever" is not just a catchphrase. Perhaps starting with Samuel de Champlain's "Order of Good Cheer," which got the first settlers in New France through their first harsh winter by encouraging them to party hearty, Canadians have learned to cope with the cold by seeking diversions. And no one likes to party more than a curler. There is no more sociable, gregarious animal on the planet. A brutal cold snap could interrupt, curtail, but never stop their parade to the ice. Not everyone had the luxury of skates, but every home had a broom. And finding rocks—be they river stones or hardwood blocks—did not present much of a challenge in the wilderness. It could be argued that had the Scots not invented the game, the Canadians would have.

Perhaps the best evidence of the role curling played in westward expansion are a few tantalizing snapshots of early Mounties posing in group shots, staring sternly into the camera with their trademark Stetsons, primitive straw brooms raised at the ready. At a higher level, one of the most famous photographs in Canadian history, recording the driving of the Last Spike to link Canada by rail, has at least one prominent curler in the near background—Sandford Fleming, later knighted for, among other things, devising an international system of time zones after missing a train that ran on a different clock than his. You just know that if Fleming curled, his peers curled. The sport was not yet the great equality game, certainly not in eastern Canada, that it would become in the prairies before backtracking toward the East. Fleming, in fact, was still a member of the Ottawa Curling Club when he helped start the Rideau Curling Club—raising a few eyebrows at this apparent conflict of interest.

If Fleming is among the best-known early curlers, he was by no means the first. The Earl of Dalhousie was listed as a member of the Quebec City Curling Club as early as 1828, and from that time curling has boasted its share of famous figures, including such powerful men as Sir John A. Macdonald, Lord Aberdeen, and Lord Strathcona—all of them, according to some accounts, Scots pursuing an ethnic interest. The *Canadian Encyclopedia* claims that the viceregal support of the Governors General was especially significant, noting that Lord Dufferin, who held that post from 1872 to 1878, was a particularly ardent exponent. He promoted curling in Russia when he was Ambassador at the Court of the Czar in St. Petersburg and even had a rink built at his own expense at Rideau Hall, the official residence of the Governor General in Canada. In 1875 he instituted the Governor General's Prize, one of Canada's coveted curling trophies. (The reception and trophy and medal presentations were traditionally held at Government House.) His successors continued to sponsor the roaring game, adding to its prestige.

There has been some confusion between the Branch Governor General's and the Ontario Curling Association's event of the same name. Research by John Falkingham, a past president of the Manotick Curling Center near Ottawa, has determined that two competitions were established in 1879—one for "iron" rocks and one for stone "granites," with the Branch hosting the former and the forerunner of the OCA hosting the latter. Even the Branch switched to granite when irons were essentially abolished in 1953. The double-team format of the competition means that you can lose your game badly and still advance if your partner team demolishes their opponent. Then again, you can win your game and still lose that matchup if your partner team tanks.

Early notes uncovered by Falkingham say the "original General's competition is still one of the most prestigious

Canadian Branch event [sic], whereas the Ontario Curling Association Governor General's competition is rather secondary in their calendar." In fact, the GG event seems to have vanished from the OCA calendar and website. The notes record that, in 1970, the Governor General's Curling Club, the OCA, and the Branch talked about combining the events. The GG had proposed withdrawing the present trophies ("trophies" perhaps including the Lady Tweedsmuir) and presenting a new one for a national championship. The idea fell through because provincial associations outside Ontario and Quebec showed little interest, further complicated by the fact that the Governor General designation could not appear with a commercially sponsored event.

Once the epitome of Canadian curling, the Branch retains five zones with only one in Ontario. The four Quebec zones play off with the winner meeting the Ontario champion. The final is always played in an Ottawa area curling club since the Rideau Hall curling rink was demolished in 1939. The Governor General's is still actively played but is no longer as well known.

The first Scottish curling tour, in the winter of 1902–03, is credited with providing an international stimulus to the sport. Playing in eleven cities from Halifax to Winnipeg, then visiting six American cities, the touring Scots lost more matches than they won, but reportedly returned home "tremendously impressed with the status and progress of curling in the Dominion." Returning the favour in 1908, the first Canadian squad to tour Scotland won twenty-three of twenty-six matches, including three international contests, to claim the Strathcona Cup.

But aside from these well-documented events and the references, however brief, to at least some of the rich and famous curlers, there are only vague references to the fur traders, trappers, outpost factors, and Mounties, all of whom presumably endured the long winter months and the isolation of the Prairies by tossing stones or wooden blocks along frozen ponds and lakes. The maddening scarcity of details and frustrating lack of evidence for tracking the lesser-known curling pioneers as they carried the game westward leaves us with the (faint) hope that surely, somewhere, given that commerce pushed back the wilderness in Canada, detailed social accounts exist alongside the balance sheets, a treasure trove of cached archives of the business enterprises and our national police force—a bonanza of diaries, reports, journals, and letters that attest to the popularity and pervasiveness of the roaring game—that predate the Confederation of Canada in 1867.

The expansion of rail and roads in Canada allowed curlers to travel farther to compete in bonspiels, carrying their personal curling stones or wooden blocks with them, packed safely, perhaps crated where possible, in ox carts, stages, and trains. The national dream to link Canada opened the door to inter-club rivalry and healthy municipal competition across the Dominion. If the path of the curling rock remains properly obscured, there are enough snippets to allow common sense and mild conjecture to suggest there is a trove of materials just waiting for historians to dust off and display. What history there is dates back to a group of Highland soldiers tossing melted cannonballs down the St. Charles River. Just as the bagpipe is the only musical instrument to be deemed "a weapon of war," curling in Canada began as an adjunct to war.

The story is well known, and oft told, but usually oversimplified: The Fraser Highlanders asked permission of their commander to melt down cannonballs after the fall of Quebec in 1759. Generations of Canadians, raised on tales of the daring, valour, and the untimely deaths of Wolfe and Montcalm, learned that the Grey Nuns knitted leggings for the suffering Scots, who, once warmed, took to the ice. The story was blindly accepted for centuries. But revisionist historians have never found a myth they didn't want to debunk. Noting the absence of any written chronicle of that historic first curling match, they argue that Highland soldiers would not be as well versed with curling as Lowland Scots and that no military commander worth his haggis would allow his troops to alter munitions for sport in a time of war. All very logical, and all very neatly overlooking some facts of genealogy and history.

Mortally wounded in the Battle of the Plains of Abraham, General James Wolfe was succeeded by General James Murray, a Lowlander from Elibank who almost certainly was familiar with the game and may well have had a passion for it. So the Highland troops were led by a Lowlander. Certainly one or the other knew the game well enough to know all they needed was ice—no problem in any Canadian winter—and curling stones or irons. Revisionists who argue that no commander would allow his troops to alter or destroy munitions like cannonballs when encamped amid a potentially hostile populace ignore the standard military practice of going into winter quarters—a strategy dating to the Caesars, virtually unchanged in cold climes until the First World War. Military commissions were often purchased back then, and no gentleman would have been keen to lead men into the heat of battle in freezing weather. Presumably, there was no shortage of cannonballs. Contemporary accounts estimate that as many as forty thousand cannonballs were fired into the city; even the cautious CBC acknowledges there were at least twenty thousand. The city and countryside would have been littered with them and photos exist of cannonballs stuck in trees. Melting a few dozen would not put the British Empire at risk.

Thus, everything seems to have been in place for a curling game: a Lowlander in charge of bored troops; a pacified, or at least hibernating, population; and little chance of renewed hostilities before the spring thaw, if ever. So, what really happened that first harsh winter credited with the first curling game in Canada? Bruce D. Bolton, director of the David M. Stewart Foundation and past director of the Stewart Museum at Fort Ile-Ste-Hélène, Montreal, and an authority on the reconstituted Seventy-eighth Fraser Highlander re-enactors, explained:

> Tradition has it that the Scottish soldiers in Wolfe's
> army, over the winter of 1759–60 had a lot of time on
> their hands, although it was a rather difficult winter. The
> only Highland Regiment in Wolfe's army was the 78th
> Regiment, Fraser's Highlanders.... Stones, iron, wood
> could be used for the game, it was highly improvisa-
> tional. Cannon balls were there by the thousands and
> they could be cut in half. All this was available that win-
> ter in the Quebec City area. This being said, I am not
> aware of any eyewitness or written account that says
> that it actually did happen.

Despite the lack of any formal documented account of that first game, the tale persists. Certainly no one has proved that it didn't happen. And, if it is myth, the current anachronistic crop of Seventy-eighth Fraser Highlanders have gone to a lot of trouble, and endured not insignificant discomfort, to preserve its memory and significance to Canadian history and curling folklore. The regiment was revived by volunteer re-enactors in the 1970s, Bolton explained, and when they were looking for a winter event, curling was suggested. A natural rink was made on the parade square of the fort, on Montreal's St. Helen's Island, and turn-of-the-century stones were borrowed from the Royal Montreal Curling Club. Thus began their annual bonspiels on natural ice. Just how dependent they are on the weather is illustrated by their 2004 outing, as recorded by Highlander Captain Bill Campbell in the *Journal of the St. Andrew's Society of Montreal* and paraphrased here.

With the temperature hovering around freezing, the curling irons, melted-down cannonballs, would not move. Neither light nor heavy irons could travel more than a foot down the "lumpy, sticky" ice, no matter how hard they were thrown. But then the curling gods intervened, the temperature dropped, and the game was on—imperfect but at least possible to play with the lighter irons. The Highlanders, outfitted in period red tunics, broadswords dragging on the ice, were complemented by Barbara Mason's Hudson Legion curlers, resplendent in long red skirts and plaid sashes. And if having women on the ice tinkered with history, so too did the Australian team iced by Dr. John Jones from Champlain College, but then the game had also been moved to Montreal from Quebec City. The Highlanders—Montreal Police Constable Claude Larocque, just back from a United Nations mission to East Timor, teamed with Ian Aitken, Andy Melville, and Major Okill Stuart, the new garrison commander—carried the day, winning the coveted Lieutenant Keith Hutchison Trophy.

Whatever the historic alterations on the ice, the event was capped with an authentic eighteenth-century meal of "thick pea soup, awash with bacon, chunks of hams and several huge ham bones lurking in the bottom of the pot." You can almost hear the rocks roll and the arteries harden. The menu was completed with servings of half-loaves of bread and huge bowls of venison stew ladled from a huge pot that had simmered all afternoon over an open fire. As Captain Campbell cheerfully reported, the wine and the conversation flowed.

The Seventy-eighth Fraser Highlanders would never have been there in Quebec in 1759 to fight the battle had it not been for Wolfe. When concerns were raised about recruiting 1,500 clansmen from the ranks of the Jacobite army that had earlier fought to return Bonnie Prince Charlie to the Scottish throne, Wolfe, who had refused to participate in the wanton murder of the Scottish wounded at Culloden, replied calmly, "If a Highlander gives his oath, he can be completely trusted." If that was good enough for an astute judge of character like Wolfe, it should be good enough for the rest of us to accept any claim by the Seventy-eighth Highlanders that they curled that day in the bitter cold on the St. Charles River. For those remaining skeptics who demand documentary evidence or artists' renditions to believe the 1759 tale, suffice it to say that curling was the first sport to have its own play-by-play and colour commentator. There is a written record clearly chronicling the reaction of a bemused *habitant* farmer who watched Scots take to the ice near Quebec City in 1821, who commented, "*J'ai vu aujourdui une bande d'Ecossais qui j'etaient des grandes boules de fer, faites commes des bombes, sur la glace; apres quoi, ils criaient 'soupe, soupe'; ensuite, ils riaient, comme des foux; je crois bien qu'ils sont vraiment foux.*"

For the benefit of our Alberta readers, allow me to translate: "Today, I saw a band of Scotsmen who were throwing big iron balls like bombs on the ice; after which they cried 'soop, soop,' and then laughed like mad; I truly think they are mad." It may not rival vintage primetime Vic Rauter or Don Wittman, but you get the gist. Wherever curling originated, it does not appear to have been in France.

There were, as always, more poetic accounts of the game; James Graeme penned his tribute to curling, "1773," about the time Mackenzie was making his way to the Pacific. Poetry aside, the public record, and certainly the membership lists of pioneering curling clubs, further confirms the significance of curling to Canadian history, if only by its attraction to many high-profile

Canadians who played significant roles as builders and players in our past. The cream of society who were swept off their feet by curling included players like Macdonald and Fleming alongside regal agents who lent their names to curling supremacy. Lord Tweedsmuir curled and lent his name to the trophy he donated to mark curling supremacy in eastern Ontario and Quebec. Lord Stanley also curled but is better known for his trophy for hockey supremacy—or to the last team still standing in today's professional shinny league. But with or without documented evidence on the Seventy-eighth Fraser Highlanders—and having dampened "Fast Eddie" Lukowich's theory that would favour the Vikings at L'Anse-aux-Meadows, Newfoundland—no one disputes that the first curling club outside Europe was created in Montreal.

The Montreal Curling Club was established on January 22, 1807, by twenty prosperous merchants who had been curling behind Molson's Brewery on the icebound St. Lawrence River. Honoured as the first curling club in North America, it was awarded the "Royal" appellation in 1924, further enhancing an already distinguished heritage. Early rules were quite simple, and no doubt popular, at least for winning teams; the losers were required to treat them to a bowl of whiskey toddy. In keeping with the history of the Frasers' cannonballs, and likely because of the lack of quality rocks in the area, the club curlers cast irons, not stones. Quebec City also chose irons when it formed its curling club in 1821. Competition may have flourished at the club level, but impassable wilderness tracts delayed the first inter-club bonspiel for fifteen years. In 1836, curlers braved the elements and the forest paths to meet halfway, at Trois-Rivières, to curl on the frozen St. Lawrence. Quebec won that historic first bonspiel 31–23; Montreal paid for dinner.

When the Grand Caledonian Club, founded in Scotland in 1838, became the Royal Caledonian in 1843, both Canadian clubs requested affiliation. Accepted into the fold by the new mother club, they created the Canadian Branch of the Royal Caledonian Curling Club in 1852. It was based in Montreal and, more than 150 years later, continues today to be the governing body for curling in parts of Quebec and the Ottawa Valley in eastern Ontario.

In his succinct on-line history of curling in Nova Scotia (at www.maritimecurling.info), John Murphy records that curling developed slowly in the Maritimes as the sport spread eastward. In a province dubbed New Scotland, Scottish coal miners, hauling their stones across the Atlantic, created the Halifax Curling Club in 1824. The Pictou Curling Club followed five years later. Murphy also credits the Scots—final apologies to the Viking hordes—with introducing curling to Newfoundland. They formed their first club in St. John's in 1843, now home to the Olympic champion Gushue team and Jack MacDuff's bronzed curling boots in perpetual tribute for first "rocking the Rock" by bringing home the 1976 Brier title. New Brunswickers were hooked after reading the details of the 1853 Grand Match at Carsebreck, Scotland—so impressed that they imported curling stones, tried curling, liked it a lot, and formed their first club in 1854. The pattern continued. Roughly 150 years after that experimental genesis, Ontario skip Russ Howard moved to Moncton and brought home his Olympic gold medal, playing for Gushue's rock stars. In addition to holding the record for most Briers attended as a competitor, he is in the running for oldest Olympic competitor and medal winner—a title with other challengers and complicated by the IOC's recent decision to declare that curling was actually a medal sport in the 1924 Olympics.

Prince Edward Island, perhaps too busy being the cradle of Confederation, finally caught the curling craze and founded a club in Charlottetown in 1887. But most of the action in the East seemed to be in Nova Scotia back then. Following Quebec's lead, the Halifax Curling Club petitioned for branch powers from the Royal Caledonian. That request was granted in 1851. Murphy notes that Halifax surrendered that title to form a Nova Scotia Branch with the Halifax Thistle Curling Club and the Dartmouth Curling Club. The Pictou Curling Club joined early in the next year, followed by the Pictou New Caledonian Curling Club and the New Glasgow Curling Club in 1854 and Antigonish in 1856. The Nova Scotia Branch lasted another six years, then became inactive from 1863 until 1867, when it held a few executive meetings, and then disappeared until it was revived in 1904, two years after the first Scottish tour breezed into the province. In its early years, the Nova Scotia Branch arranged the first curling game of record, involving teams from the Halifax, Thistle, and Dartmouth clubs, on a Dartmouth lake on January 12, 1851. Nearly two years to the day later, it scheduled a match between the Halifax and the Dartmouth clubs to compete for a district medal sponsored by the Royal Caledonian Curling Club. It's unclear why the Thistle club was omitted, but its days were numbered. In 1874, that club amalgamated with the Halifax Curling Club. The result was the province's first indoor rink, built on Tower Road.

The original Halifax Curling Club was the inevitable result of the presence of Houston Stewart, a British naval commander stationed in that port city, who had initiated outdoor curling on local ponds and lakes—with descriptive monikers like Chocolate Lake and Hospital Pond. To honour him, the club adopted the Stewart tartan. When the club moved indoors, its two-sheet rink was hailed as a state-of-the-art facility, but neither that nor its adoption of the kingfisher for its club crest from the City of Halifax crest was much help when it hit financial troubles. What was couched as "unpleasant but not unusual" became terminal when, in 1892, the city sold the club to collect back taxes.

Returning temporarily to the local ponds, a second Halifax Curling Club was opened in 1899, boasting three sheets of natural ice and a bowling alley. On December 30, 1902, the indoor club hosted the official debut match of the first Scottish curling tour. Gracious to a fault, the Haligonians lost 84–78, but great events and better times beckoned, capped, in 1927, when they won the first men's national curling championship that would, under various sponsors, remain known simply as the Brier.

Authors Doug Maxwell and Bob Weeks have both documented the history of the Brier, with the former concentrating on its first fifty years dating to 1927. As curling fans—particularly western curling fans—are aware, the Canadian men's championship has been dominated by teams from Manitoba, Saskatchewan, and Alberta, but Nova Scotia won the very first. Interestingly, that first Tankard was won by a club that had not won its provincial championship. Indeed, it is written that, prior to stepping onto the ice at the Toronto Granite Club, the foursome from the Halifax Curling Club—Murray Macneill, J. Alfred MacInnes, Clifford Torey, and James Donahoe—had never curled together. That's a far cry from the team building that occurs today at the elite levels, for both men and women, but was apparently a recipe for success for the roaring game in the Roaring Twenties. For some reason, the champion provincial team could not make the journey to Toronto (all early Briers were held in Hogtown), so Macneill, a professor at Dalhousie University, was instructed to pick a team to represent the province. He selected curlers from his home club and apparently chose wisely, sweeping the ice with everyone except New Brunswick to win the first national title with a near-perfect 6–1 record. There were no playoffs back then. Macneill returned to the Brier three more times over the next decade (1930, 1932, and 1936) but was never to sip from the Tankard again.

In the interim, the Halifax Curling Club became, in 1928, the first Maritime club to install artificial ice. The club represented the province at the Brier again that year with a team that included two of Macneill's winning team. The Second World War disrupted Brier play for the duration, delaying until 1948 the appearance of Halifax club skip Gerry Glinz, who posted consecutive provincial championships in 1944 and 1945. Third time was a charm for his foursome—G.K. MacIntosh, J.A. Snow, and H.A.Williams—who made their national debut with a different skip in 1946 when the Brier had resumed play. Glinz eventually made the trip, too, but skipping teams from Sydney in 1948 and for Truro in 1955 and 1956. In 1974, its 150th anniversary, the Halifax Curling Club nearly burned down. Whether celebrating the former in any way sparked the latter is unclear, but the club was rebuilt on the same site.

Moving west from Quebec, curling quickly established a foothold in Ontario. Nearly forty thousand people, most of them Scots, settled in Ontario between 1816 and 1823. Some were stonemasons and made their curling stones from granite. Ontario's first curling club was established in Kingston in 1820, and within five years, the game's popularity had spread to Toronto. Curling clubs sprouted all over the province, and the founding of the Toronto Curling Club in 1837 foreshadowed that city's becoming the centre of curling in Ontario. Competition between Quebec and Ontario curlers grew, and in 1859, with the coming of the Grand Trunk Railway, curlers no longer had to travel days by horse and wagon to compete. The only problem was that Quebec curlers insisted on competing with their irons (used widely in Montreal until 1954), while Ontario curlers wanted to use granite rocks. They compromised by playing separate matches using irons against irons and rocks against rocks. Quebec invariably won the games using irons and Ontario the games played with rocks.

Curling spread fairly quickly throughout Ontario in the early part of the nineteenth century. But even though Ontario curling clubs had three times the membership of Quebec clubs, they remained without a policy-making voice until 1874, when they united and joined the Royal Club as the branch of the Province of Ontario.

While the Scottish influence was obviously still felt, as evidenced by the success of their first tour in 1902, its dominance ebbed as other nations grew more involved. When a Canadian-born curler, William Reynolds, won the Denham Medal in 1843, a Toronto newspaper claimed, "Curling may now be considered in this Province a Canadian rather than a Scottish game." That sentiment was echoed in Quebec in 1861, when a French-Canadian (Benjamin Rousseau) won that province's first gold medal in a major curling competition. Even the Scots kept close tabs on the progress and successes of non-Scottish "barbarians" against their clubs. It has been suggested that some of the Canadian curlers nursed a grudge and were highly motivated to defeat the "socially superior and influential" Scots. If so, it's quite probable such motivation increased with the game's westward expansion, where farmers and settlers were as apt to start curling clubs and make it more an equality game than it may have been in the early days back east when merchants and pillars of society dominated the curling scene. If such sentiments grew deeper with each new generation of native-born Canadians, the rules and etiquette of curling ensured that rivalries never led to rifts or rowdiness more closely associated with hockey and other team sports. With each step west, curling just grew more democratic.

There was unbridled passion for curling in the west, where club founders were as likely to be farmers as merchants. Compared to the hazards of pioneer life, and some other sports, curling posed a remarkably low risk to life and limb—provided you didn't go through the ice on a lake—that got even safer when the sport moved indoors. With medical help a long way off, that was a genuine concern for folks who survived by their wits and their labour. Curling was a bit of exercise, a lot of socializing, and unlikely to impair anyone's livelihood. That also meant that the elitism that could sometimes accompany early clubs in Ontario and Quebec gave way to curling as an equality game, which anyone could play, and, increasingly, nearly everyone did.

Manitoba's first settlers arrived in the region in 1812, on the eve of the war against the Americans. With Napoleon Bonaparte running amok in Europe, Canada became a fringe theatre of war. And if loyalty to the British Empire was assumed, Manitobans were about to literally carve their own empire—a curling empire—that remains strong after nearly two hundred years. Taking a page from the Ontario curling book, they carved their first wooden curling stones, substituting hardy oak for the bounteous maple that proved so popular—and durable—in Fergus and other Ontario curling hotbeds.

With more clubs in Manitoba than in Quebec and Ontario combined, the Manitoba Branch of the Royal Caledonian was established in 1888, and curlers from all parts of Canada and the United States flocked to the Winnipeg Curling Club: sixty-two teams participated in the bonspiel that year. As Winnipeg evolved in the geographic centre of the continent, it laid claim to being the centre of the curling universe. Certainly, it seemed at times to virtually own the men's national championship, winning the Brier so many times that Manitoba became known as "a hard province to come out of," meaning simply that there was so much talent there that squads that could have excelled in many other provinces were simply not able to grasp the gold ring on the day it was up for grabs. Winning the Brier, some said, was easier than winning Manitoba. Part of that province's allure lay with clubs like Deer

Lodge, organized in 1918 and quickly known for its "tricky ice." It became the home of the Dominion curling champions in 1947.

Small clubs began to pop up all over Saskatchewan after about 1880. They catered to farmers and featured thatched wooden huts to protect curlers and the natural ice from the snow and wind. Before long, Saskatchewan had more curlers than any other province. Early clubs in Saskatchewan, Alberta, and British Columbia looked to the Manitoba Branch for guidance. Cold winters drove curling indoors, and the bigger clubs began to build indoor rinks after 1840. By 1900, Canadian curling clubs had moved almost exclusively indoors. Indoor rinks and, later, modern ice-making technology brought the sport closer to an art form, eliminating snow, ice bumps, and much of the luck that had previously made up the game.

The *Canadian Encyclopedia* notes that by 1839, when more clubs had been formed, locally made granite curling stones were being advertised in Toronto at $8 a pair. A year later the first book on curling in Canada was published—James Bicket's *The Canadian Curler's Manual*. Intercity matches began in 1835, expanding to interprovincial in 1858. In 1865, at the end of the U.S. Civil War, the first international bonspiel was held between American and Canadian clubs in Buffalo, New York. Much of this progress was aided by the long, cold winters and the availability of innumerable lakes and rivers, ensuring abundant and safe ice on which to enjoy curling. Indeed, these conditions surpassed even those in Scotland, an unusual occurrence for a transplanted sport. In fact, it was often too cold to participate outdoors, and curling fanatics took their sport indoors; members of the Montreal Curling Club were likely the first to do this in 1837. The neighbouring Thistle club constructed an enclosed rink seven years later. Toronto built its first indoor facility in 1859, and others became common across Canada.

During the 1880s and 1890s, until hockey arenas were created, these rinks were used by many fledgling ice hockey teams. By 1910 almost every town in the West had an arena, and Winnipeg was the acknowledged curling centre of Canada. In 1950 it had more curling clubs than Montreal and Toronto combined, and Manitoba had more clubs than Ontario and Quebec. The Flin Flon club was the largest in the world, with more than fifty rinks.

At different points along that timeline, curling became as enlightened as it was equal. If the "copious quantities of whiskey" reputedly consumed at bonspiels were blamed for the delay in welcoming women to curling, several ladies' clubs had sprung up across Canada, dating to 1894 in Montreal. That same year, the Fergus Curling Club celebrated its sixtieth anniversary as the longest continuously operating curling club in Ontario—cited by authors, historians, and the media as a quintessential small-town curling club. Its house has been home to history, tradition, and many, many thousands of local, touring, and guest curlers.

IN THE HACK

HOME SWEEP HOME

I am sitting behind the glass in the Fergus Curling Club with Hugh Black. The morning senior curlers have just left the ice and are mingling with those preparing for the annual Sweetheart Bonspiel, played every Valentine's weekend. I learn that Scottish curlers will be stopping in to play as part of their goodwill tour. But my focus is history, and Black, though not the formal club historian, knows his family tree. In Fergus, that amounts to the same thing. Black is the namesake, four generations removed, of the original Hugh Black who, at age fifty-seven, bundled his wife and thirteen children off to build a new life in a new world and, once here, discovered by accident that maple blocks curl well. He also reasoned that the best place to curl in a wilderness town is on the main street—especially if the main street runs right in front of your tavern. Curlers are a thirsty clan, especially when the temperature dips to –30 degrees Fahrenheit.

Despite his lineage, the Black I am interviewing was not genetically drawn to the sport. He neither curled nor golfed growing up in the most Scottish of Scottish settlements, content to play hockey and baseball. In fact, he was sixty-four when he cast his first stone, drawn to the game by a friend at work who needed a replacement for his team. Black arrived more curious than enthused. He left addicted. A decade later, he plays at every opportunity, a confirmed second-rock man who loves "throwing takeouts" to knock the opponent's rock out of the coloured rings of the target house. Don't we all? Lead players rarely throw take-outs anymore, thanks to the free-guard zone rule, first implemented by the CCA in 1994 and then modified to conform to World Federation standards nearly ten years later. The rule forbids taking out rocks between the hog line and the house until after each side has thrown two rocks, an effort to deter blank ends, when no one counts, to make the game more exciting for the fans and TV audiences. Seconds, however, often get to glee-fully throw the "high hard one" as a result of this rule, as do skips like Harry Fendley, who sniffed at "parking lot weight" and threw "freight train," advising his sweepers, "Sit down, boys, you'll never catch her." We sat. He was right. It was my first inkling, prior to *Men with Brooms*, that granite might shat-ter on impact.

As Black documents seven generations of Black curlers, famil-iar faces pass through the club. George Thomas, who personifies grace and finesse on the ice, and is unflappable under pressure, lobbied many years ago for my schoolboy team to curl as a squad in the men's league. I owe him much. Jim Carter, a former defen-sive lacrosse stalwart, is now the resident pin collector, boasting many thousands and logging as many miles flying and driving to Briers. Club website designer George Loney owns a jacket signed by Shorty Jenkins, the ice-making "King of Swing." His son mocks him as the only parent on the planet who goes to a rock concert and gets the roadie's autograph. Loney shrugs. Others whisper he was at the "real" Woodstock. He knows his rock stars. All urge me to get a copy of Emery Nelson's club history. The former school inspector is in his nineties now and still curl-ing. He is less scary now than when I was seven.

Not all is bliss at the Fergus club. Sam Harrop, whose team, including a blind lead, won the club's 2007 seniors title, laments ice number 8 in a four-sheet club. The lifelong dairy farmer and long-time piper in the town's highland band, who has dabbled in local politics, now makes the ice. His job is to keep three hundred club curlers and their guests happy, a tall order, he deadpans, when you have to replace an entire ice sheet. Harrop lists a seemingly endless litany of woes that befell ice number 2; heart-rending stories of the effort required to tow it out and tow in ice number 8—kept in reserve for just such an emergency. Those failing to grasp that the sheets are numbered 1, 8, 3, and 4 to commemorate the club's founding year are bombarded mercilessly with good-natured ribbing. It's their way of having some fun while sharing their proud history. And everyone feels a little more at home in the house. Ah, yes: "We are curlers, hear us laugh!"

THE THIRD END
ROCKS OF AGES

*C*urling histories dating to the 1930s often cite the Fergus club's contributions to the sport. Some just mention its founding in 1834 and move on, but many provide elaborate details and ascribe great significance to the club's role in the genesis and evolution of the roaring game. It helps to know a little about the Scots who came to the Canadian wilderness to carve out their own Utopia.

Early waves of Scottish immigrants were driven to North America by desperation. The economic depression resulting from the Napoleonic Wars, combined with the sometimes brutal Highland clearances that drove Scottish crofters and farmers into the teeming cities, was a recipe for despair. The gentry members of the Highland Society, based in Edinburgh, sympathized with their plight and worried that many were heading to Canada and the United States lacking any knowledge of what awaited them or the resources they would need to survive. Society member Adam Fergusson, a "gentleman" who enjoyed calling himself a farmer while admitting his tenants actually worked the farm, resolved to visit North America to see for himself what the Scots would find and what they would need. He set sail in February 1831 and kept a journal of his experiences and the cost of his journey in exacting detail. His published journals offered the first glimpse of what awaited the Scots immigrants. In 1833, Fergusson returned to Canada to found a utopia, even if he wasn't exactly sure just where. At first attracted to a low tract on the southern shore of Lake Michigan, he rejected it for being too marshy and being outside the Empire. Sailing east from what would become the city of Chicago, he headed up the Grand River and decided to found his idyll and name it Small Falls for the cataract he found. The settlement was renamed Fergus, in his honour, and that "wee toon," not the Windy City, would cast the first stone in the wilderness.

With the site selected, the Highland Society devoted itself to selecting the right people to populate Fergusson's inland Eden— those most likely to survive, settle, and expand the British Empire in North America were educated, hardworking, prolific, and pious men of good character, and their families. Hugh Black, a successful farmer with a brood of thirteen children, fit the bill on all counts. Arriving in Fergus with more furniture than any other immigrant, Black was persuaded, perhaps with some difficulty, to forsake agriculture for ales and bitters. As every schoolchild educated in Fergus into the middle of the twentieth century knows, Black's tavern was the first building to grace the landscape, just as the Beatty factory produced the most washing machines, and the Tweddle chick hatchery the most hatchlings, in the British Empire. Local lore includes the reputedly likeable young wastrel George Clephane, "the Black Sheep" immortalized by his sister's popular elegy, "The Ninety and Nine," after he fell off his horse (drunk or sober is debated) and died while in the process of turning his life around.

The Anglican church in nearby Elora, whose curling club opened five years after its upstream neighbour's, is home to the silver tea-serving set given by Florence Nightingale to her missionary cousin. Forbidden to marry, he fled to the New World to preach the Good Book; she went to the Crimea to tend wounded troops as the first war nurse.

Fergus men took up arms during the Fenian threat, and Thomson Beattie added his own tragic chapter. After relocating to

Winnipeg, he later toured Europe and the Middle East. At the last minute, he cancelled his return berth on the *Mauritania* to sail home on the unsinkable *Titanic*. One of the few plucked into a lifeboat from the sea, he died of exposure awaiting rescue.

The need for shelter was clear to the pioneering Scots in Fergus in 1834. First to rise was the tavern, followed by the Presbyterian church. The logic to building the tavern first was to provide food and shelter to the tradesmen who were building the town—and a stiff belt on rainy days when they were not. There seems to be some question as to just how much the lodgers enjoyed the Blacks' furniture, as the design of the two-storey log house was altered with an eye to common sense more than comfort. Early accounts recall the workmen taking their meals on the dining room floor. Sitting cross-legged got uncomfortable, so they simply lifted a line of floorboards so they could sit on the floor and dangle their legs through the hole. The floorboard across the gap became their table. Then again, as local historian A.E. Byerly describes the saloon antics in his book *Fergus*, the publican may have had legitimate reasons for keeping his furniture out of sight and his family out of harm's way. All seemed tranquil on sunny days when the tradesmen were able to work, but on rainy days, the bar was crowded and the partying continued long into the night. That was further complicated by a bartender known only as "the Major," who had a knack for inciting arguments and fights among the patrons without ever engaging in the frays he ignited. He is also credited with restoring order and resolving the fracas with an amicable round of drinks. The Major may have been good for business, but, Byerly observes, "He was a dangerous associate for idle young men."

Those antics did nothing to undermine the plan to give Fergus the best possible start by enticing the best possible people. Overall, the evidence suggested that the Highland Society had chosen well. The first settlers were industrious, compassionate to less fortunate Scots who passed through en route to other settlements, and loyal, taking up arms against the rebels in 1837 and the Fenians in 1866. They are also credited by some historians as being, by accident or design, the best curlers on the continent. The first stone was actually made of wood in the debut match played that severe first winter, marked by prolonged cold snaps down to −30 degrees Fahrenheit and four-foot snow drifts. Curling provided an escape from the dreary reality of Canadian winters, just as Samuel de Champlain's "Company of Good Cheer" had helped the early arrivals in New France endure their bleak days and nights. But that curling began as soon as it did may have been dumb luck or happy coincidence.

Curling in Fergus began during a barn-raising bee for Black. The tavern keeper idly tossed a block of maple across the ice and apparently marvelled at its sliding abilities. The first match was staged in front of his tavern—Black was nobody's fool when it came to smart business—with players navigating their stanes through the maze of tree stumps dotting the main street. In his history booklet *One Hundred and Fifty Years of Curling*, published in 1984 to mark the sesquicentennial of the town and the Fergus Curling Club, Emery Nelson notes the first crude blocks, hewn from trees, were later replaced by "bird's-eye" maple fashioned by James Perry on his lathe. Perry fitted the blocks with handles and, when they wore down, weighted them with pieces of iron. In the end, the wooden stones proved more durable than the soft stones collected from the Grand River.

A formal club was formed in 1834. Black was voted charter president, but he stepped aside the following year as he led the drive to make Fergusson president for life. Although the village founder had moved to Waterdown, past Hamilton, initially a four-day stage ride away, Fergusson returned annually to Fergus to compete in a major bonspiel that always seems to have been scheduled for his arrival. Elected club president from 1836 to 1838, he was returned in 1840 as the Hon. Adam Fergusson. Skipping a year, he was then acclaimed perpetual president in 1843, a title he held until 1858. At that point he was named club patron. He died in 1862.

At its creation, the club capped its membership at twenty— roughly a third of the entire village population of seventy—and much of that first curling fraternity was also true family. The Black family had nearly enough children to ice its own eight-curler teams; the club signed up four of Black's sons and two of his sons-in-law. Among the others was James Dinwoodie, perhaps the most ardent curler on the continent, and possibly in the world, as he routinely walked the seven miles from his farm to play, and then returned home the same distance. And even back then, in the dark ages a century before television, there were young people dismissing the sport as "an old man's game." Young Alex Ferrier took to skating, as he never thought he would take to curling. He held out for four years but joined the curling club in 1838. Membership inevitably expanded, but joining the Fergus Curling Club, and at least some of the others that sprung up in Upper Canada in the next few years, was more involved than making a request and paying your dues.

Historian John A. Stevenson's *Curling in Ontario: 1846–1946* chronicles an almost closed society, complete with password and secret handshake. Curling in the nineteenth century was almost exclusively a male domain, bordering on a fraternal secret society. Stevenson states, "A century ago, an aspirant for membership in a club had to be formally proposed by an initiated brother and undergo a scrutiny of his worthiness for admission to the brotherhood," explaining that the candidate had to appear before a "court of initiation" where a "duly qualified brother" read a digest of the "obligations incumbent upon every genuine curler." Upon faithfully swearing his solemn promise, the new brother was advised orally of the "curler's word"—Stevenson said it was never to be written—and a demonstration of the secret handshake known as the "curler's grip" before being formally admitted to the brotherhood of curlers. Fergus was apparently no exception.

Citing club records, Stevenson confirms that "the prescribed ritual was faithfully observed in that stronghold of curling." As evidence, he recounts a resolution on the rules that came out of a meeting held on January 3, 1837: "If at any meeting a member shall be unable when called on to give the curling word and sign, he shall be fined as the majority see fit." The motion carried. The Fergus club was just three years old at that time, and its fraternal brotherhood was underscored six years later by further resolutions passed at the meeting of January 31, 1843:

> That new members (uninitiated) who have not attended this meeting be fined sixpence and old (initiated) one shilling.
>
> That at 10 a.m. on the day of the annual game, the players will meet and be examined as to word and sign in the house, where the dinner is ordered.
>
> Also, that the secretary write the word and a concise description of the sign on a slip of paper, that the same be sealed in the presence of the meeting after having been examined and approved of by the examiners and entrusted to the secretary's care, to be opened for the purpose of verifying the sign at the time and place specified in the previous resolution.

Four years later, the record shows that at the general club meeting of Friday, January 8, 1847, "it was resolved that a grip be introduced into the Society to be held as sacred as the word and sign: likewise that each member on meeting another club for a match at curling must shoulder his broom on the left shoulder."

Lest any of this seem too sinister or elitist, the Fergus records also underscore the club's morality, documenting fines levied against members for on-ice profanity. Fines were imposed per curse with no apparent maximum. Nelson's club history offers the best evidence that blue language was common on the open ice when the curlers moved to the river from the main street.

In 1836, Fergusson was elected club president. After two years, the growing interest in the club was sufficient to warrant drawing up rules, determining the size of the rinks, who had the power to call meetings and admit new members, and who qualified for which type of membership—ordinary and honorary. Winning teams (usually eight to a side, each curler throwing one rock) were the first to score thirty-one points. The club also established rules of conduct for players and decreed that curlers were to provide their own stones, brooms, and shovels.

"Any member conducting himself [all members were male] in an irregular manner or using unbecoming language when engaged in playing shall be fined a penalty not exceeding 2/6 as the majority of the club present may deem right to inflict, and may be prohibited from playing or from joining the club in any way until the same is paid to the secretary," according to Nelson's review of the club minutes. Evidently, the one-cent fine levied at the club's charter meeting two years earlier was not doing much to curtail the profanity, as this marked a significant increase just two years later. The fine would rise again in the near future, another indication that no imposed morality, no financial penalty, no Temperance Hall or movement was going to squeeze temperance from any intemperate Scot. Certainly there was precedent that accepted "a wee dram" of whiskey as readily as outlawing profanity. As the first matches on the main street were played directly in front of Black's tavern, to ease the biting chill, curlers would adjourn to the bar every few ends to enjoy the heat of the fire and a glass of firewater. When the games moved, first to the beaver meadow behind St. Andrew's church, then to the Washing Green (where the sheep were washed before shearing) on the river, the curlers began secreting their own bottles, bringing their creature comforts of home to the house. Indeed, more than one member is said to have paid his dues in hard liquor rather than cold cash.

Beyond those house records and local histories, the Fergus club's contribution to curling in Canada has been chronicled by several independent authors and historians, notably David B. Smith with his illustrated history of the game and earlier works, including Robin Welsh's international history of curling, and Stevenson's celebration of the first hundred years of curling in Ontario, written immediately after the Second World War. Ironically, that classic work begins at 1846—a dozen years after the first maple block sailed through the tree stumps still dotting the town's main street.

"The Fergus Club...is worthy of more particular notice," Smith wrote in his international history of curling. Noting that the hardwood blocks were "turned to the proper shape," he said they were "found to answer the purpose, except when the ice is dull." He also applauded the experiment to load them with lead, saying that "decided improvement" gave them size and weight consistent with actual curling stones.

"The example of the Curlers in Fergus, in constituting a club, ought to be followed in every neighbourhood where there are players sufficient for one rink," Smith concluded. "The permanency of the game and the opportunities of playing, may thus be secured in places where, without such arrangement, the greatest difficulty might be experienced in bringing the players together."

And the Fergus curlers never seemed to lack an occasion to get together to throw rocks. For years, the first match held on the day of the club's annual meeting was between the town's bachelors and its benedicts (married men). Black the tavern keeper later donated a pair of curling handles, and Fergusson awarded a medal to heighten the competition. The losers paid for the traditional meal of "beef and greens" at the tavern, where the curlers could replay their games and extol their play and that of their opponents in post-meal speeches. One address is particularly memorable for its poignancy and for its tragic ending.

In 1847, a schism in the town church divided the congregation. Once passions had cooled, a New Year's Day bonspiel became an annual event between the Auld Kirk (now St. Andrew's Presbyterian) and the Free Kirk (now Melville United). At stake was a barrel of oatmeal, which was to be distributed to the poor with the loser bearing the cost. As for the curlers, winners and losers sat down to a more traditional meal of beef and greens. William Weems, a shepherd in Scotland's Grampian Mountains before landing in Fergus, skipped the Auld Kirk team. Described as "a fine specimen of a breed of men noted for their intelligence and courage," he was reportedly recognized by Fergusson and others of high standing as a man of "genuine worth." He was an ardent curler and often proved his worth on the ice, no doubt a striking figure in his long beard and tartan plaid. In the early 1850s, Weems won the annual match with a fine shot on his last rock in the final end. Following the banquet that night, he replied to a toast by Fergusson with a passion that hushed the boisterous crowd of curlers.

> Sir Adam Drummond and friends, I hae tae thank you. I am gettin' gey auld and stiffand yeken I'm no guid at speakin'. The tapple-tursie o' work has been mine maist

of ma days with aday's play moo and then—wi' the
bools in simmer and the curlin' in winter. And of a' the
money games I hae played since comin' tae this country,
this day's game caps them a' for rale curling. The ice
was fine and the drawin' grand. And of a' the shots for
steady winnin' gie me a canny draw. I'll no misca a
frisky run whiles, if we could a' dae it like Whistlewood
of Mattha there. And let me tell you there were no mony
chips or wicks missed by either of them this day. The
game was oors at the end, to be sure, but with naething
to brag o'. Anither breath and the Free Kirk would be
sitting here and us there the nicht. There's nae game like
curling. It's an honest sensible game. It's an honest
couthie game is curling, that we Kirk folk are a better
for taking a spiel at whiles.

And forbye there's muckle o' life to learn frae it. We
a' ken the slipls and fa's in it, the chancy shots and a'
that. When ower muckle room is gi'en a stane and it
gangs birling awa' through the hoose, a waif strae whiles
will grip the bottom o't and drag it to a stop on the
snuff. We've a' seen that. Anither stane cast asklant will
whiles lose its turn and wind in shankshaped tae the
very bit. But anither stane cast exactly tae the broom
will no come near the bit. And whiles the maist carefu'
o' curlers will slip their foot oot o' the hackie and spil a'.
(Ay, said the Minister, taking a pinch of snuff from
Wallfield's box.) Thae things hae happened this day and
it's my belief that sic mishaps are aye gaun on ilka day in
the game o' life. As Robbie Burns says, "The best laid
plans o' mice and men gang aft agley." Aye dae they.
Aye, my friends, like the game o' life, the game of curling is a chancy struggle at best. In the middle of the

game o' life we meet wi' disappointments, we fecht
for bread, we wrangle, we play pranks and we chase
baubles. Near the end o't, in the glimmer o' auld age,
we dream dreams o' the game we hae played. At last we
slip awa' like the snaw in the thaw: to foregather aroon
the Great Tee abune, and oor ain bit place here is kent
nae mair forever.

At the end of his moving speech, Weems sang his favourite
song, "The Land o' the Leal," wiped his brow, and slowly sat
down to thunderous applause for his analogy of the games of life,
and of curling. The old shepherd's comment that both were
chancy proved tragically prophetic. Walking home alone after
midnight, within steps of the humble cottage he had shared with
his wife until her death, Weems was struck a mortal blow by a
cutter sled's runner when the horse bolted. Knocked into a snow-
bank, he stumbled to his home and slumped into his armchair
near the fireplace. He was later found dead in the chair, clutching
a portrait of his wife.

"Such was the touching and dramatic end of a grand old Scot
and one of the best curlers of Fergus in its early days," Stevenson
concludes.

If the tragedy dampened the spirits of the curlers, it did not
deter the spirit of competition. The Kirk rivalry eventually lapsed
but was revived by both congregations for the club's sesquicentennial celebration in 1984. On other earlier occasions, Tories
curled against Grits in a presumably good-natured political arena,
and, in 1883, the local bankers challenged the doctors and
lawyers. The latter, calling themselves "the Professionals," won
that match, then defended their title successfully against a challenge from the tavern and hotel owners. Fergus was becoming the
model for other clubs, but if it stood first in those hearts, if it

could claim to be a premier, even a pre-eminent club, it could not claim to be the first in the province.

While Kingston has the unarguable claim to being the oldest curling club in Ontario, and has been granted the "Royal" appellation, Fergus has squeezed its way into the record books by claiming to be the longest continuously operating club. The story goes that Kingston briefly closed its doors at some point for some reason. Details remain sketchy, but it left a port for the Fergus club to sail through. In the wake of those two historic clubs, others sprang up in Flamborough (1835); Toronto and Milton (1836); Galt, Guelph, and Scarborough (1838); Paris (1843); and Elora (1839), about five miles downstream from Fergus. Others followed in Bowmanville, Ancaster, Hamilton, Woodbridge, and Dundas.

Citing these fifteen clubs as the provincial pioneers, Stevenson notes that Galt was nearly as purely Scottish as Fergus and cites an early account by contemporary historian James Young to show that the virtual neighbours in the wilderness had something else in common—their first stones were actually wooden. Young offered a brief glimpse of that first game, curled on Altrive Lake, about two miles west of Galt: "They made blocks out of the maple tree, putting in pieces of iron as handles and, although labouring under some disadvantages, the survivors describe it as a jolly and long-to-be-remembered meeting." It echoed the earlier Fergus experience. In fact, the reputation of the town's wooden blocks was so good that the record shows curlers in Hamilton ordered a sheet of them.

As road and rail transportation improved, clubs could travel to more distant bonspiels. Fergus sent five squads to the first large-scale bonspiel, played on Toronto Bay in 1859. The event drew teams from London to Montreal, and the Fergus contingent was larger than some from far larger centres. In the early years, Fergus curlers lost the occasional game but rarely lost a match.

Even when outlying clubs improved enough to become serious competition, Stevenson confirms they continued to win more than they lost, posting a record of sixty-eight wins and forty-nine losses between 1858 and 1900.

In 1869, the Fergus club, which predated the creation of Scotland's Grand Caledonian Club, joined the Canadian Branch of the mother club.

There were other international links to Fergus, as local four-somes first competed against U.S. teams in 1865, during a break between the American Civil War and the Fenian raids into Canada. Often successful at the regional and district levels, the club's greatest triumph came at the close of the century, when David Mennie, John Graham, Robert Kerr, John Bayne, W.A. Richardson, Thomas J. Hamilton, John Mennie, and H.S. Michie won the 1899 Ontario Tankard, back then the symbol of curling supremacy. Stevenson reports, in his history of Ontario curling, that, when the victorious team arrived home, the entire village turned out to cheer them at the train station. Stevenson records the town's "great day" in his history of Ontario curling, writing, "Preceded by the town's brass band and escorted by 100 torch-bearers, they marched to the town hall, where they were raised shoulder high by strong arms and carried to a platform amid the tumultuous cheers of the assembled crowd." A sumptuous banquet followed at the American Hotel and "a mighty spate of oratory" gushed for hours.

"It was the greatest day of glory in the history of Fergus," Stevenson concluded, "and, if in the shades of old Adam Fergusson, Hugh Black and other founding fathers of the club, were able to observe the rejoicings, they must have felt that their pioneer labours had borne rich fruit."

While interpreting the sentiments of the spirit world can be chancy at best, there seems no doubt that the Fergus Curling Club had produced men with stamina equal to their skill. Hamilton was seventy-seven and Kerr seventy-three, but both were still curling when the club celebrated its centennial in 1934, skipped by elder statesman James Anderson, who at age eighty-four was the oldest competitor on the ice. Their squad was rounded out by Andrew C. Steele, a mere kid of sixty-nine. The club celebrated its first one hundred years by winning its own grand bonspiel against teams from thirty-eight other clubs. The win came on a spectacular shot. Trailing Durham 12–9 in the final end, with the three of the visitors' stones in the house, skip E.C. Codling threw a triple takeout to score five and win by two rocks.

The intervening century had done nothing to dim the town's pride in its curling club. Just as many prairie towns would later claim, the club was one of the first buildings to go up in the new settlement. In fact, in Fergus, it seems to have been built second only to Black's tavern. "Before Fergus had a church, a school or an industry of any kind, the first sporting association was formed," wrote local historian Hugh Templin, noting that it was still alive and thriving.

The club continues to attract members and media notice seventy years later. Both TVO and CanWest Global have produced recent television documentaries on the Fergus Curling Club. That may be flattering to the locals, and informative for many across the rest of the country, but Fergus curlers have visible reminders of their heritage. Today, as in the beginning, there is a Hugh Black, generations removed from the original but an equally avid curler. In the end, the longevity of his family may be the most compelling statement on the success of curling in that "wee toon" astride the Grand River in southern Ontario. To put the Fergus curling experience and significance into broad perspective, consider the scores of clubs across Canada celebrating significant anniversaries measured in decades. In Fergus, they count their past glories by generations. Juniors Tayler and Adam Black are the seventh generation of family curlers, dating to the original Hugh. Given time, and the laws of nature, his great-great-great-great-grandsons will introduce an eighth generation to their ancestral home in the house.

If they do, they'll find better ice and warmer quarters than old Hugh could have ever imagined; the indoor club, first discussed in 1870, was built in 1879. The club moved to its current location, originally adjacent to the arena, which was touted, in its heyday, as the best box lacrosse arena in the country, next to Maple Leaf Gardens. The next generation will also find competitors that the charter club members did not envision. Sir Walter Scott and Robbie Burns may have indeed proclaimed curling to be "a manly sport," but the descendants of the Scots in Fergus have shown their enlightenment. After a mere 120 years, the men of the Fergus Curling Club invited women to join in 1954. Few had curled and a couple of the men offered to teach them the game, prompting the editorial writer at the weekly *Fergus News Record* to joke about the prospect of men teaching women how to sweep. It was all, like the game itself, good fun. Scott, who penned *Ivanhoe*, may have been particularly cheered to see that chivalry was not dead in Adam Fergusson's Utopia. Perhaps just a tad slow in coming.

Women had curled against the touring Scotsmen on their first North American visit in 1903. The women won. Those goodwill tours continue to this day, with Scottish teams visiting Fergus and Fergus curlers travelling there, most often touring with Rotarians. But the goodwill doesn't stop there. Bill Thompson and his wife, Helen, have been fixtures at the Fergus club for decades. He began curling in 1947, and he is still curling nearly sixty years later, still hitting the broom. All that changed is that he can't see the broom anymore. Thompson is legally blind, robbed of his sight by vascular degeneration. In just three months, his vision plummeted from 20/20 to 20/400. It looked like his curling would bottom out nearly as fast. Then someone got the idea to hold the broom in the near house, close to the hack. Thompson worried more about hitting him than hitting the broom, something that didn't help him concentrate on his shot. The answer came from another blind curler at a bonspiel in nearby Ayr, who approached Fergus skip Jack Duthie and offered to buy him the drink he owed him. Duthie was confused. He told the man he had not played against him. The errant curler chuckled and apologized, explaining, "Yep, I'm blind."

That accidental encounter led to a conversation. Duthie learned that the blind curler could distinguish a flashlight beam held on a broomstick wrapped with florescent tape. He coaxed Thompson to come back out to try this latest solution. Indeed, he could see the light beam. And he continues to curl. He may be unique in Fergus, but he's far from alone in the curling world. In fact, the house is full of curlers proving they can compete with anyone, given a fair shot.

IN THE HACK

A SENSE OF COMMUNITY

$\mathscr{I}$am attending my first national curling championship, where I meet on-ice official Lynne Jambor. She has a treasure trove of curling anecdotes, including the time she had to double as a play-by-play announcer. She recounts the event in fine dramatic fashion, her excitement building as she details the progress of the rock. It is a difficult shot—to be perfect, the rock must wick off another stone to roll into the house. As the drama built, her fever-ish monologue proved too much for the shooter to bear. Throwing his arms in the air, he covered his eyes, yelling, "I can't watch! I can't watch!"

The overwrought curler has been blind since birth.

It's a great story and a glowing testament to the hearts and humour of all curlers who find that setbacks can make things harder, but not impossible. A lost sense can inspire an indomitable spirit, and while those thus deprived may concede it can be harder, most refuse to accept that life dealing you cards off the bottom of the deck makes things impossible. Perhaps more than any other group, those deemed "disabled" parlay their challenges into a marvellous sense of humour. It helps sustain them and others, like Jambor, who rejoice in their company.

I've been on the ice with curlers who are blind or have intellectual disabilities. What I learned there has prompted me to attend this national championship for deaf curlers. Jambor—who has worked across much of Canada with curlers who are blind, deaf, use a wheelchair, or have intellectual disabilities—confirms everything I have learned to love and respect about these curlers. She admires their abilities, their accomplishments, and, above all, their marvellous sense of humour. These qualities are not confined to Canadians or to curlers. Check out the U.S. Amputee Hockey website and you'll see kids in full gear, grinning ear to ear over their motto: "Some assembly required."

The overall message is clear: just give them a chance. That's underscored by Jambor and Jim Barber, the head official, and his wife, Helen, who have flown in from Vancouver. Helen is descended from the Curling Campbells (Ontario Clan), one of whom bequeathed gin breakfasts to the Brier. All know their curling. Both agree with Jambor that you bandy about labels like "challenged" or "disabled" at your peril with these athletes. They are curlers. Period. If you don't believe it, challenge them to a game. Wheelchair curlers in particular have kicked some pretty elite ass over the years.

There is little difference between this deaf championship and any other national bonspiel. Fewer voices, perhaps, but the banter is there and it's just as lively. The rocks rumble, the brushes scour, and the pipers are cued to open and close the event. Front ends accompany the rocks down the ice, glancing at the house for the skip's commands, conveyed by hand or broom motion. The intensity mirrors that of any other major bonspiel. The smiles are as infectious, the grins as broad, the frowns as deep, the pressure as palpable, and the shrieks of joy or sighs of lament just as evident. All the familiar noises are there, plus one—the humming air turbulence in the clubhouse where scores of speeding hands sign some very animated conversations. If anyone is out of place in this curling clubhouse, it's me. Yet, I'm welcomed warmly by the organizers, the officials, and the curlers, and gain a healthy new respect for yet another group who ask only for the chance to compete.

THE FOURTH END

A LEVEL PLAYING FIELD

A state-of-the-art Paralympic training centre:	$3.9 million
One wheelchair modified for curling:	$5,000 to $7,000
Transatlantic airfare to Italy:	Likely less than Toronto to Moncton
One Paralympic gold medal:	Priceless!

The IX Winter Paralympic Games, hosted by Turin, with wheelchair curling played in the new centre at nearby Pinerolo, confirmed once and for all that athletes can rise to any challenge. The glory is no less warming, the achievement no less thrilling, for those unable to crouch in a hack or stand atop a podium. Canada's gold-medal performance in curling's Paralympic Games debut was cheered and toasted throughout the curling world. Certainly the Canadian curling nation took great pride that Canada won gold, but everyone rejoiced that another international venue had opened its house to curling and welcomed home curlers who just happen to shoot from an elevated hack.

The 7–6 win over Scotland in the traditional six ends was "third time's a charm" for Canadian Chris Daw, from London, Ontario, on the heels of edging Norway 5–4 in the semifinal. (Sweden then beat Norway 10–3 to win bronze.) The veteran skip has been a fixture on the team, along with alternate Karen

Blachford, also from London, since the debut 2002 World Wheelchair Championships in Sursee, Switzerland. Canada won silver that first year—falling just short of gold when Britain drew to the button for the 7–6 win on its last rock. The Canadians won bronze in 2004 on their second outing to Sursee, where coach Amy McAninch iced an entire team of London curlers—Daw, Blachford, Bruce McAninch, and Jim Primavera—to edge England 6–5. Frank Duffy's Scottish squad capped an undefeated appearance by doubling up 6–3 on the defending champions from Switzerland.

In Italy, the team iced by coach Joe Rea—Daw and Blachford from London (equipment manager Trevor Kerr was also from London), and Gary Cormack, Gerald Austgarden, and Sonja Gaudet, all from British Columbia—led by two and stole another in the last end to win gold when defending world champion Duffy missed his last-rock takeout and a possible four-ender. This was a rare miss for the defending world champion who had won his second consecutive title scoring two with the hammer in the final end to edge Denmark 7–5 at the Braehead Curling Club in Glasgow. Canada missed the podium for the first time that year, so the gold must have felt particularly good this time out. Daw admitted it was the highlight of his thirty-seven years—not a bad record for someone expected to live six weeks at birth. "That's curling," he told Canadian Press. "On any given day a stone can do what it's supposed to do...or what it's not supposed to do." Yes, that certainly sounds like curling as all curlers have come to love it.

Curling is just the latest in a list of sports Daw has tackled in a career that listed him as the "fastest wheelchair athlete on the planet" in 1986. He told the media that he will continue with curling because it's a sport you can play forever. Daw may have a special interest in qualifying again for Vancouver in 2010—his parents and three children may finally see him compete internationally. It augurs well that Vancouver Mayor Sam Sullivan joined Whistler Mayor Ken Melamed at the Paralympic Closing Ceremonies in Turin—marking the first time that two mayors accepted the official handover of the Paralympic flag. Melamed flew the flag in Whistler on March 24. Sullivan seems equally supportive of the Paralympic movement—unfurling the Paralympic flag atop a special eighty-foot pole beside the Olympic flag at Vancouver City Hall in June, where they will fly side by side until the 2010 Olympic and Paralympic Winter Games. Vancouver is the first host city to honour the Paralympic movement in this visible way.

The addition of wheelchair curling to the existing Paralympic winter venues—Alpine and Nordic skiing as well as ice-sledge hockey—had been in the works for some time and seems a natural extension from the earlier world championships. A Canadian national championship debuted in November 2003, and wheelchair curling made its first appearance at the B.C. Winter Games hosted by the town of Greater Trail in February 2006. But the 2010 Games have given unprecedented impetus to drive the program forward. The sport is played in sixteen countries. The key requirements are that the teams comprise men and women and that the game must be played without sweeping. Wheelchair curling proved to be a popular debut sport in Turin, and supporters in British Columbia seem determined to build on that early success. The provincial government granted $3.9 million to the City of Kimberley to build a state-of-the-art Paralympic athletic training centre. It will be the first in Canada and one of the few in the world. Kimberley mayor Jim Ogilvie told the media that the city will also upgrade a ski run and improve other facilities to meet Paralympic standards for all five sanctioned sports, as the biathlon will make its debut at the Whistler Paralympic Games.

These changes should increase the number of participants from the twelve hundred—six hundred of them athletes—from forty countries that were at Turin. All projects are to be completed by 2008. The Royal Canadian Mint also waded in, producing athlete medals and coins. Curling was the first sport to be featured at the February 2007 product launch; a coin for wheelchair curling was released in July.

Another sign that the Paralympic Games are hitting the mainstream is that the athletes now have their own hall of fame. Well, like the Canadian Curling Hall of Fame, it exists only in cyberspace. It may pose no threat yet to the vast holdings of the Turner Curling Museum in Weyburn, Saskatchewan, but the Paralympic Hall of Fame is sponsored by Visa, so presumably there is money available to expand as more athletes are enshrined. No curlers yet, but then they've played at only one Paralympic Games so far. It's all in keeping with the forward-looking motto devised by Sir Philip Craven, president of the International Paralympic Committee: "We can only make progress if we ensure that the athletes are at the centre of everything we do."

The future bodes well for international curling, with Daw and Brad Gushue each winning gold and Calgary's Shannon Kleibrink chipping in a bronze medal at Turin. Daw's gold was one of thirteen medals won by Canadian Paralympic athletes—good enough to finish in the top six; Gushue's and Kleibrink's medals were two of twenty-four Canadian medals, our highest medal count ever in a Winter Olympics, good enough to rank third among all nations. Those impressive numbers led to a formal federal reception for the Canadian Olympic and Paralympic athletes and the personal heartfelt appreciation of Prime Minister Stephen Harper, Sport Minister Michael Chong, and Minister of International Trade, the Pacific Gateway and the Vancouver–Whistler Olympics David Emerson. There is still work to be done. Canadian Paralympic

Committee President Henry Wohler hopes to get more athletes involved and more fans in the stands. He'll likely do it. The Paralympians are getting very good at getting their message out; the Canadian Public Relations Society named the association's Turin promotion—"FEEL THE RUSH"—one of the best marketing communications programs of the past year.

Globe and Mail curling columnist Bob Weeks, who has also authored a couple of popular books on the sport, had written prior to the 2004 Nokia Brier that curling was becoming more accessible, citing the "championship runs" by Special Olympics and wheelchair curlers playing out behind the scenes of better publicized provincial playdowns in Saskatoon.

"They're not likely to receive the same coverage or play to sold-out arenas, as will the Brier participants in Saskatoon next month," Weeks wrote, "but they are evidence that curling is spreading beyond its traditional boundaries."

In fact, history would be made the following week when curling made its debut as a medal sport at the Canadian Special Olympics hosted by Prince Edward Island, what Weeks termed "a testament to how fast the roaring game is growing among Special Olympians." Not bad for a program that had been formalized fewer than five years earlier. With support and formal assistance from the national office of the CCA right up to chief executive Dave Parkes—his daughter, Allyson, was then curling with the Special Olympics athletes at the City View and other Ottawa curling clubs—the effort received a further boost when the Ontario Curling Association came on board, giving the athletes access to other clubs in the province. Increasingly, Special Olympics athletes were finding a house to call home.

The social aspect was important, but Weeks also saw a perfect match between event and athlete "because the game is easy to learn, not overly taxing physically and takes place in a confined, safe area." Noting its blend of social and competitive opportunities, Parkes agreed, noting that curling was "perfectly suited for Special Olympians for the same reasons it's well-suited for all Canadians."

Allyson Parkes and her teammates had been the subject of a newspaper feature article a few years earlier as they prepared to head to the Special Olympics in Charlottetown. The story made it clear that while winning was important, for the curlers and their coaches it was just part of the larger thrill of competing, just being on the ice, feeling welcomed at the club by the other members. To be sure, there were frowns and frustrations with missed shots and lost ends, but the smiles that first flashed during the warm-ups never disappeared for long. These young athletes were having a ball, learning a game, and playing it well.

Every week for two years, those pioneering teams of aspiring Special Olympics athletes had stretched and swayed to thumping rock music at the City View and the Ottawa Curling Club clubhouses before heading onto the ice. Marian Dupont had started the City View program after volunteering at the 2000 Canada Winter Games, hosted by Ottawa. That experience made her aware that programs existed for curlers with intellectual disabilities, but also that none existed in Ottawa. Back then, six provinces iced teams. Both Ontario squads came from the north; there were no other programs in the province. Dupont didn't read too much into that, figuring it was likely just a case that no one had thought to start it elsewhere.

An avid curler since she was lured to the sport in Quebec City years earlier by husband Pierre, Dupont set to rectify the oversight. The early results were very gratifying and the growth amazing, as both participation and popularity soared. The number of Ottawa curlers mushroomed from five, in 2001, to nearly forty within a few years. That's enough for local competition, but there are now also enough curlers and clubs in nearby centres for each to host its own bonspiel. The Ottawa curlers began travelling across Eastern Ontario—to Pembroke, Kingston, and Belleville. And they loved it. Each squad played two games, then everyone adjourned off-ice to savour the post-match socializing that is the hallmark of the sport and one of the key aspects that sets it apart from all other competitive contests.

Whatever unique challenges these curlers may face, they share what seem to be the twin universal loves of all curlers at all skill levels everywhere—bonspiels and takeout weight. It is their love of the latter that routinely prompted Dupont to clarify, before those early sessions to practise their robust takeouts, that she was looking for weight that knocks the rock out of the house—not across the parking lot. The curlers laughed in chorus, a few tossing back their own one-liners, before dutifully trooping out onto the ice with the Duponts and the other volunteer coaches. All of the coaches have taken the Special Olympics instructional course; Marian and Gord Stockdale are also certified by the CCA, through the Curl Ontario provincial body, to teach the sport. Back then, Gord Stockdale candidly admitted he was enjoying the experience, but had one eye on the future when he could start curling with his first granddaughter, probably by age six.

In a way, they're all family on the ice in this program. There's a special bond between the athletes and their coaches. In his second year of curling, Douglas Beckett named them as the major reason he kept coming back each week, saying, "They make it fun." The coaches are equally fond of their charges and that has extended to the club at large. Dupont—"Coach Marian"—had initially asked for free ice from City View. That was granted, but once the curlers showed up, their enjoyment was so infectious that the club promptly adopted them as members—right down to a special fee for all the aspiring Special Olympics athletes.

That sense of family assumes a more literal application for some. Scott McEwen liked all the coaches but admitted harbouring a special bond with one of the new instructors—his dad, Norm. Then in his fourth year of curling, Scott explained that he began after watching his father curl at Lansdowne Park years earlier. His dad seemed to enjoy it and he grabbed his chance when Dupont started the program, allowing father and son to curl together at a time when the Ottawa curlers were preparing to make history at the Ontario Winter Games, in Barrie – the first event to officially recognize curling as a Special Olympics event. That set the stage for the 2004 Canada Games slated for Charlottetown, when a full slate of teams from across Canada was possible for the first time. While everyone wanted to be picked to curl at Barrie, those who missed the cut were philosophical. There would be another time and they'd try again. In fact, opportunities seem to be expanding faster than anyone had initially thought possible.

If social curling had been the foundation of the program, there was also true competition. Between draws at the 2004 Ontario men's final in Owen Sound, Special Olympics athletes vied for their own trophy. The ultimate goal is to get curling accepted as a medal sport at an International Special Olympics. The organizers of the 2005 Special Olympics Winter Games held in Nagano, Japan, declined the opportunity to launch curling in the Special Olympics as Nagano did for the Olympic Games in 1998. Dupont pinned her hopes on the top contenders for the 2009 Special Olympics.

After Charlottetown, where Ontario contributed four of the sixteen Special Olympics curling teams that competed, Dupont took a breather and headed for the world championships in Europe, then continued on to Moscow. The Russians were delighted to have a Canadian curling delegation visit their two-sheet club. In one of those "small world" moments, she heard her name called as she entered the Ice Plant, the only true curling club in all of Russia, among numerous converted hockey arenas, and turned to see Fred Boyce from the Canadian Embassy. They had worked together years earlier when he was involved with the junior program at the Richmond Curling Club, just south of Ottawa. That's where she had also met Richard Fraser and had encouraged him to become involved in wheelchair curling after a tree-cutting accident had cost him the use of his legs.

Fraser began curling about thirty years ago, when he was in his mid-twenties. A devoted farmer, his introduction to the sport came through a local junior farmers program that rented ice each Sunday evening in the Metcalfe Curling Club, less than an hour's drive east of Richmond. He learned to love the game as much as he loved farming and began coaching when his son and daughter began curling at the Richmond club. There was no master plan, he explained; he was just another parent getting involved with his kids' sport. Some dads coach hockey or ball; he coached curling. All went well until Boxing Day 1997, when he decided it was time to cut down a tree on his property. The last thing he remembers is the tree falling in the direction he had planned; he recalls nothing of the next four days. He was told by his family and the doctors that a large branch had caught him from behind, striking him just below the shoulders. In medical terms, he had a T5 fracture of the spine; in plain English, he had two smashed vertebrae—a broken back. Fraser could still use his arms, but he couldn't move his legs. He accepted that he would never curl again.

Fraser was still trying to run the family farm with his two brothers, an expansive two thousand acres where they milked about 170 dairy cattle and grew various cash crops. Everyone urged him to slow down, take life a little easier. He'd worked hard all his life; it was time now to learn to relax. Dupont figured it was also a good time for him to learn how to curl from a wheel-chair. Fraser wasn't sure what to think when she first broached the idea. She explained that the sport was becoming popular in Europe and there was a movement to get it established in Canada. She knew Fraser primarily through his work with the Richmond juniors and thought him a good candidate. That was in late 1998. "Then," Fraser says, chuckling, "Marian disappeared." When he heard back from her in the fall of 2001, much had happened. The Europeans had staged a successful World Games for wheelchair curlers and had invited Canada to assemble a team for the 2004 competition. Dupont advised Fraser that there was a movement to form a team under the auspices of the Ontario and Canadian Curling associations. The event would be staged in 2002 in Switzerland, and, if he made the team, it would be all expenses paid. She urged him to get involved. Fraser agreed to give it a try.

Tom Ward and Pat Reid arrived from Toronto to explain the process and to meet potential team members. Those who made the cut would be playing six-end games. There would be no sweepers. Ward would coach. It was the first time Fraser had met him, but he knew Reid, a former president of the CCA through her work with the junior program back when he was coaching in Richmond. The rest of the team—Daw, Blachford, Primavera, and Don Bell—hailed from London, Sarnia, and Toronto, making it easiest for them to train in centrally located London. Fraser, the sole selection from Eastern Ontario, was too far away to make as many of the sessions. That logistical problem pales by Turin standards, when curlers from Ontario and British Columbia tried out for the Paralympic team. But back then, it was enough to relegate Fraser to fifth-player status when they headed overseas. It's a compliment to the man that not only was he content just to have made the team, but also paid to have his family accompany him as he embarked on an adventure beyond anything he had imagined in his earlier curling days. The Canadians won silver—an incredible feat for five individuals thrown together just months before the event.

By any standard, the final game played in Sursee in January 2002 against the host team was a thriller. Leading the Swiss team 6–4 heading into the final end, Daw drew twenty centimetres too far, leaving the door open for Swiss skip Urs Bucher to draw for three, upsetting Canada 7–6. Scotland won bronze, blanking Sweden 6–0, and returned to Sursee to become world wheelchair champions in 2004. The Canadians won bronze.

Fraser identified a distinct difference in techniques in 2002. Based on his observations, the fact the Swiss had to draw rather than make a takeout may have helped them win the gold medal. The Canadian and American teams used the curling stick to make their shots. The Europeans leaned over the lowered arm of their wheelchair to deliver by hand. Each had its strengths and weaknesses. Using the stick, Fraser found, allowed him to line up his rock on the skip's broom and any rocks in the house. He favoured an extended stick, which allowed him to grip the shaft with both hands, raise his arms over his head to pull the stick back, and shove from there to give his shots greater force. The leverage of the stick allowed the Canadians to dominate the takeout game. For the Europeans pushing their rocks, throwing takeout often meant losing their line and missing their shot.

Basically, wheelchair curlers have a three-foot arc, and getting the same force that a curler standing in the hack can produce with a push-off is possible, but difficult. Upper body strength becomes a huge factor for heavy throwing weight, particularly when there are no sweepers to help the rock along. Those who consistently make their shots must be among the best shooters in the world because they get no help to compensate for line or speed as their rock curls down the ice.

Fraser played in a couple of the games to the delight of his family in the stands. Whether he ever gets to take a second shot, he has happily resumed playing on weekend afternoons at the Ottawa Recreation Association facility. He's even dabbled with trying to improve the game. With no sweeping, basically curlers shoot their two rocks, then "sit around and freeze" until their next shots are played. Fraser experimented with pairing up two wheelchair curlers with two able-bodied curlers to make the game go faster and to add another dimension to the sport. It seemed to work well but he admits he has no way of knowing if his idea will catch on with the powers that be. Fraser isn't alone in trying to think of ways to speed up the game and broaden its appeal, particularly at the grassroots level. Kelowna, British Columbia, has explored new formats in its "Sweepless in Seattle" bonspiel.

Event organizer Eric Eales concluded a few things in the wake of the October 2005 bonspiel, which featured the debut of two Alberta teams playing against squads from the B.C. lower mainland and the Okanagan. In the two-on-two tournament, each pair played four one-hour, four-end games, earning ten points for a win, five points for a tie, and one point for each end won and each point scored. It was a big hit, and while Eales conceded that able-bodied teams have natural roles for four curlers, pairs works well for wheelchair curling, "especially if members of the other team are prepared to assist with rock wrangling and chair bracing." He also found that having curlers throw four rocks each allowed non-skips to become more involved in the game, causing less sitting around. In short, the game moved faster. "Perhaps team formation and different formats will help our game grow," he says, "and success at the elite level will come from strong grassroots participation." Bottom line, Eales likely speaks for many when he concludes, "It is my hope that as more competitive events are held, and social bonds established, we will continue to work together to grow our sport."

Like Fraser's, the idea seems sound, and a possible solution to one of the problems inherent with wheelchair curling. With little or no sensation in their lower extremities, curlers run the risk of freezing without realizing they are cold. That's just one of the messages hammered home in the detailed coaching manual produced by Curl Ontario and Curl B.C. Those provinces staged the first Canadian national championships in December 2003, pitting two teams from the East against two from the West. The Canadian curlers reportedly practise three or four times a week, honing their skills and strategy by playing in a club league near London. There was interplay in Fraser's time too as Mike Harris, George Karrys, and other Olympic curlers dropped by for an exhibition match. Harris also recalls the event, conceding the wheelchair curlers kicked his butt.

Both the Special Olympics and wheelchair curling movements are growing, across Canada and around the world. The Canadian Spinal Research Organization (CSRO) and its flagship "Shoot for a Cure" fundraising campaign originally focused on hockey, in partnership with big-name NHL superstars. Now, there is an entire Shoot for a Cure Curling division, aiming at drawing more support from Canada's 1,100 curling clubs. In early 2004, Bruno Schallberger, chairman of the World Wheelchair Curling Championship, confirmed the worldwide numbers—Korea had ten wheelchair curlers; Canada and the United States had twelve each; Sweden had ten; Norway, Finland, and England had fifteen each; Wales and Italy had eight each; Germany had six; Australia and Bulgaria had seven each; and Russia had twelve. Switzerland, the first champions, had thirty, and Scotland, home of the 2004 world wheelchair champions, had fifty. That growth no doubt played a role in wheelchair curling's making its full-medal debut at the 2006 Turin Paralympic Games. Weeks spoke for many when he wrote in his *Globe and Mail* column, "Making an old game accessible to those with disabilities is an important step. And although it's taken a while to open the doors, it shows again the wide appeal of the game."

The same broad appeal extends to the deaf and blind curling communities as the latter reached its goal of having its own national championship.

What began in Alberta as a "funspiel" between sighted members of the Calmar Lions Club more than thirty years ago has evolved into an annual competition among blind and visually impaired teams from across western Canada. Lions Clubs continue to sponsor the event, a legacy from the Calmar Lions who took to the ice blindfolded to curl against the Edmonton Blind Curling Club back in the winter of 1971–72. In 1979, Calmar hosted the first Western Blind Curling Championships, drawing players from all four provinces west of Ontario. Alberta continued to host the event until the 1990s, when the championship began to rotate among the four western provinces. When hosting duties for the 2003 thirty-first blind championship were awarded to Lac du Bonnet, a ninety-minute drive north of Winnipeg, the local Lions Club began its preparations in February 2001, working with the Western Blind Curling Association to organize, raise funds, line up local and corporate sponsors, arrange for all meals and accommodations for the curlers, and ensure that any special needs were met. As for the curlers, their road to the championship starts with provincial playdowns. The two teams from each province that emerge at the end are allowed to take designated sighted sweepers to the finals.

Writing for the *Winnipeg Sun*, Jim Bender found that some blind curling teams play in the gigantic Manitoba Curling Association bonspiel in preparation for their own Western championship. Some are veterans, all are competitive, and none seemed overly sensitive to the good-natured barbs that sailed their way from sighted competitors. Laughter becomes a survival skill when life deals to you from the bottom of the deck, but the genuine humour comes from the athletes themselves, who are genuinely happy to be on the ice, to be able to compete, and who make the most of the opportunity to demonstrate what they can do, given the chance. The house is a home to them, too. And the ice is a level playing field for people who sometimes have to trudge just a little harder uphill than the rest of us. They are the same as anyone else, whether nine or ninety, throwing Little Rocks or using a curling stick. They all curl because they can. The fact they enjoy it so much is a tremendous bonus.

On the ice at the Winnipeg tournament in 2001, Bender chatted with Norm Lyons, who back then was a fifty-year-old skip teamed with two blind curlers, one sighted curler, one sighted designated sweeper, and a spare with an artificial leg. You sense from the article that the squad, competing in what has been called "the world's biggest bonspiel," doesn't win many games at that level of competition. It doesn't seem to matter. Lyons was philosophical, noting that the consolation for losing is that the winners buy the first round of beer. There likely isn't a sighted curler in the world who hasn't taken similar consolation on a night when the curling gods won't give him a break.

There were no youngsters on Lyon's five-man squad. His blind curlers were his youngest and oldest players—Paul Hogue was forty-five and Harold Thorvaldson was sixty-four—while his sighted curler and designated sweeper were both in their fifties. Spare George Horning, the sighted curler with the artificial leg, was also the president of the Winnipeg Blind Curling Club. Its eighteen members play at the Manitoba mother club. Different curlers use different styles to compensate for their limited or extinguished vision. Some, like Bill Thompson, the only blind curler at Fergus, rely on flashlight beams to line up their shots; others have a teammate place the broom just beyond the tee line or at the near edge of the house.

Lyons, who has 4 per cent vision in his left eye and 5 per cent in his right, took to the ice in 1967 and has represented Manitoba at the Western Blind Curling Championship seventeen times since 1971. His best finish was third. He seems to want to do better: he told Bender that while he loves the camaraderie and the competition that curling affords, he figured he'd "be right up there"—if he could just master the skills.

Bender brings a unique perspective to his reporting—he knows first-hand what it's like to curl blind. Oh, he can see all right, but in a George Plimpton-ish outing at the Grain Exchange Curling Club, he joined with his media colleagues to stage a celebrity game against Lyons and the blind curlers. His experiences serve as an eye-opener for those of us who remain uninitiated. To level the playing field, the sighted journalists were required to wear vision-impairing goggles. The options ranged from something resembling squinting through smeared glass to total, disorienting darkness. Sighted coaches helped both sides line up their shots, guiding them by voice or by holding their broom at the near hog line. Bender's account suggests all went well, until the totally blacked-out goggles went on—each sighted curler then proceeded to throw a rock into the boards. When the blind curlers stole three from the sighted team, Bender was compelled to report the rare instance of, you guessed it: "Yup, the blind stole from the sighted."

Staged to kick off White Cane Week, the game was an effort to promote public awareness of blind curling. The Winnipeg Blind Curling Club, operating out of the Valour Road Curling Club, was down to seven members at the time, symptomatic of a larger general membership decline that led to the sale of the building to a private interest in 2005. But the renamed Asham Arena was still home to Lyons and his team as they prepared for the Western Blind Curling Championships in Lac du Bonnet. Lucy Chase seemed to sum up the can-do attitude of the blind curlers when she said, "The only limitations are the ones we put on ourselves." The sighted media celebrities apparently came from behind to tie the game 8–8—after removing their goggles to steal four.

A similar story unfolds at the Vancouver Curling Club, where VancouverCourier.com writer Bob Mackin found blind curlers honing their skills for the 2001 Western Blind Curling Championships in their allotted Wednesday afternoon slot—just one more group taking to the same ice that is reserved at different times for ministers, pharmacists, businesswomen, and gay and lesbian curlers. That year's competition, in Stony Plain, near Edmonton, was significant for team spare Nick Lutz, who doubled as president of the local blind curling league. He was considering retiring the next year, when he turned seventy-five. On the other hand, Mackin noted, Lutz's curling had improved as his vision deteriorated. Diagnosed with glaucoma more than thirty years earlier, his failing eyesight had left him with tunnel vision in his right eye, and no depth perception. He had been totally blind in his left eye for more than two decades. As for curling a heavy rock down a slippery surface toward a distant target you may not see clearly, if at all, Lutz comments that while the odd curler may lose balance and topple, no one has ever been injured curling.

The Vancouver Curling Club, sponsored by the local Metro Monarch Lions Club, was just one of seven B.C. clubs to have blind curling in 2003. Victoria, Nanaimo, Chilliwack, Kelowna, Kamloops, and Prince George all iced blind teams and made the necessary alterations to make the curlers safe and welcome in the clubs. Common sense can reduce most issues to little more than considerations. Clubs offering ice to blind curlers will ideally provide a spare sheet the curlers can use to walk up and down without worrying whether the rock they hear roaring along the ice is, in fact, rumbling toward them. Players should be allowed to use their broom or white cane to get them safely from end to end during the game. Blind curlers can decide which colours are easiest to distinguish for use as markings. Using coloured duct tape to mark stairs, handrails, backboards, and anything else they need to navigate to get to the ice provides safe access. Curlers should determine where the markings should be. It's as simple as asking them what they need.

To some extent, the story is the same as you move east across Canada. In Ottawa, Moe Aubry, a retired police sergeant, has championed the rights of the blind, in part because he wanted to continue to golf; curling came later. Aubry can be a rather determined fellow; when he learned there were efforts afoot to ease him out of an upcoming golf tournament, for what he considered to be the lame excuse that he couldn't see, he insisted he could still hit the green and sink the ball as well as any sighted duffer. Aubry challenged anyone who wanted him out of the tournament to accompany him onto the links. His challenge was accepted, but if the sighted golfer had any initial fear of hurting Aubry's feelings, he quickly relaxed, then had to concentrate on his own game rather than on the blind man's so-called impediment. Aubry was two strokes back after nine holes. He got to play in the tournament.

Aubry lost his sight when he was struck on the head with a crowbar when he interrupted a burglary in progress. He shrugs off any sympathy for his misfortune, happy to be alive and still active. And just as the Lions Club has played a huge role in blind curling in western Canada, a member of another service club got the ball rolling, and the stone curling, in Ottawa. Aubry credits Kiwanian

Ted Anderson for approaching the Canadian National Institute for the Blind (CNIB) in 1978 to seek their guidance on how best to involve some of their members in a recreational sport.

About the same time, Richard St. Germain, another Kiwanian who had lost his sight, discovered blind curling. With assistance from CNIB administrator Gord Sheppard and Betty Reid, who was working with blind curlers in Kingston, Ontario, the Ottawa Blind Curling Club cast its first stone at Lansdowne Park on ice provided free by the city. In 1990, they moved briefly to the Granite Curling Club before landing at the City View rink, their home since 1992. The local blind curlers have excelled at the sport, winning a medal at almost every provincial championship since 1979. The most successful skips have been St. Germain and Aubry. The latter has been the perennial club president and has won three gold, three silver, and six bronze medals. He jokes that he wears his history on his hat, a reference to his pin-laden tam.

Blind curling may vary slightly across the country, but the overall approach and net effect are the same. Blind curlers will aim toward the skip's voice or at a distant flashlight or a nearby broom. But what happens when the skip is also blind? In that case, at least in Ottawa, sighted coaches are allowed to help the skips place the broom and offer verbal clues or a corrective touch to help the shooter aim the rock. But from there on, it's all up to the curler. Similarly, Ottawa allows blind curlers to sweep in tandem with sighted coaches. But most clubs also seem willing to allow blind sweepers who can see the dark rock to sweep with a little verbal help from a sighted coach.

The Saskatchewan Blind Sports Association's rules for curling are typical, noting that the game is played by the same rules as regulation curling. Teams consist of three blind or visually impaired athletes and one sighted athlete. During competitions, the sighted person plays the lead position. Curlers may use flashlights or monoculars (like miniature telescopes), plus verbal directions from teammates. Created in 1978, the association exists to assist people who are blind or have visual impairments to achieve excellence in sport, satisfaction in recreation, independence, self-reliance, and full community participation.

The most pressing problem for blind curling seems to be membership. The Blind Curling Association operating out of the Valour Road Curling Club in Winnipeg is not alone in suffering low numbers. In Ottawa, where club members sport colourful jackets graced with crossed brooms and a white cane, an aggressive membership drive edged them up to sixteen members from thirteen, but they're always on the prowl for more. Blind curling also seems limited compared to other curling groups. Despite ongoing efforts to institute a national championship by the Canadian Council of the Blind—the self-proclaimed "Voice of the Blind in Canada"—no Canadian title for blind curlers was ever sanctioned by the CCA, dating to the first invitational bonspiel that was held in Regina in 1990. That was a one-time deal for more than a decade, leaving them confined to regional or provincial championships until 2007.

Michael Hayes, president of the Ontario Blind Curling Association, has been nudging the movement forward for the past several years. His efforts paid off with the first White Cane Week National Blind Curling Championship at the Ottawa Curling Club. Kicked off the week of February 4, 2007, competitors were piped onto the ice by Rod McNeil of the Ottawa Police Pipe Band, and escorted by a police colour guard composed of officers from that city force, the Ontario Provincial Police, and the Royal Canadian Mounted Police. The event, held during Ottawa's annual Winterlude party and sponsored by the Canadian Council of the Blind, also drew ambassadors from three countries with varying involvement with curling. The championship was a spiritual and personal triumph for Hayes as his team won the bronze medal behind traditional powerhouse Kelowna, BC, (gold) and Edmonton (silver).

Hayes, who lost his sight to a rare disease, has a clear vision of where he believes blind curling can go and the faith to get it there. With about twenty blind curlers now competing in blind and sighted leagues in Ottawa and perhaps seventy across Ontario, his goal is to get one thousand out on the ice nationwide. The trick is to get them out of their homes and into the curling house. That's not as simple as it might sound. "You can deal with the physical impact of losing your sight," he explains. "It's the emotional consequences that really screw you."

The problem can become chicken-and-egg, with neither going first. Hayes says a lot of potential blind curlers confine themselves in their own homes, unwilling to venture out because they don't want to become objects of pity. "We just have to find ways to make people happier," he says, explaining that happy people are sociable people who enjoy good times and good company. What better cure for the blues than curling, where the camaraderie lends itself to a sense of community among like-minded and similarly challenged athletes?

Hayes joined the Ottawa Blind Curling Club in 2002. A year later, he was attending the annual general meeting, excused himself to visit the washroom, and returned to find himself elected president. The curling bug had bitten. Within his first two seasons on the ice, Hayes was on the team that won the Ontario blind championship, and the sighted team he played for won the Ottawa Curling Club seniors league title. Off the ice, he pitched his idea for a national championship to the Canadian Council of the Blind. They promptly lived up to their motto—"A lack of sight is not a lack of vision"—by agreeing to stage their first title tournament in 2005.

The first national invitational—meaning teams participated according to finances more than on merit, Hayes explained, chuckling—boasted some high-profile guests. Hayes and Danny Lamoureux, manager of club development for the CCA, swept the first ceremonial stone thrown by Ontario women's champion Jenn Hanna to then Governor General Adrienne Clarkson, standing in the house at the other end of the sheet of ice. All had been piped onto the ice by a volunteer piper arranged by Hayes's younger brother, Pat, who was the pipe major of the Ottawa Police Pipe Band until his untimely death a short time later. Teams came from across Canada, from Newfoundland to British Columbia, and Kelowna, BC, took home the trophy. The event repeated a year later (it's always played during White Cane Week) as part of Ottawa's official Winterlude celebrations. Unseasonably mild weather dashed hopes to play on the frozen Rideau Canal—the world's largest outdoor skating rink—and Ed Werenich threw the first ceremonial stone, again swept by Hayes and Lamoureux, in the Ottawa Curling Club. Once again, there were ten teams and Kelowna repeated as the winner. Newfoundland took a pass that year but Hayes correctly predicted they'd return in 2007. He's still trying to attract his first blind team from the rest of the Maritimes and hopes he's found a staunch ally in the region after discussing his dream with former Canadian and World champion Colleen Jones at the 2007 event in Ottawa. In the meantime, he continues his quest to raise funds for the national championship. Among the possibilities is a blind (or blindfolded) Draw to the Button competition for a healthy purse—that could then be donated back to help fund the event. Having now pulled off a three-peat tournament success, including the first formal national competition, Hayes hopes that corporate sponsors will begin to see more clearly the value of getting more blind and visually impaired individuals out of their homes and into the curling house. He's getting help from the CCA on that front. In May 2007, Lamoureux confirmed plans to build on the success of the CCB's National Invitational and move its agenda forward to build the sport for visually impaired Canadians (among other groups). The action plan for a four-year campaign aimed at broadening the profile of the Canadian curler was timed for launch in June 2007. Donors were already stepping forward, most notably via Barry Winfield, of the Canadian Paralympics Foundation, who was instrumental in arranging a $400,000 donation from the Toronto Stock Exchange to be shared among blind, disabled, and wheelchair curlers. And Hayes shows no signs of stopping. He and the CCA's Lamoureux are hoping to stage the first international blind competition in 2008 with a formal international championship to follow in 2009.

By contrast, deaf curlers have competed nationally for decades (Winnipeg hosted the twenty-ninth Canadian Deaf Curling Championships in 2007 for mens, mixed, and seniors) and globally in the IOC–sanctioned Deaflympics dating to 1924. (Salt Lake City hosted the sixteenth Games in 2007.) Wheelchair curlers and Special Olympics athletes also compete at the world and Paralympic and Special Olympic Games. Doors are opening wider for curlers with intellectual disabilities, who crossed the brink to international competition with curling's inclusion in the Special Olympics, and curlers with physical disabilities, who made their international debut at the Paralympic Games in Turin. The neglect of blind curling may be nothing that a major sponsor can't fix. Until then, the rocks will roar and the curlers will laugh, playing whenever and wherever the opportunity presents itself. Regardless of the barriers to a national competition, blind curlers share across the land share humour, determination, and the spirit of the game.

But of all the tight curling communities, the deaf may be the most insistent that they are not disabled in any way when it comes to playing the sport. Nor are they new to the game, having been playing for trophies since 1979, when the British Columbia Deaf Sports Federation hosted men's and women's teams from the four western provinces at Port Moody, British Columbia. That same year, Daniel Wojcik conceived the idea of a curling club for the deaf in Ottawa. The first mixed bonspiel at the Nepean Sportsplex drew six entries. The Ottawa Silent Athletic Club— Curling was created after this successful experiment. Twenty-five years later, Bruce Ullett, a founding member and perennial club champion, was the point man on the national deaf bonspiel in Ottawa, a tribute to his staying power, his dedication, and the need for a venue for deaf curlers.

While there is a great deal of statistical and chronological data available on several websites regarding the history of deaf curling, an article detailing the importance of curling for deaf schoolchildren in northern Minnesota may offer the most poignant insight to something as simple as just wanting to belong. Headlined "Deaf, hard of hearing enjoy a day of curling," in the March 27, 2004, *Mesabi Daily News*, the article by Angie Riebe described what community can be, and what it can mean to those who never take it for granted. The local Lions Clubs and veterans' organization funded the event and lunch. University of Minnesota-Duluth sign-language students played games with the kids while presenters spoke briefly to parents and adults before the kids hit the ice. The novice curlers, aged four to nineteen, had hearing impairment ranging from total deafness to partial hearing assisted by hearing aids or cochlear electronic implants. Some signed messages with their fingers, while others read lips. Most of them were curling for the first time. All of them loved it.

EVELETH—More than a dozen rosy-cheeked children
smiled and giggled while taking turns sliding rocks down

the ice at the Range Recreation Civic Center Curling Club Saturday.

For many, like 9-year-old Brady Mistic of Saginaw, Minn., it was their first time curling. Brady excitedly followed his rock down to the house, proud to show his mother, Cindy Bruning, his new skill.

But the afternoon of curling was more than just a Saturday activity for the kids and adults who attended the event. It was a chance for families with deaf and hard of hearing children, and deaf and hard of hearing adults, to socialize, learn about new tools and resources for those so impaired and share information with each other.

The event, in its 20th year, began as a group of parents in northeastern Minnesota decided to gather annually so their children could play with other children with hearing difficulties. For years they met at the Chisholm recreation center to swim and socialize. But recently, the event was moved to the curling club so the kids could try a new activity.

Curlers who are blind or deaf, use a wheelchair, or have physical or intellectual disabilities all find a community on the ice that is equal and supportive. Others find their support rooted deeply in what is perhaps the strongest bond of all—family.

Ghislain Lascelles began curling at Hawkesbury Secondary School in eastern Ontario in the 1970s, at age thirteen. Over the years, he rose from schoolboy lead to successful skip. He also took up golf. His parents urged him to try everything, to fear nothing. It never occurred to him not to try anything that appealed to him just because he was a thalidomide baby. Missing a finger on each hand at the end of arms that are roughly half their normal length has done nothing to deter him from his passions in life. He has adapted a few things, using a longer shaft on his golf clubs, wearing a toe slider to allow him to make his delivery almost flat out against the ice, but he competes as an equal and returns the support he has always received from his family. With four sisters and two brothers in a curling family, the Lascelles could ice two teams should the need arise. And it would be a close game. Two Lascelles sisters—Nathalie, playing third in 1990, and Dominique, skipping in 1994—made it as far as the Canadian junior playoffs. Both finished or tied for fourth at a time when only the top three teams went on to try to qualify for the world junior championship.

Given all these family accomplishments, you get the impression from Ghislain that his success is not all that remarkable. Encouraged by his parents from a young age, supported by his siblings along the way, he has found another home in the house. Competitors pay him tribute as "a fine curler," noting his unique curling style almost as an afterthought. That acceptance may be one reason he continues to curl. But he also curls because he enjoys it. And because he can. And, yes, he just happens to be very, very good. He finished third at the 2006 Quebec men's provincials, playing for skip Simon Dupuis. The winner? Jean-Michel Menard, who went on to win the 2006 Brier—only the second time Quebec has achieved this—and finished second at the world championship in Lowell, Massachusetts.

For a lot of people, the simple act of competing can be as rewarding as winning. Those who make their mark on the ice simply by strolling or rolling into the house perhaps demonstrate most clearly that curling is truly the universal sport. It is also the emancipating sport, perhaps the only one that allows anyone and everyone to compete on the same playing field, almost always by the same rules, using the same tools. Any specific modification is rooted in reality and a sense of safety, but the game remains essentially the same—curlers throwing stones and being made to feel at home in the house.

IN THE HACK

IN THE COMPANY OF ICE MEN

I am sitting in the Ottawa Curling Club, where it seems you can't throw a rock without hitting a Merklinger. Anne is there with her brothers Bill and Dave. The stories and the beer flow. Earle Morris buys me a drink as I chat with Anne and Marian Dupont, who is just back from a holiday at the world championships and a side trip to Russia where she has been most warmly received. She has lost none of her zeal for promoting the Special Olympics and blind and deaf curling. Also huddled at the table are some of the greatest ice technicians on the planet—Shorty Jenkins ("the King of Swing"), Kirk Smyth ("the Ice King of Europe"), the nomadic Ian MacAulay, and guest of honour Dave Merklinger. (Lou Anne Pauhl, the icemaker at the Brantford Golf and Country Club, would be the first to crack this all-male fraternity in 2007, admitting to *Hamilton Spectator* scribe Steve Buist it was "pretty cool" being certified the first—and at this writing, the only—woman in the world to be certified a Level IV curling ice technician.)

I chat with them all, but MacAulay, who recently curled in the Brier, made ice in Eurasia, and is just back from Cuba, catches my attention. I did not know they curled in Cuba. I scribble furiously as he details his time there, waiting to hear the curling parts. He eventually admits surprise that I care this much about him taking his wife south. I finally realize he's telling me about his family vacation. It was apparently their first vacation in a while, but still—I am an idiot.

My time interviewing has breached curling etiquette. I scan the room, but Earle Morris has left before I can repay the drink he bought me. I feel bad. If he reads this, he should call me. I'm in the book.

While the ice technicians chat, I ask Shorty's daughter just how much coffee her dad drinks. She estimates five a day. I'm unsure if she means cups or pots. Depends who makes it. As you will learn later, it should not be me.

THE FIFTH END

SHORTY JENKINS—
"THE KING OF SWING"

*C*larence "Shorty" Jenkins is undeniably the most colourful character in curling, a flamboyant icon with a rebellious streak who pebbles to a different drum. He earned his nickname at age seventeen for the small BSA motorcycle he rode as a member of the Royal Victoria Motorcycle Club, and although his bikes got bigger as his wallet got fatter, the moniker stuck like a curling rock on frosty ice. It was just that type of slow ice that led to a disappointing experience curling at the 1974 Ontario men's championship. Shorty's disappointment at losing his shot at the Brier was secondary to his distress that bad ice could ruin such a memorable event. He tried hard not to complain—he was just so darned happy to be there—but was stunned to hear the other curlers say that the ice was relatively good, compared to other venues.

Shorty left that qualifier determined to find a better way to make ice. In short order, he revolutionized curling with a stopwatch and his powers of observation and common sense. He concluded that "a curling rock is smarter than a human being," and he shares that epiphany in ice-making courses he teaches around the world. While good skips can unerringly "read" the ice, rocks "feel" it, reacting immediately to any change, no matter how great or small. That may not sound like rocket science, but before Shorty, no one had discovered or articulated that basic fact of physics and common sense. No superlative adequately describes the global impact on the roaring game of that epiphany by the man exalted by curling icon Doug Maxwell in the *Canadian Curling News* as the "King of Swing"—homage to a great icemaker making great ice for the 1996 Brier in Kamloops, just a year after what was labelled the "Bad-Ice Brier" in Halifax.

As the man most responsible for the evolution of curling from the Stone Age to the Ice Age, Jenkins became visible early for his flamboyant, vividly hued curling outfits, topped off with his trademark Stetson. The outfits were designed and created by Johanna, his wife of nearly fifty years, to add some colour to the game, but the colourful character they adorn is pure Shorty. Curling is a better sport for everything Jenkins brought to it. His efforts have inspired skips to call ever more daring shots that are made frequently and with amazing accuracy by club and elite curlers. Honoured as a curling pioneer, inducted into the Canadian Curling Hall of Fame, he has been further enshrined in pop culture, on television, and the big screen: he was satirized on the *Royal Canadian Air Farce*, played himself in a national ad plugging Tim Hortons coffee, and made a cameo appearance in *Men with Brooms*. In the process, he breathed fresh air into a traditionally staid sport and, without stealing the thunder of the on-ice stars of the roaring game, has perhaps transformed the sport further, and faster, than any other.

The first breakthrough was the realization that the temperature outside the curling rink could directly influence the quality of the ice inside the club. The ideal range for ice temperature seems to be between 16 and 20 degrees Fahrenheit. Any colder and the ice becomes so sleek that it minimizes the curl of the rocks; any warmer and the frost that forms will stop a rock dead in its path. Both create fewer options and less enjoyment for curlers. By contrast, anyone throwing a rock on Shorty's ice could expect it to swing (curl) a good five feet, game after game, day after day, for the duration of a major national or world championship. That created more options, made the game more exciting, and no doubt played a vital role in attracting expanded television coverage. Under his guidance, and following his lead, everyone from a Nobel Prize–winning scientist and university engineers to chemists and clubhouse icemakers have revolutionized the sport in ways no one had dreamed possible. In fact, for years, an awful lot of people in the curling hierarchy didn't even see that the game could, and perhaps needed to, be improved. Shorty changed all that by showing what stones and sheets could do if you just gave them a chance. The journey was neither short nor direct; it almost didn't happen. He was turned down flat the first time he applied for a job making curling ice. But he persisted, and the rest is history.

Born in 1935 in Hanna, Alberta, a village of maybe five hundred back then, Jenkins was the oldest of five brothers. George William Jenkins had emigrated from England in 1919 and found work above ground at the nearby coal mines. He met his wife, Laura, a stunning young nightclub singer eighteen years his junior, after watching her perform. Shorty was the inevitable result. When Shorty was five, the family moved to Calgary. George was rejected for military service in the Second World War because of his gas-seared lungs from the First World War. Settling in Victoria two years later, both parents landed jobs in the shipyards. George went to sea, while Laura welded hulls. Both survived the war; their marriage did not.

With five boys to support, no family nearby, and a job that took him to sea, often for days at a time, George saw no option but to place the four younger brothers in an orphanage. Shorty stayed home, but he was nine and lonely. He asked to join his brothers. Wish granted.

A child's only options for escape from an orphanage were to be adopted, turn fifteen, or find a job. Shorty found an early-morning paper route to earn his keep and help make ends meet. Since he had to rise at 3:00 a.m. to deliver the papers when they arrived an hour later, he was given his own room on the top floor of the orphanage to avoid disturbing the others with his early departures—one of the bonuses of the job, besides the pocket change he earned. Shorty managed to divert some of his earnings to buy firecrackers to celebrate Halloween—strictly taboo to the religious order operating the orphanage. He was caught with his explosive contraband, and his father was summoned. While George and Matron consulted in her office, Shorty found himself alone and bored in the hall. As luck would have it, Matron had not confiscated all of his fireworks. Shorty lit and tossed one, and was lighting the second when an errant spark ignited the remaining fireworks crammed into his bulging pocket. They exploded, setting his pants on fire. Drawn by his son's screams, George beat at the flames, his own clothes catching fire as he wrestled desperately to strip off Shorty's burning clothing. The early prognosis was not good. The burns were severe enough to put Shorty into shock, and there were early fears that he would lose his leg. Shorty battled back and, with extensive loonie-sized skin grafts from his left leg, his damaged limb was saved. He was soon back riding a bike.

After a stint delivering messages for the CPR—his father's employer—Shorty followed George's footsteps to sea. Sailing aboard the HMS *Laymore*, he quickly rose from mess boy to steward. It was a great way to be sixteen, at least until one horrifying voyage cast grave doubt that he'd live to see seventeen. While the *Laymore* was shipping home from San Francisco, where it had picked up a load of blast sand used to scour ships' keels, a terrible gale blew in, tossing the ship like a toy boat. Eventually, the sand shifted, and for a few anxious minutes it seemed the ship was going to turn turtle or sink. But the crisis passed and Shorty lived to tell the tale—one more to add to the list.

On September 27, 1952, Shorty turned seventeen, the minimum age to join the military, and promptly enlisted with the Royal Canadian Air Force. Posted to CFB Trenton, in southeastern Ontario, he was trained in munitions and weapons. Four months later, he was arming and maintaining Lancaster bombers at CFB Greenwood, Nova Scotia. Following a stint at CFB Summerside, Prince Edward Island, he was shipped overseas. Arriving in Germany on April 11, 1955, the young airman was excited at his life's latest turn, blissfully unaware that his footloose bachelor days were numbered.

Overseeing quality control for maintaining the Sabre and F-100 jet fighters did not appeal to the gregarious airman. Pointing out everyone's mistakes was a poor way to make friends. There were exceptions, of course, and, on the eve of a close friend's wedding to a Dutch woman from Arnhem, Shorty and his pals took the groom out on the town in Amsterdam for the bachelor's final fling. Somehow, during the course of the revelries, Shorty was lured away from the party. He awoke the next morning to find the woman, his vest, and his money gone. It wasn't the first time he'd been robbed—he'd been "rolled" at a USO club in London's Piccadilly Circus on New Year's Eve—but at least there he could ask for help and be understood. This time, his fate was complicated by being stranded alone in a city where he did not speak the local language.

Rightly assuming that his friends had returned to Arnhem without him, Shorty grappled to find a Plan B. Never shy to show initiative, he wandered into the street to get his bearings and chart his path to Arnhem. Once oriented, he prepared to thumb a ride, aware that hitchhiking was illegal in Holland. That simple plan was short-circuited by two Dutch police officers parked nearby in a white Volkswagen who seemed to be uncomfortably interested in him. Unsure what else to do, he relied on instinct, smiled, and lied, assuring the police his friends were coming to meet him at the bridge. To his dismay, the police proved happy to aid a stranded Canadian airman. They motioned him into their car and drove him to the nearest bridge. Likely to no one's great surprise, no one showed up. The police took it well. Motioning Shorty out of their car, one of the officers jerked his thumb in the universal language for hitching a ride. Relieved, Shorty soldiered on.

Arriving in Arnhem too late to attend his friend's wedding, Shorty hopped a ride to the address he had for the reception. That seemed simple enough, but when he asked his driver to drop him at an address on Erica, he was dismayed to learn there were *three* Ericas, roughly equivalent to street, boulevard, and lane. Either Shorty guessed right, or they found the place by process of elimination, and he was dropped at his rendezvous before the wedding party arrived. Alone in the house with a woman who was scrambling to prepare a large meal. Shorty, ever thoughtful, gestured his willingness to help. Whether the woman didn't understand or simply wanted no part of the scruffy Canadian intruder in her home, she made no welcoming gesture to him to join in. No more successful in conveying his desire to shave and shower, he was still trying to get his message across when his now-married friend arrived with his wife and her girlfriend.

Shocked by Shorty's dishevelled appearance, his friend stated the obvious, telling him he needed to get cleaned up. Shorty agreed, and the wife's friend, Johanna, the daughter of the woman preparing the meal, helped him find a razor and soap. After eating, he and Johanna took the bride's German aunt, who was a bit under the weather, for a walk. He learned that Johanna was fluent in speaking and writing three languages. It was love at first sight. They were married in Arnhem on August 3, 1957. Their daughter, Kitty, was born in Germany two years later.

Returning to Canada in October 1959, Shorty ended up at CFB Cold Lake, north of Edmonton, needing a car to get to work and a place for his young family to call home. Lacking the points to qualify for base housing, or even a home in the military trailer park, he bought a trailer in Edmonton. It was nice but it wasn't cheap, and he could no longer afford to keep the car on the road. When the family was finally admitted to the trailer camp, their monthly rent dropped from $100 to $5. Son Kiet arrived in April 1961.

Posted back to Germany in 1962, Shorty accompanied the advance party to prepare the base for the arrival of the Hercules aircraft. When U.S. President John F. Kennedy was shot dead in Dallas, the assassination troubled Shorty more deeply than suddenly being ordered to arm Canadian aircraft with lethal weaponry. Growing increasingly despondent, he was transferred to the National Defence Military Centre in Ottawa. The doctors suggested he request outside work or get out of the military. The air force offered him an indoor supply clerk's job, prompting Shorty to resign in March 1967. Back on civvie street, he managed a couple of Sunoco gas stations. Sunoco eventually sent him to Toronto, but his life veered once again when he returned to Trenton to play in a golf tournament. This time he would drag along the curling world with him.

The Trenton Golf and Curling Club was one entity back then, and it was while golfing that Shorty noticed the club's greenskeeper had packed it in. Shorty decided immediately that he wanted the job. It was outdoors. Fresh air. Not Toronto. What more could he ask? He knew the club was not rolling in dough, and the dollar-an-hour pay would have to be spread thin to raise his growing family. Still. He got the job. And, after his first week, he got a hefty raise—to the more princely $1.50 an hour. There were lots of hours spent maintaining the course to get it to the level he wanted, and although the work was seasonal, Shorty didn't have to look far for winter work. The former greenskeeper had also been the icemaker at the curling club. Shorty applied for the job—and was turned down flat.

Those who know Shorty well, and especially those who knew him back then, agree that he is an animated character, a human dynamo in constant motion—presumably fuelled at least in part by his chronic caffeine intake. While such traits may be assets for traversing the wide-open spaces of a golf course, club president Harold Hemstead perceived them as very definite liabilities within the confines of a curling rink. As Shorty recalls the exchange, Hemstead refused him the icemaker's job because he was "too hyper" and "wound up." But Shorty had never been quick to grasp the word "no." When the job was advertised, he applied again. And was turned down, again. But there was a catch. No one else had applied. Shorty, believing there is no problem that cannot be fixed, asked to be allowed to try doing the job. If either he or Hemstead was unhappy, he'd quit and there'd be no hard feelings. The offer must have seemed particularly appealing in the absence of other applicants. Shorty got the job, kept the job, and transformed the job and the roaring game when he hit the first bump in the ice.

As soon as he knew he had the job, Shorty sped along Highway 401, making stops from Kingston to Whitby to talk with icemakers he knew had reputations for making curlers happy. He picked their brains and was confident he could do the job by the time he was to install the ice in Trenton. All seemed well. Everyone seemed happy. Until the night someone commented to him that his ice was a lot slower than it had been the night before. Shorty scoffed at the idea. He had done nothing different from one night to the next. That's when he got the idea to use a stopwatch. He could time the rocks as they slid down the ice and prove the ice was the same. It was a lesson he'd learned helping a friend who built and drove Formula V race cars to ensure the cars were still as fast, or faster, after any adjustment. Timing a rock as it slid down the ice confirmed that it was curling slower, although Shorty had changed nothing. Yet something was evidently affecting the ice. He quickly deduced that if everything was the same inside, it had to be the weather outside the rink that was playing havoc with the sheets. The ice was just reacting naturally to external forces. That epiphany gave Shorty his new mantra: "Ice is smarter than people."

Quite simply, the outside air temperature had dropped dramatically, dragging the inside temperature down with it, from what was then considered an ideal 23 degrees Fahrenheit to a chillier 17 degrees. That created frost, which created slower ice. No one was taking ice temperatures back then, allowing Shorty to take the first step toward converting the art of ice making to pure science. He gives great credit to the rock, explaining it will find every little fall in the ice and react immediately to any temperature change.

Shorty wasn't a curler before he started making ice in Trenton. No one in his family had played, and although he had curled in one military bonspiel while he was posted to Germany, it had been a party-hearty affair. To this day, he has no idea how well or poorly he curled in his debut. All that changed when he got involved in the Trenton club, but not all the bumps were on the ice. No one was initially keen to take him on as a teammate. But, once given a chance, he quickly proved he could play the game. Two years later, he was skipping, and although he recalls that Paul Savage—an elite curler who has been at the Brier, Worlds, and Olympics—"thumped [my] ass" in his debut, within two years he was knocking off some name curlers. He reached the Ontario finals for the first time in 1974. Among the names he remembers from those early years was a talented vice-skip named

Al Gilchrist, who went on to become president of Nokia, an eventual Brier sponsor.

For years, the Brier remained an elusive dream for Shorty. His failure to qualify at the 1974 Ontario Curling Association's play-off left him determined to find a way to provide consistently good ice. As more and more Ontario curlers played on his "swing" ice, the demand grew for better ice at the national level. Paul Savage was among the first to realize what Shorty was on to, and lobbied, with others, to allow him to make the ice for the Brier. Their arguments failed to impress what some Ontario curlers refer to as the "Western Mafia," who, they say, believed then and possibly now, that they were the superior curling authority, based on their overwhelming number of Brier victories since its founding in 1927. The Ontario skips conceded that point but continued lobbying to play on the best possible ice. Savage recalls that, in those days, it was heartbreaking to determine the Ontario championship on magnificent swing ice, then proceed to play for the Brier on demonstrably poor ice. Eventually, their arguments were heard and their cause prevailed. Shorty's ice quickly became both popular and award winning as he rose to the top of his field, making ice for every major national and international championship for years following his disappointing experience at the 1974 Ontario championship. He never claimed it was perfect, citing the simple theory that all curlers curled differently and therefore had different preferences. What he sought to achieve, with scientific certainty, was to make any shot playable.

Since Shorty undertook his mission, there has been no shortage of science applied to the art of curling. We have come a long way from 1962, when the federal government got involved to try to resolve the problems of condensation and dripping pipes. Citing the growing popularity of the sport that was leading to a rash of new curling clubs, G.O. Handegord and C.R. Crocker tackled the issue of controlling condensation in curling rinks in an article they co-authored in the National Research Council's *Canadian Building Digest* (CBD-35):

> The growing popularity in recent years of curling as a winter sport in Canada has led to the construction of an increasing number of new buildings for curling rinks and to the renovation and improvement of existing ones. Mechanical refrigeration equipment is now normally provided to ensure a more uniform ice surface and to extend the curling season from early fall to late spring. These changes, coupled with increased serious interest in the game, have brought about a growing awareness and concern for problems associated with the performance of curling rinks, particularly the problem of "dripping" on the ice surface.
>
> Dripping describes the condition arising from the melting of frost that has accumulated on the underside of the rink roof or ceiling. Frost forms during the curling season and subsequently melts in mild weather, dripping to the ice sheets where it refreezes and forms undesirable "bumps." Under normal weather conditions on the Prairies the problem occurs only in the spring, but in regions of Canada having more moderate or variable winters it may occur frequently. In natural ice curling rinks the curling season was more closely related to the outside weather, and although dripping was a problem in the spring the season was almost at an end and the ice itself beginning to show other signs of deterioration.
>
> The accumulation of frost on the ceiling of a curling rink is the result of the condensation of moisture originating from flooding and "pebbling" operations, from

the curlers and spectators, and from the ice surface itself. These sources of moisture tend to produce high humidity conditions within a rink, resulting in dew-point temperatures approaching the interior air temperature. Under cold weather conditions the interior surfaces of the rink enclosure will be at a temperature lower than that of the air. If these temperatures fall below the dew-point temperature, condensation results.

It is evident that any efforts to lower the humidity and hence the interior dew-point temperature will reduce the possibility of condensation. It is also apparent that raising the temperature of interior surfaces will serve a similar purpose. Consideration of these two principles is essential in any attempt to reduce or eliminate condensation.

Condensation normally occurs as frost in a curling rink because of the temperature levels involved. The frost itself is not objectionable, as it might be in other buildings, nor is the subsequent melting of the frost of concern provided that it does not fall or drip onto the ice surface. The problem is in this way unique from the practical point of view, and suggests yet another solution involving proper control of condensed moisture during the curling season.

Any veteran curler can probably recall playing on (or around) bumpy ice, often resorting to crushing the blemishes with the broom handles. Early solutions ranged from installing fans and dehumidifiers to spraying the metal roofs with water-absorbent materials. Now, compare that annoyance with the problems confronted by today's ice technicians who must make and maintain playing surfaces in heated arenas filled with thousands of cheering fans, their breath mixing with the steady heat projected by television lights at major events.

Prior to the 2002 Calgary Brier, chief icemaker Hans Wuthrich acknowledged to the media that it would be difficult to keep the ice in top shape toward the weekend playoffs when crowds of seventeen thousand would pack the Saddledome. He was able to hold the building temperature at 57 to 58 degrees Fahrenheit for the start of each draw by opening the air-handling units in the building to bring in outside cold air. Even then, the temperature would have risen to about 68 degrees, which Wuthrich said was fine. The ice would be affected at 70 degrees, which would inevitably be reached with so many people in the stands. That meant opening the air-handlers during the game, which could affect the ice—and the rocks—as well, but it would be worse without them.

Wuthrich, from tiny Gimli, Manitoba, where airliners without fuel glide safely back to earth, was already among the most experienced and universally respected ice technicians at high-profile events. He had been the head icemaker for the Brier since 1998 and had eight world championships under his belt. He must have been doing something right; he was given the CCA Award of Achievement in 2003 and was named in July 2006 to a committee overseeing the curling facility for the 2010 Vancouver Olympics.

The dilemmas he faced in Calgary were common across North America and Europe for very different reasons. In Europe, the chronic lack of curling rinks often meant using arena ice. In Canada, the exploding popularity of the roaring game meant relocating to ever larger venues, beginning with the Saddledome. Thereafter, NHL arenas became the norm where they existed. Writing *Curling Ice Explained* for the World Curling Federation, Leif Ohman of Sweden and his editor, John Minnaar of Scotland, listed more than a half-dozen problems that must be overcome to convert pitted and grooved hockey ice into pristine curling sheets: among them, the ice had to be levelled and patched, and water purity and ice-surface temperature had to be monitored, controlled, and corrected.

Shorty's pioneering efforts led to a flurry of scientific papers, doctoral theses, and complex curling scenarios recreated under the controlled confines of laboratories and full-size curling rinks. All sought to prove scientifically what Shorty had determined by close observation, calculation, and common sense. Every study confirmed his findings and theories, leading to further advances but taking some of the romance out of ice science.

One thing that ice making did allow, the same as curling, was the opportunity to spend time on the ice with a loved one. However, Johanna didn't seem to find standing behind Shorty, pulling in hose for hours at a time, all that romantic. She was bored to tears and voiced her unhappiness. Shorty's solution was to change positions. At least by letting her run rather than coil the hose she had something to do—and it gave him time to step outside for a smoke. He'd return after five minutes, pull in the hose, then retreat once more behind the glass. It took two hours back then to manually scrape, flood, and pebble each sheet of ice. There were four sheets. You do the math. Even when it got to the point where Shorty and Johanna could each tend two sheets, they still had to spend four hours on the ice. Making ice for bonspiels meant going to work before the sun rose and going home after it had set—and sometimes not going home at all.

"First few nights of an event he sleeps in the machine room, right by the condenser," declares George Karrys, 1998 Olympic lead and now publisher of the *Curling News*. "Shorty likes to listen to the hum of the machinery, get used to the sound and how hard the machines are working. Anything shuts off in the middle of the night, you lose a day's curling the next morning. Not

Shorty. He may have been burned once when the power went out, but never again.

"You go into the engine room of an arena, you see bedsheets and a pillow right there on the floor, surrounded by machines. That's Shorty."

One of the first to benefit from Shorty's efforts was the Brockville Curling Club, about an hour east of Trenton along Highway 401. Shorty has always charged clubs what they can afford and accepts that there can be exceptions to hard currency. He was happy and honoured when the club named a major bonspiel for him as payment for his services. The Shorty Jenkins Classic has run annually for the past decade.

As early as 1976, the Cataraqui Golf and Country Club in Kingston tried to lure him away from the Bay of Quinte Golf and Country Club in Trenton, where he had risen to become course superintendent. Shorty declined each offer, but finally slid east down the 401, in 1991, to oversee that club. He stayed for a decade, then returned to Trenton in 2001—the same year he was inducted into the Canadian Curling Hall of Fame, complementing his 1995 Award of Achievement from the CCA. While he appreciates the efforts of those who nominated him, Shorty confesses that he doesn't get too excited about awards. He's proud of what he's done and seems happy to be judged on his accomplishments—as a crusading icemaker, a competitive curler, and a coach. Several of his students have gone on to compete at the highest levels of curling, notably the Brier, the Scott Tournament of Hearts, and the national juniors and mixed championships. He retains close ties with his earliest students and their families—a couple of air force brats named Merklinger.

If the second generation of pebblers to follow Shorty's lead are less flamboyant, they have a way of making their point succinctly. During an ice meltdown caused by an accidental equipment shutdown at the 2005 women's worlds in Paisley, Scotland, MacAulay shrugged off media critics with a terse: "Shit happens." Merklinger's actions can speak volumes. In 2007, when curlers complained of "picks" in his ice at the Hamilton Brier and Edmonton Worlds, he scraped up an assortment of human hair, brush bristles and other debris and had his crew deposit it with the complainants as evidence that the curlers, not the ice, were causing the problems. But his woes continued. A surprise visit by Prime Minister Stephen Harper, a long-time Brier fan, ended with his security entourage opening the large cavernous doors to the lower levels of Copps Coliseum, allowing uncontrollable weather to assail curling ice that must be rigidly controlled—a new stage in a saga that even some members of his clan have dubbed: "The Merklinger Curse."

IT'S RAINING MERKLINGERS

I am visiting the Navan Curling Club near Ottawa seeking family and icemakers. I find my brother John and ice technician/raconteur Doug Titus. My initial quest had been to find members of Clan Merklinger and Ian MacAulay, but this is close enough. John, my inspiration to start curling, has curled the three Ms—men's, military, and mixed—along the road from schoolboy to senior. Bypass surgery has been no deterrent. His wife, Nicole, continues to curl, jog, and cycle after recovering from a broken neck suffered in a traffic accident. They are two more who curl because they enjoy it—the competition and the camaraderie—and because they can.

Titus is a born storyteller and my best hope to hook up with MacAulay and the Merklingers, none of whom I've met at this point; all intrigue me for their diversity as elite curlers and ice-makers. Titus offers to get me their contact information. The ice technician, who is also an accomplished curler, then turns his attention to "the Norwegian" sitting at a nearby table who, in their long-ago first match, stole a victory in a game Titus was expected to win. It seems neither man will ever forget that classic upset—for very different reasons. Both regale their audience with details retold from two vastly different perspectives.

The conversation turns to the upcoming Scott Tournament of Hearts. Anne Merklinger will be there as president of the Sandra

143

Schmirler Foundation, not as a competitor, having bowed out at the provincials. Ironically, the game in which she was eliminated is replaying on the lounge television. As we watch, a man walks in, greets the room, glances at the TV, and mutters something I can't hear. He is accompanied by two teenaged girls who quickly change into curling shoes and follow him out onto the ice.

"That's Bruce Merklinger," Titus advises me. "The patriarch."

I learn the girls are his twin daughters from his second marriage. Bruce is coaching them to prepare for the upcoming junior playdowns. Pondering my next step, I am distracted by a loud groan: "That's the shot that did her in." As I glance at the TV to see why Anne Merklinger would not be curling at the Scott that year, a woman enters the lounge with a young boy in tow. She glances at the screen, winces, and mutters a line that draws an appreciative chuckle.

"That would be Anne Merklinger," says Titus, "with her son, Connor."

Connor also heads onto the ice to practise for his upcoming Little Rocks zone playoff, which falls on the same weekend that his mom will be in Red Deer, emceeing the fundraising telethon to be staged at the site of that year's Scott. Brother Dave will be making the ice.

It's raining Merklingers. The planets have aligned.

How best to accept this gift from the curling gods? Three generations of Merklingers have just shown up to coach, curl, and cheer. An impromptu interview with a writer with a beer and a notebook might not be high on their wish list. What to do? I step outside to think deep thoughts. The curling gods again intervene. A nearby SUV starts honking and flashing its lights for no apparent reason. Moments later, Bruce bursts outside, points his fob, and clicks off the alarm. He smiles, explaining that he slipped on the ice and fell on his activator. We chat. He gives me his phone number, tells me to call him later, and heads back to the ice.

One Merklinger down, a bunch more to go.

Titus does the rest, loudly suggesting I should get Anne's autograph and that she should make sure she gets into my book. Another phone number, another invitation to call. It's a good start. I will find more Merklingers than I even knew existed. Their family seems blessed, so why the whispered warnings of the "Merklinger Curse"? I will soon learn that you can inherit it, marry into it, hire it, or be blindsided just by writing about it.

THE SIXTH END

CLAN MERKLINGER—
CHIPS OFF THE
SHOT ROCK

*F*amily has been an important part of curling going back at least to Hugh Black in Fergus and the seven generations who have followed him onto the ice. Family was also key to the celebrity of Clan Richardson and the Curling Campbells, who swept out of Saskatchewan, then swept away all challengers in their path. There is a sentimental as well as social aspect to families curling together. Paul Savage dedicated his 1974 book, *Canadian Curling: Hack to House*, to those closest to him: "To my son, Bradley, who was the youngest spectator at the London Brier and to my wife, Barbara, who has watched hundreds of my curling games." In fact, Savage helped extend "family" to "families" in the memorable dream team formed in 1982. He and teammates Ed Werenich, John Kawaja, and Neil Harrison were good curlers who became good friends, as did their wives, who began socializing while their men were off contesting the most competitive bonspiels they could find across Western Canada. The wives always attended the provincial playdowns, Ontario championships, and Briers together.

Alas, Barbara Savage missed the trip to Nagano in 1998, and so there was no one to stop the effervescent veteran from baring his Olympic-tattooed buttocks to the world. Admittedly, the world press promptly took more interest in the debut full-medal sport—just one more marketing coup for the man savvy enough to help launch the Kurl for Kids charity bonspiel in Toronto at the Avonlea Curling Club and sufficiently affable to land a supply contract for, and then a speaking role in, *Men with Brooms*.

Savage played third for Werenich when they won the world championship in 1983. Calling it a day at the turn of the millennium, "the Wrench" hung up his competitive boots with ten Brier appearances and two national and world titles. But the curling bug bit again in 2003 and Werenich returned to curl with his son, Ryan. The fifty-six-year-old Toronto firefighter acclaimed for throwing the only bodycheck in the history of curling—when Glenn Howard was allegedly a tad slow getting out of his way while Ed was sweeping an opponent's stone through the house— was back, thrilling his army of fans and giving new hope to aging curlers everywhere.

Somebody always seems to have been shunting Glenn Howard aside; most often it was curling in the shadow of his older, louder brother, Russ. But when Russ published his memoirs in early 2007, recalling former Brier, world and Olympic glories, Glenn may have written the final chapter in that year's instalment of the family saga, winning the Brier, then the worlds. Winning that latter title in Edmonton, nearly ninety years to the day after the Battle of Vimy Ridge, it once again came down to the Canadians against the Germans with the whole world watching and—unlike that historic 1917 attack—anticipating a Canadian victory. Glenn and his team did not disappoint. His boyish grin adorned sports pages across Canada, welcome-home parties were planned across the Georgian Bay region, and fans swarmed him, chorusing: "Great game, *Russ!*" Glenn's grin never faltered. It can be tough to be the little brother.

The Howard brothers had been a dynamic force on the ice, winning several Brier and World titles. Russ added son Steve as his fifth player to his 2004 New Brunswick Tankard team, the year Halifax Mayflower powers Mark Dacey and Colleen Jones snagged national honours at the Brier and the Scott Tournament of Hearts. In 2006, Russ and Steve were in the stands, cheering for younger daughter/sister Ashley's national debut at the Canadian junior championship in Thunder Bay, Ontario, with Mary Jane McGuire's squad—including the skip's twin sister, Megan, playing third, while Sarah Berthelot threw lead rocks for the New Brunswick squad. And that was just the tip of the iceberg when it came to junior curlers sharing family names at the 2006 M&M Meat Shops Canadian Juniors: Kirsten and Erin Fox were there representing British Columbia; Calleen and Sabrina Neufield were there for Manitoba; Stacie and Julie Devereux curled for Newfoundland and Labrador; and Kristen Mitchell accompanied Mandy, Erin, and Megan Selzer from Saskatchewan. In men's competition, Travis and Curtis Bale headed the Manitoba foursome, Luc and Charles Savoie formed New Brunswick's front end, and Mitch and Drew Heidt were there for Saskatchewan.

Four years earlier, the media reported that Arlen and Colin Wiens qualified for the Manitoba men's junior playoffs. A year later, Arlen played third for David Kraichy in the provincial championship, losing a tiebreaker and the chance to advance to the nationals. The family carried on as Phyllis Wiens and her daughter, Vanessa Giesbrecht, headed off to the 2003 Scott.

Family connections aren't constrained by borders. On the heels of qualifying for Canada Winter Games trials, playing in her first provincial junior championship, and becoming the Manitoba representative at the 2007 Optimist International Under-17 championship, Breanne Meakin shared her dream with the

Winnipeg Sun's Jim Bender that one day her dad would coach her at the Olympics or a world championship. Dad is Rob Meakin, who, Bender noted, played second for Manitoba's Kerry Burtnyk when he won the 1995 world championship and came within a loss to Alberta's Kevin Martin of earning a berth at the 2002 Salt Lake Olympics. More recently, he helped guide Deb McCormick's American team to a silver medal at the women's world championship as the technical director for the United States Curling Association and helped guide Cassie Johnson's bid for Olympic glory at Turin in 2006.

Family is so important, for even the most accomplished couples, that clan trumps curling every time. Dave Nedohin wasted no time telling Randy Ferbey that he wouldn't be available to help the Alberta team chase the 2006 Canada Cup because his father was scheduled for major surgery. Neil Nedohin and his wife, Kris, had followed Dave and his wife, Heather, to many Brier and world championships over the years, finally moving to Edmonton from Winnipeg to be closer to their grandchildren. Neil had been his son's fifth player at the previous Canada Cup and had coached Heather's foursome. It was, Dave told the media, "a full-time job." Other elite couples have also coped with the delicate balancing act between kin and competition. Fortunately for Wayne and Sherry Middaugh, the gap between the Brier and the Scott means one watches their two young daughters and leads the cheering while the other curls for a national championship. But Wayne left no doubt of his priorities, telling the *Toronto Sun*'s Perry Lefko, "Would I rather be at the Brier, or if my kids were doing something great would I rather be with my kids? I'd rather be there for my kids. They'll always come first."

When Anne Merklinger announced her retirement from competitive curling in early 2006, she cited a desire to spend more time with her children, Meagan and Connor, who both swim competitively. Connor also curls, and Anne hoped to see more of his zone and regional Little Rock finals—not surprising for the heart of a clan rooted in family and athletics, in that order.

Over the years, Clan Merklinger has played on the ice, coached on the ice, made the ice, and at least once danced the Macarena on the ice. If that makes them unique, their saga began innocently enough.

Marj Baggs met Bruce Merklinger through her sister, who was dating him at the time. When that relationship ended, it was on such good terms that the departing sister suggested Marj start seeing her ex-boyfriend. The suggestion must have appealed to a young woman with a sense of humour inherited from a dad whom she still describes as "a great guy" from Newfoundland and a mother named Hazel who endured her nickname "Hay Baggs" with remarkable good humour. Bruce was a fighter pilot. Enough said.

Marj was a curler. A very good curler. Son Bill estimates she was possibly in the top five, certainly among the top ten, women curlers in Winnipeg, where he first got the curling bug. Bruce also curled, not surprising in a career where frequent postings made it impossible to put down roots. Curling clubs continue to hold great appeal for military members and their families, as much—perhaps more—for their social aspects and as forums for meeting new friends than for any competitive outlet. It was only natural that their kids would be introduced to the sport through their parents.

Dave, the oldest, was the first to step onto the ice. Marj took the sport seriously enough that she thought her son should look nice on the ice. And so it came to pass that Dave was outfitted in her image of what a curler should look like—a crimson curling sweater, dark stretch pants with gold piping down the legs, and cuff straps to slip under his tasselled curling shoes to keep him looking trim throughout his matches. Alas, what his mother saw as the ideal image of a curler, Dave, at age twelve, saw as "silly pants, silly red woolly sweater, and silly girly boots." His friends thought he looked like a dork, and that was the end of curling for him. Fortunately for younger brother Bill, Marj had realized that her good intentions had backfired ("Terrible what scars a mother can leave on her little children," she would lament forty years later, while still insisting she thought Dave looked great). Bill was free to dress as he chose. Free from any wardrobe distraction, he was able to focus on curling. When he brought home his first trophy, Dave headed back to the rink. While prepared to accept that his kid brother was the academic in the family, there was no way he was willing to concede that Bill was also the better athlete.

Sibling rivalry chilled on the ice as the brothers soon learned they curled well together. Their teamwork got a further boost when Bruce asked Shorty Jenkins to coach his sons, to make them truly good curlers. It wasn't that big a stretch for Dave. Never all that keen about school, he recalls that he attended Grade 13 "on a curling scholarship." In other words, he stayed in school to curl, not to cram. He was hanging around the curling club so much by then that Shorty, beyond coaching the Merklinger brothers, took the rink rat under his wing, showing him how to make good ice. But the early emphasis was on transforming the brothers into truly competitive curlers.

The results were immediate and promising, as Shorty guided his young charges to the 1972 provincial schoolboy playdowns, representing Trenton High School. A year later, with Bill skipping and Dave throwing third rocks, they finished third. That same year, the Merklinger brothers defeated the Howard brothers en route to winning the Ontario Junior Tankard. Following their father's posting to Ottawa, the air force brats, representing

Laurentian High School, finished second at the schoolboy provincials, losing to Brampton's Peter File. The Merklinger team dissolved when Bruce was posted to Prince Edward Island. Bill and his younger sister, Anne, followed their father, while Marj and Dave stayed in Ottawa.

Bill and Anne joined ranks and met with remarkable early success. In 1975, they both represented Prince Edward Island at the Canada Winter Games in Lethbridge, Alberta, where Anne won bronze and Bill missed the final cut with a 6–5 record. A year later, at age seventeen, Anne lost the final game in the provincial junior ladies championship. Her father coached her, and that bridesmaid finish may have been the genesis of what Bruce would later term the "Merklinger Curse." As for Anne, her only recollection of that memorable event was losing the last game.

Bill continued to excel, winning the 1982 provincial mixed championship and advancing to the nationals in Timmins, Ontario, bowing out to Saskatchewan's Rick Folk in the semifinals. Back in Ottawa, Dave was being tutored in ice making by Shorty Jenkins, but still curling well enough to reach the elite level of men's curling. In 1977, he was runner-up in the Ontario playdowns, a win away from going to the Brier. He came up short again in 1981 but finally made it to the big show with skip Earle Morris in 1985. They finished with five wins and six losses, respectable but not enough to advance to the playoff round. In 1990, Dave was reunited with Bill and they came within a hair of returning to the Brier. Literally.

Down to final skip rocks in the final end of the semifinal game in Trenton, Ontario, the Merklinger brothers seemed to have clinched the game against the Howard brothers. Dave's final rock picked up a hair from a brush and veered sharply out of play. Legend has it that Russ Howard's final stone also picked up a hair, altering it enough to steal an end, the game, and the Brier berth. Whether it was a great or a lucky shot, Marj, who still has her "Mother Merk" sweater, applies a uniquely colourful expletive to describe it. But were the Howards blessed by the curling gods or were the Merklingers cursed?

Bill says he initially handled his deep disappointment well, but acknowledges that his mood changed abruptly. Competing teams shared a common dressing room back then, and while the two skips changed into their street clothes without exchanging a word, Bill recalls overhearing a member of the Howard team chirp, "You didn't really expect to win, did you?" That struck the younger brother as a particularly cruel breach of the curlers' code, and he rose to the occasion, prepared to make curling a true contact sport. Crossing the room toward the Howard team, mayhem clearly on his mind, he was intercepted, and cooler heads prevailed. Glenn Howard doesn't recall that incident, but remembers the game vividly. Dave, though obviously disappointed at the time, was philosophical in recalling the defeat fifteen years later, chuckling that there was actually a third hair that day—floating in his post-game beer. As he savoured the irony—and the beer—the Howards went on to beat Ed Werenich to advance to the Brier and the worlds.

The final showdown for the Merklinger brothers pitted them against each other at the 1993 Ontario mixed championship in Peterborough, Ontario. It was a true family affair for both brothers; Dave's team included then-wife Janet, a recreational curler who played at their club once a week, while sister Anne played third for Bill. Both brothers viewed her as the possible ringer, fresh from winning the Ontario women's title the week before and earning her first trip to the Scott Tournament of Hearts. Dave admits candidly that he never expected to advance beyond the provincials playing with two club-level curlers but after dropping their first five games, his team, and his own hand in particular, got hot, winning their final six games, including the round-robin match against his kid brother and sister. "We got better when they stopped worrying about their shooting statistics," Dave recalls, adding, "Stats are for losers." If he thought that reaching the finals was the pinnacle of his mixed curling career, he hadn't counted on ever beating his siblings' squad, clearly superior on paper. Bill and Anne could handle any situation and outshoot his foursome end after end. So Dave killed them with junk.

Since this was before the free guard zone rule, Dave filled the ice in front of the house, then claimed end after end by throwing perfect shots. Bill recalls that he and Anne switched their strategy and tried to put pressure on their brother's third—their sister-in-law at the time—believing that she would crack under the strain. She didn't. In fact, she curled better in that tournament than anyone had ever seen her curl before, making several double takeouts, difficult raises, and on and on. Dave beat his siblings in the round robin, then again in the championship game. More than a decade later, Anne jokes that she still bears the scars from that championship, before confessing, "It was fun." After a moment's pause, she adds, "Well, for Dave."

Big brother took his team to the Canadian mixed championship in Swift Current, Saskatchewan. On the eve of competition, he poured his players a drink, then stunned them by announcing he was disbanding them for the next season, reasoning, "It was never going to get better than this." The magic faltered, and they promptly lost their first six games, then rebounded to win their final five matches, including an upset against the eventual national championship team from Nova Scotia. Dave and Anne were reunited five years later at the Scott Tournament of Hearts, where she played on the ice he made. Once again, the improbable happened. First, she skipped her squad to victory over the powerful Sandra Schmirler team—

twice—to advance to the final game. Having staged apparent back-to-back miracles in the round robin and semifinal games, and trailing Alberta's Cathy Borst 5–2 after five ends, Anne narrowed the gap then delighted the 7,373 spectators at the Regina Agridome by drawing for two in the tenth to force the game into an extra end. Borst, who had lost only one game all week, drew to the back of the four-foot circle to win 7–6 in eleven ends.

Anne has made several appearances at the Scott since then, each time coming up short but making her mark in other ways. Twice named to skip the second all-star team, in 1998 and 2000, she was honoured those same years with the Marj Mitchell Award, the sportsmanship trophy—named for the woman who skipped Canada to its first world title in 1981 and died tragically young of cancer at age thirty-five—presented to the curler who best embodies the spirit of curling.

There are indelible images of Anne at the Scott Tournament of Hearts over the years—dancing the Macarena with her opposing skip during a lull in the action; sliding down the ice after winning a crucial game; draping a comforting arm around the shoulder of a dejected young skip, as if to remind her that her day will come in a game where all things are possible, where anyone can beat anyone else on any given day. There are the smiles of victory and satisfaction with a good shot, no matter who made it, and the stoic stare when a hometown crowd erupts for her opponent, cheering their local hero's biting six-ender. But the Merklinger clan knows perhaps better than most that the greatest accomplishments often occur far from the limelight. They learned early the magic that curling can cast over a kid who never seemed to have much of a future in athletics. For all her accomplishments and near misses, Anne's greatest achievement may simply be her ability to walk onto an ice sheet—a testament to the courage of a young girl with a limp who wouldn't quit.

She rates her parents as her greatest influences in her formative years for instilling in her the importance of giving back to others and doing your best, no matter what the task. That "acceptable standard" was challenged occasionally by obstacles that rose along the way; "little bumps," as she called them, "that made sure you still had to give your best effort at everything you did." Anne had more than her share of bumps; the most dramatic was being diagnosed as a child with a "slipped epiphysis" in both hips. The congenital disorder is marked by deferred pain to the knee from the slippage in the hip joint. Both her legs hurt, but the pain in the right knee was more severe. The doctors operated soon after diagnosing the problem, leaving Anne with childhood memories of being in traction and a "loooooong" time on crutches. Months of therapy followed. The entire clan seems to recall watching her do constant leg raises with five-pound bags of peas strapped to her ankles.

Despite the successful surgery and Anne's determined therapy program, the doctor warned that she might suffer a permanent limp. He encouraged Anne to "work real hard" to make it less noticeable. Swimming was the recommended therapy, and she quickly found one stroke that she could do very well—the breaststroke. This "bit of a fluke" proved providential. She excised all traces of her limp and was soon excelling. She added "whip quick" with front crawl and butterfly and was soon competing at the provincial level, enjoying unusually early success while somehow avoiding the burnout that often accompanied it.

Attending the University of South Carolina on full scholarship, she continued her successes right up to the Olympic Trials for the 1980 Moscow Summer Games. Anne finished third in the breaststroke, one spot shy of an Olympic berth. Any disappointment she might have felt was eased by advance knowledge that Canada, along with many other Western nations, planned to boycott the Games to protest the Soviet invasion of Afghanistan.

If Anne was graceful and skilled in the water, she had taken her first shot at curling with no more promise than any other eight-year-old in the era of wrestling full-weight rocks down the sheet—two hands on the handle, push hard out of the hack, shove the rock, and belly flop on the ice. Her reward then was not that she did it well—but that she could do it at all. She never forgot what she had endured to come within a stroke of the Olympics, and quite possibly the medal podium. Nor did she forget those who, like her, just need a chance, maybe a helping hand, to compete. She would pass on the support she had received, share her good fortune with others who might lack a sense or a limb but whose spirits were intact, and encourage them to strive, to compete, to achieve. She would be there for others, as others had been there for her, including extended "family."

It is no accident that Anne has headed the Sandra Schmirler Foundation since its inception. It is no secret that the mutual respect between those elite curlers led to a personal friendship. Rivals on the ice, they shared a special bond off the ice. The example most cited was the Schmirler team's unusual, perhaps unprecedented, invitation to the Merklinger team to join them in their dressing room for a drink at the end of a major competition. Their bond was strengthened when Sandra confided to Anne that she had been diagnosed with cancer. Doodling on a napkin at sportswriter Barre Campbell's wedding a short time later, Anne designed the four clasped hands—the fireman's grip known for its unbreakable strength—that would evolve into the logo of the charitable foundation for sick children that was created after Schmirler's untimely death. But there is more to the story.

For six years, Anne worked with the Canadian Paralympic Committee, lobbying with the Canadian Federation of Sport for the Disabled to include their athletes in full-medal competition for field events. In 1990, she joined Rick Hansen—who was concluding his wheelchair world tour—to help him create his Man in Motion Foundation, which funded the Commission for Inclusion of Athletes with Disabilities. Their efforts led to the debut of the 800- and 1,500-metre wheelchair races at the 1994 Commonwealth Games in Victoria. They were granted full-medal status at the 2006 Turin Olympic Winter Games and Canada Summer Games. Her efforts to help others, greatly motivated by her own experiences, also hit closer to home.

In 1982, Anne met world-class paddler Don Michie at the Rideau Canoe Club. They were married in 1984. Anne spent much of the next decade travelling the world to lobby for Paralympic athletes, and then started a family. Meagan and Connor both swim competitive breaststroke. Like her mom, Meagan has overcome some obstacles to achieve what she has. Diagnosed at the age of one with the genetic disorder Prader-Willi syndrome, she attends high school and has distinguished herself with her swimming at provincial championships, has met and exceeded national standards, and qualified for both the 2003 Special Olympics and the Physically Disabled Games. Meagan was also eligible for the Paralympic Games and competed for the Canadian team at the 2006 swimming trials in San Antonio, Texas—one month after competing at the Special Olympics in Brandon, Manitoba. Her future looks bright, as does her brother Connor's; he continues to excel in swimming and curling, laying the groundwork that same year at a summer curling camp in Guelph, Ontario, for future regional success.

So what does an elite curler, a recreational paddler, an international advocate for people with disabilities, and a mother/wife and coach/fan do with the rest of her time? Anne parlayed a six-month stint with the Canadian Synchronized Swimming Association into her current post as director general of the

Canadian Canoe Association, and she has paddled into the semi-pro ranks after ten years with the sport.

She dismisses her achievements as "nothing too serious," and considers husband Don to be quite remarkable as both a world-class athlete and a skilled tradesman. He continues to pursue both those loves, despite injuries suffered in an industrial accident that would have stopped lesser mortals. While he was working at home alone with Connor, then eighteen months old, resting nearby in his crib, Don's left hand slipped into a saw, severing all his fingers. Bleeding profusely, he staunched the flow as best he could, calmly scooped his digits into an ice-filled plastic bag, grabbed Connor from his crib, loaded the family van, and drove himself to hospital where he promptly passed out from blood loss. The surgeons were able to reattach or rebuild his thumb and three fingers but could not save his index finger. The fingers work "okay" but if they slow his work, they haven't affected his paddling. The affected hand is his lower pulling hand on the paddle, apparently causing fewer problems than if it were the top hand. "As long as he can paddle, he's okay," Anne concludes philosophically. "He could easily have packed in his profession but he never gave up. He does amazingly well and never, ever complains."

Noting that Don was raised with the same strong work ethic instilled in the Merklinger kids, Anne considers her "amazing guy" to be a great athlete, partner, and parent, as well as a true artist...and far too modest. Those romantic sentiments seem to embrace the whole family at different times. Anne's divorced parents both met their current spouses through curling—Bruce on the ice at a mixed bonspiel, Marj in the clubhouse when asked for the loan of a slider.

Bruce stayed on the ice, coaching twin daughters, Lee and Breanne toward junior supremacy. Their quest failed in 2004—losing in the final game as they did in 2003—but there are signs

"Peelers" on Parade: World champion Colleen Jones lamented that women would have to curl naked to retain their audience if their World Championships were split from the men's. It didn't quite come to that, but women curlers from around the world did shed their clothes in 2006 and again in 2007 for the women's fundraising curling calendar.
PHOTO: ANA ARCE, *THE CURLING NEWS*

A Sweeping Success: Curling has become a big-money game for elite curlers who draw big crowds to fill huge hockey stadiums. Television ratings are equally impressive for major national, world and Olympic bonspiels. The challenge will be to sustain its popularity to the next generations.
PHOTO: *THE CURLING NEWS*

Tornado Tragedy: Of all the disasters to befall curling clubs, the Windsor tornado was the most deadly, peeling back the roof while curlers were on the ice. This chaotic scene of the interior of the Windsor Curling Club leaves little doubt of the carnage left by the tornado that killed nearly a dozen curlers, and injured many more caught on the ice and in the clubhouse, in 1974. PHOTO: *THE WINDSOR STAR*

Wrenching Welcome: The 415 residents of Benito, Manitoba, lay proud claim to native son and curling legend Ed Werenich—a big guy from a small town whose intensity led to the only body check in curling history.

I'll Take Curling Hosts, Alex: Before hosting the popular game show, Jeopardy, Alex Trebek (left) was swept away by curling as much as his CBC colleagues Doug Maxwell (centre) and Don Chevrier (right). PHOTO: ROBERT C. RAGSDALE, LTD.

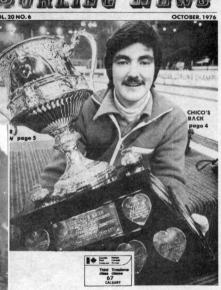

CANADIAN CURLING NEWS

VOL. 20 NO. 6 OCTOBER, 1976

CHICO'S BACK page 4

Rocking the Rock: Newfoundland's Jack MacDuff pictured with the Brier Tankard on the 1976 cover of *Canadian Curling News* (now *The Curling News*), thirty years before Brad Gushue's "rock stars" won Olympic gold. PHOTO: *THE CURLING NEWS*

Ice Breaker: Curling's debut as a demonstration sport at the 1924 Olympics was retroactively upgraded to full-medal status in 2007. PHOTO: IOC/OLYMPIC MUSEUM COLLECTION

Shooting Blind: Three-time world champion Randy Ferbey dons vision-impairing goggles in a 2006 exhibition "blind curling" match in Gander, Newfoundland. PHOTO: SCOTT COOK

Paralympian: Gold-medal skip Chris Daw uses a curling stick to throw his rock from his wheelchair while training for the 2006 Paralympic Games in Pinerolo, Italy. PHOTO: BENOIT BELOSSE. USED WITH PERMISSION OF THE CANADIAN PARALYMPIC COMMITTEE

Gold-Medal Victory: Team Canada celebrates their gold-medal victory in wheelchair curling at the 2006 Paralympic Winter Games in Pinerolo, Italy. PHOTO: BENOIT BELOSSE. USED WITH PERMISSION OF THE CANADIAN PARALYMPIC COMMITTEE

Cool Sport: The Tragically Hip made curling "cool," recording the soundtrack for the movie, *Men With Brooms*, and making a cameo appearance as a curling team. They are ardent curlers who, some say, schedule their tours around the curling season.

PHOTO: MICHAEL GIBSON, USED WITH PERMISSION OF SERENDIPITY POINT FILMS

Curling Rocks: On the set of *Rock Stars: The World of Curling* at 2002 Olympic venue. From left: Colleen Jones, Leslie Nielsen, Paul Gross, and George Karrys.

PHOTO: *THE CURLING NEWS*

Lights, Camera, Laughter: Veteran Canadian actor Leslie Nielsen as Gordon Cutter, is surrounded by the cast of *Men with Brooms*. From left: Paul Gross as Chris Cutter, Jed Rees as Eddie Strombeck, James Allodi as Neil Bucyk, and Polly Shannon as Joanne.

PHOTO: MICHAEL GIBSON, USED WITH PERMISSION OF SERENDIPITY POINT FILMS

Future Olympian?: Sandra Schmirler with four-month-old Joey, son of Olympian Richard Hart at the 1998 Nagano Winter Olympics. Schmirler the Curler evolved from a sports legend to Canada's Sweetheart for winning the gold medal in Japan and for her courageous battle against cancer. Her funeral was televised nationally. PHOTO: *THE CURLING NEWS*

Kamikaze Kanucks: When not defying death sliding down ice hills or curling for silver at the 1998 Nagano Olympics, the men's curling team—(left to right) Skip Mike Harris, Richard Hart, George Karrys, and Collin Mitchell—toured the sights. PHOTO: *THE CURLING NEWS*

Great Ones: The 1998 Nagano Olympic welcomed curlers to their first Olympiad. Enroute to winning a gold medal, curlers Joan McKusker, Marcia Geudereit, and Jan Betker of Team Schmirler socialized at the Athlete's Village with hockey stars Theoren Fleury and Wayne Gretzky. PHOTO: *THE CURLING NEWS*

Team Merk: From left to right, Anne Merklinger, Theresa Breen, Patti McKnight, and Audrey Reddick helped pioneer an aggressive style of women's curling. Clan Merklinger has contributed to the roaring game at all levels, and in a host of ways: as athletes, organizers, and ice makers. Anne, in particular, has been an ambassador for the sport and a champion for worthy causes on and off the ice. PHOTO: USED WITH PERMISSION OF KRUGER PRODUCTS/ONTARIO CURLING ASSOCIATION

Party Hearty: World champion Glenn Howard (left) and future Olympian Paul Savage (right) flank Chris Berlette, the top junior fundraiser at the 1993 Heart to Heart charity bonspiel, in Thunder Bay, Ontario. PHOTO: *THE CURLING NEWS*

The Ice Man: Clarence "Shorty" Jenkins' legendary "swing" ice revolutionized curling. The flamboyant dynamo has been lauded and lampooned in movies and on television. PHOTO: USED WITH PERMISSION OF MCCAIN FOODS, LTD.

Sibling Rivalry: Anne and Dave Merklinger can't help smiling whenever they're on the ice together, even when preparing to cast stones in a Battle of the Sexes promotional event. PHOTO: *THE CURLING NEWS*

that the "Merklinger Curse," if it exists, may be lifting. Playing in the 2004 Ontario mixed junior championship at the London Curling Club, the team, which included two members of what *Free Press* reporter Steve Green dubbed "Ottawa's first family of curling," held off a late charge by Derek Abbotts' Sarnia rink to win the clan's twelfth provincial championship, 9–7. There's little doubt that Bruce must have endured some nervous moments as Abbotts clawed back from a 7–3 deficit after seven ends to count three in the eighth and steal another in the ninth. The twins' team finished 6–1 in the round robin, thus avoiding a sudden-death playoff game and no doubt bringing relief to their coach. But a playoff game was never an option for Breanne, who told Green she had an essay due the following Monday and a mid-term to write on Tuesday. Both twins, then nineteen, were attending the University of Ottawa. As far as they were concerned, there was simply no time for an extra game.

London was their second Ontario crown and, with Lee throwing last rock and Breanne shooting second, the first junior mixed title won by a female skip. Those titles are added to the ten won by Anne, Dave, and Bill. The twins also credit their half-sister for inspiring them, telling the press she gave them pep talks before every bonspiel. Her message was constant: "One shot at a time, one end at a time, one game at a time." They also credit Anne with teaching them "a lot" about respect—for their teammates and for their opponents.

Until Anne announced her retirement from elite curling in early 2006, there were those who imagined seeing her and the twins curling and standing together on the Olympic podium. That's unlikely to happen after the twins joined Janet McGhee's Uxbridge-based team; Lee has joined Jenn Hanna's team for 2007–08. Anne plans to curl recreationally a couple of nights a week at the Ottawa Rideau Club, leaving more time to spend with her family. Even a curling clan like the Amazing Merklingers have lives away from the ice and for years enjoyed a family diversion that would make Fast Eddie Lukowich, the Vikings' last champion, smile: Dragon Boat racing.

Bill Merklinger was the first to discover the passion and was soon joined on the oars by his brother-in-law Don and niece Jennifer (Dave's daughter, a schoolteacher and an internationally acclaimed dancer). Meagan, perched high in the prow, would beat the drum to set their pace. The rest of the clan cheered them on.

But the Merklingers will always be best remembered for their contributions to curling—reading the ice, sweeping the ice, and making the ice. Everyone agrees Anne and her long-time teammates—Theresa Breen, Patti McKnight, Susan Froud, and Audrey Reddick—had a great run. They represented Ontario at the Scott Tournament of Hearts in 1993, 1994, 1998, and 2000, twice reaching the final game. The national title eluded them, as did their one shot at an Olympic berth. But Anne has been credited with changing the game, making it more exciting for those on the ice, in the stands, and watching on television. Long-time friend and competitor Joan McCusker, the Olympic gold medallist–cum–CBC curling commentator, praised her "feisty" aggressive style to the media, claiming it forced competitors, often reluctantly, to put more rocks in the house to compete. That, she conceded, probably made the game more entertaining, perhaps more for the fans than for Anne's opponents. Yet Anne's impact on the roaring game may continue. At this writing, she may have a chance to build on those early achievements in a new—and potentially very powerful—venue. Her name is whispered to be on a fairly short list of possible replacements for CCA executive director Dave Parkes, who retired in May 2007, months earlier than expected.

In 2002, Anne finally got to an Olympiad, joining CBC at the Salt Lake Olympics as a spotter—the eyes and ears of the producers and directors in the trucks who beam the images to a worldwide audience. It was a little overwhelming for a single set of eyes and ears, so George Karrys was brought in to help ease the load at Turin in 2006. Karrys claims that he thinks he and she spotted the streaker at the curling venue at the same moment, but he willingly concedes that she was the first to slam an elbow into the producer's ribs. However that worked out—and we must give Anne the nod for the alleged elbow that may become known in some curling circles as the Merklinger-Werenich manoeuvre—spotting that naked man racing across the rink may have answered a lingering mystery, less to do with curling than with the Scots who created the sport. The media reported that the sole clue to the stripped speedster's identity or even nationality was the strong brogue with which he asked someone to bring him his "troosers" as he was escorted off the ice by security. Assuming the interloper—much enjoyed by most if not all in attendance—was indeed Scottish, the flopping adornment he had tied around his waist for modesty may finally answer the perennial question: What does a Scot wear under his kilt?

Apparently, it's poultry.

If that seems unseemly to any self-respecting Scot, they can relax. George Karrys determined that the streaker was in fact an Englishman, Mark Roberts—*The* Streaker—who has bared his all from the Super Bowl to golf greens and nearly every major sport in between.

Several months after the Turin Olympics, the CCA terminated an unhappy marriage to the CBC and awarded full curling coverage to TSN. That likely had nothing to do with the CBC's hiring Anne or the alleged "Merklinger Curse." In fact, all went well at Salt Lake, raising the spectre of a "Karrys Kurse," as he was not in Utah.

Then again, history has not always been kind to curling or curlers. The roaring game has had its share of dark times, black ice, true tragedy, tears, and death.

IN THE HACK

TWISTER

*I*t is Wednesday, April 3, 1974—another tropical night in Canada's banana belt in southwestern Ontario. I savour the air conditioning, listening to the nearby radio console as I police (dust and tidy) the upstairs lounge and crew quarters at Arbour's Chatham Ambulance Service. While I toil in solitude, the two-man crews are downstairs checking the vehicles to ensure that everything they could possibly need over the next fourteen hours is stocked or replenished—splints, oxygen tanks, portable ventilators, back boards, cervical collars, extrication gear, even Band-Aids. An hour west down Highway 401, the border city of Windsor is living up to its claim of being the thunderstorm capital of the world. Even by banana-belt standards, this has been a stifling day. The humidity seems thick enough to slice. In hindsight, perhaps that should have given some early warning of what was to come.

The radio crackles a jarring, urgent message from Windsor dispatch, advising me that a tornado has just struck the Windsor Curling Club, where an unknown number of curlers were on the ice and are now trapped under the rubble. Casualties are assumed, but the number and extent of their injuries are undetermined. I am asked to send help. Stat!

I dispatch both duty crews as my supervisor instructs me to start moving ambulances from other services to the east of us and to call in backup crews to cover local calls. I request help from London. The call is relayed east to Woodstock, Kitchener, and Milton until I can no longer hear the distant dispatchers as they move beyond our transmission range.

Our first-run crew is racing to Windsor with lights flashing, sirens blazing. The second crew is to stand by at Tilbury, which has already dispatched its ambulance west. This same "backfilling" will play out in much the same way as outlying volunteer services rushed into New York City on September 11, 2001, to respond to calls and crises while Manhattan squads dashed to the burning towers. Both disasters, one natural, the other man-made, will end in death.

My only link to the disaster is radio chatter, like an old wartime movie where controllers and senior officers stand helplessly by, listening to the distant battle chatter. The sense of dread is compounded by an inability to do anything more to help.

By the time our first crew arrives on the scene, the survivors have been rescued or at least located. It takes longer to locate and identify the dead. The toll is high—nine killed, dozens injured—in what must certainly be the greatest tragedy in curling history. That it could have been worse offers little consolation.

I will never forget that night. Of the thousands of curling clubs that dot the Canadian landscape, my most vivid memory is of one I never visited and which, in little more than an instant of terror, ceased to exist.

THE SEVENTH END
BLACK ICE

*O*n June 9, 2006, American faux-news commentator Jon Stewart, star of *The Daily Show* and the host at that year's Academy Awards, became the latest American late-night television celebrity to take his shot at Canadians and curling. Applauding Canada for arresting alleged homegrown terrorists a few days earlier, he welcomed us as a fellow target for terrorists, but was at a loss to fathom their logic. Hating Canada, he told the 5,200 people packed into Casino Rama near Orillia, Ontario, was like hating toast. Or curling. It reportedly generated a big laugh.

Two days later, someone did take an apparent dislike to curling and torched the historic Winnipeg Thistle Curling Club, destroying it. Club president Laurie Baudreau reportedly took home the sole charred surviving trophy to polish it. A suspected arsonist was arrested within days. In May 2007, Ashley Prest reported in the *Winnipeg Free Press* that the Thistle would rise from the ashes by merging with the Valour Road Curling Club, which had continued to operate out of the building it had sold to a private interest in 2005.

Once again, curlers were left wondering whether to rebuild, likely worrying if they could afford to. It's a scene that's too often been played out over the years across Canada. The Windsor club may be the worst, but is certainly not the first, nor will it be the last, to be hit by disaster. Google "curling club + disaster" and you may be shocked at the number of clubs that have burned down or been crushed to the ground by the snow on their roofs. Over the centuries, curlers have fallen through lake ice, been shipwrecked, and had their curling stones torpedoed at sea. Curling has links to major calamities over the years. The Mayflower Curling Club in Halifax and the local club in Lockerbie, Scotland, were transformed into temporary morgues for the dead of the *Titanic* and Pan Am Flight 109, respectively.

On January 29, 1946, Angus Walters, who skippered the working schooner *Bluenose* to the coveted International Fisherman's Trophy—and onto the Canadian dime and a commemorative stamp—was curling, presumably at the Bluenose Curling Club in Lunenburg, when he learned that his beloved ship had struck a reef off Haiti and sank.

While some disasters can be ascribed to human error—like when the Rossland, British Columbia, club replaced its 1898 rink with a new five-sheet rink in 1914 on a creek that was undermined by local beavers (shades of *Men with Brooms*)—fire and weather are more likely culprits. Dozens of clubs have burned down or collapsed under the weight of snow on the roof. A random sampling from British Columbia is enough to give you an idea of the scope of the losses. Most of the following clubs were replaced or rebuilt:

- Curling began in the Alberni Valley in 1953 when the old Royal Canadian Electrical and Mechanical Engineers (RCEME) maintenance building of the Greenwood Army Barracks was reconstructed into a curling facility. In 1962, the building was destroyed by fire.
- The Ashcroft and District Curling Club was founded in 1896, and its first building was erected in 1899 and rebuilt in 1912. That building was demolished in the summer of 1954, and a new two-sheet club opened two years later. In

1966, the club expanded to four sheets. In 1968, it burned
down. Today the club is adorned with a mural depicting a
turn-of-the-century curling scene painted by the local high
school art class.

- The Burns Lake Curling Club officially opened in October
  1951. It burned down the next spring; only the ice plant was
  salvaged.
- The Creston Curling Club was created in 1925 and built a
  two-sheet rink the next year. The club burned down in
  1968.
- The Fort St. John Curling Club was founded in 1946 when
  it took over an old U.S. Army building in the Peace area of
  British Columbia. The six-sheet rink built in 1960 was
  destroyed by fire in 1978.
- The Grand Forks Curling Club opened in 1909 with three
  sheets of natural ice. The roof of the building collapsed
  under heavy snow in 1928.
- The original Howe Sound Curling Club opened in
  Valleycliffe, in Squamish Valley, in 1964 and burned down
  twenty years later.
- Founded in 1959, the Hope Curling Club was the focal
  point of the B.C. town in the early years. In January 1976,
  the club was destroyed by fire.
- In 1893, Kaslo became the first community in British
  Columbia to organize a curling club. Its original arena clubhouse, built in 1896, was crushed by a heavy snow
  accumulation in the 1930s. The clubhouse built for the
  Rainbow Curling Club in 1963 also collapsed under a heavy
  snowfall soon after.
- The Mission City Curling Club opened in 1954. The curling
  facility did exceptionally well until the building was
  destroyed by fire in 1967. Rebuilt on land donated by the

city, the four-sheet rink was renamed the Mission Granite
Curling Club.

- The Revelstoke Curling Club was founded in 1899 and its
  facility was completed in early 1900. The original curling
  club burned down in its second decade, and for ten years
  Revelstoke had only open-air skating and curling. The next
  curling club was built in 1924 and operated until 1962,
  when it was condemned and closed. The present four-sheet
  club was opened in 1964.
- In 1893, S.E. Elliot built a private curling rink at the Vernon
  Hotel. In 1912, the club moved to a modern six-sheet natu-
  ral-ice building at Polson Park. The Vernon Curling Club
  burned to the ground in 1926. It was rebuilt with eight
  sheets.

Fortunately, there was no loss of life reported in any of the
British Columbia destructions, although the province's oldest
curling club came close to setting a lethal precedent. The Golden
Curling Club hosted its first game on December 11, 1893, using
two sixteen-by-eighty-foot tents placed end to end to cover one
sheet of ice. Officially opened in October 1894, it was replaced in
1967 by the Golden and Districts Centennial Arena. In 1972, the
curling portion of the complex collapsed just moments after a regular women's draw had been completed. The facility was repaired
and curling continues to this day. But the disasters continue. In
April 2007, the roof of the Fort Nelson Community Centre,
which houses the local curling club, collapsed "like a deck of
cards" under the weight of heavy snow that had piled up for a
week. There were no injuries. Others have not escaped so lightly.

On April 3, 1974, 323 people died when a series of tornadoes
struck eleven states in the United States, and Ontario, within an
eight-hour period. The tornadoes caused more than $1 billion in

damage. In Windsor, one funnel cloud touched down at several locations, taking nine lives at the Windsor Curling Club. Dozens were injured. The following front-page account by police reporter Blair Crawford appeared on Saturday, April 3, 1999, as part of the *Windsor Star*'s twenty-fifth anniversary coverage:

Tornado Nightmares Linger

After 25 years, the nightmares have faded, but Fred Wilkinson will never forget the night a man died in his arms.

Wilkinson was on his hands and knees, picking his way through a treacherous jumble of shattered concrete and smooth granite curling rocks.

On April 3, 1974, beneath the tornado-flattened rubble of the Windsor Curling Club, eight of Windsor's most prominent citizens lay dead or dying. A ninth would linger in hospital for nearly nine months before succumbing to his injuries.

Wilkinson was one of dozens of rescuers who plunged into the chaos, crawling through the rubble with only the pitiful cries of the injured to guide them through the blackness.

Wilkinson found one man, pulled away some rubble to make him more comfortable, then slid his leg beneath the man's head to act as a pillow.

"He was pleading for help," Wilkinson recalled. "He told me his name. He wanted help in such a bad way, but all I could do was talk to him and try to make him as comfortable as I could."

They were still waiting for an ambulance when he felt the man slip away.

"It's something you never forget," he said.

Wednesday, April 3 was muggy and eerily warm—
close to 18 C. While Windsorites basked in the weather
and dreamed of summer, somewhere over the American
Midwest a natural disaster was being born. Displaced by
an advancing cold front, a huge mass of warm, moist air
began to rise, shedding rainfall as it did.

The rising air column began to rotate, picking up
speed and spawning violent thunderstorms. As the storm
front moved northeast, clusters of tornadoes formed
along its trailing edge, twisting destruction from
Alabama to Ontario. More than 300 people had been
killed and thousands more were homeless as the killer
storm rolled toward Ontario. It was the deadliest tornado swarm in 50 years.

At the Windsor Curling Club on Central Avenue it
was the night of the Chrysler Blue Broom Bonspiel. Storm
warnings had been broadcast throughout the day, but few
thought them serious enough to change their plans.

Grace McLaren and her husband Allister noted the
peculiar sky as they made their way to the bonspiel.

"We should never have gone," she said. "But we did.
Now, whenever there's a storm I look at the sky. I know
what to look for now—it was yellow-green—but back
then we had no idea what it meant."

It began to rain at about 5 p.m., slackened off 30
minutes later, then struck with fury at 6:30 p.m. Curlers
inside the club could hear the rumble of thunder even
over the booming slap of curling brooms.

Punishing winds lashed the city and rain fell in tor-
rents. Fifteen-year-old Don Strilchuk was running home
from a friend's house when he stopped to take shelter
under a tree near the curling club.

He heard a deafening roar and looked up between two houses and watched, astonished, as the west wall of the curling club crumbled. He sprinted to the scene.

"I didn't see a funnel cloud. I just remember the sound it made," Strilchuk said. "It was incredibly loud."

Fire Lt. Joseph Kato and his partner Marcel Fields were on their way to another call when their heavy rescue squad was lifted from the roadway.

"Marcel was turning the wheel every which way and it didn't make a difference," said Kato, 67, now retired and living near Sturgeon Falls.

"He said 'Joe you won't believe this. I can't steer. The whole front end's off the ground.' We must have driven right through it."

Inside the club, the lights flickered. Stunned curlers watched the wall waver, then begin to fall as the roof peeled back, in the words of one witness, "like a sardine can."

"We all looked up and something made my husband start to run," McLaren recalled. "He got hit by a brick as it fell. The man a few feet behind him didn't make it."

By chance, the tornado struck when the skips were standing at the west end of the ice sheet with their backs to the wall. All of the casualties came from that end of the building. Had it happened a few minutes later there could have been dozens more curlers caught in the avalanche of concrete.

"The noise was deafening," said another curler, who asked her name not be used. To spare other victims, she volunteered to handle many of the media interviews after the disaster and she still feels embarrassed about the attention she received.

"I happened to turn around and look up and I saw it coming down," she said. "We were yelling at the skips, but they couldn't see what was happening behind them. They didn't know what to do."

"Then the ceiling went off and the lights went out."

Across the street, at the French Canadian Club, 31-year-old Fred Wilkinson and his fellow Chrysler workers were on break downing glasses of draft beer when the lights flickered and the emergency lights came on. Then a man burst in shouting the curling club had been hit. Debris was still raining from the sky when Wilkinson and the other rescuers reached the club across Central Avenue.

The rescuers ran to the rear of the club, and stepped through the gaping wall and into the darkness.

"There was just a bit of light. You couldn't see much, but we could hear the moaning and crying," he said. "Everyone was so focussed. We just starting uncovering every voice we could hear.

"Everyone was running on adrenaline. They were hard-working factory workers and they just wanted to help."

Don Strilchuk, now a Windsor police detective, remembers the nightmarish scene—arms and legs protruding from the debris. Bodies and blood. Like dozens of others, he began clawing at the rubble.

"It was like a scene from a movie," he said. "All these people wandering around in a daze, bleeding."

Grace and Allister McLaren were among the curlers who pitched in with the rescue. Allister, still in shock and bleeding from where he'd been struck on the head, helped lead several people to safety. He remembered none of it the next day.

"I helped dig out three men who I thought I'd saved," Grace said. "They were all still breathing, but they all died later. We lost eight friends that night."

A week after the disaster Allister's hair turned white, she said. Three years later he died at age 45. "I think it killed him," she said. "I think Al was the 10th victim of the tornado."

Bob Gammon was on duty at the ambulance base at Metropolitan Hospital when the call came for both units to roll. Gammon hadn't even got out of the ambulance when a woman came up to say a wall and the ceiling had collapsed. There were many injured inside, she said.

Gammon radioed his dispatcher: "You better send everything."

Gammon and his partner, Gerry Valente, stepped through the wall and into inky blackness. Rain poured through the open roof. They began groping their way forward, without even a penlight to show the way. It didn't take long to realize the scope of the disaster. The first "four or five" victims Gammon found were VSA—vital signs absent.

"Then we came upon a lady who was still breathing and I realized we had to get her transported," he said. "I thought, these other people we're not going to be able to help, but she's one we can."

The police and fire department still hadn't arrived when Gammon and Valente loaded their patient and headed for Met Hospital. They were at the hospital in barely two minutes, but it was of no use. Their patient died.

By then the emergency response was in full swing. The fire department had brought emergency lights to the scene. Off-duty police officers had been called in. When Gammon and Valente returned to the club, a line of 18 ambulances—some from as far away as Chatham—jammed Central Avenue.

Fearful of more collapse, police cleared the club of everyone but emergency workers. Retired *Windsor Star* photographer Walter Jackson captured the devastation with a front-page picture of Lt. Kato standing in the rubble between two shrouded bodies.

Jackson and *Star* reporter Greg Parent were the first on the scene. Jackson had photographed events at the club often and knew the building well. He walked through the darkness to where he knew the ice surface was, focussed his camera at about 12 feet, then fired blindly into the darkness.

He didn't know what he had photographed until he saw it develop in the darkroom.

"Kato's expression said it all," Jackson said. "He was standing there with his hands out as if he was saying 'What can you do?'"

Dennis Ducharme, then 23, was a young constable with less than a year on the job when his brother called him at home to tell him all off-duty officers were needed. Ducharme put on his heavy black police raincoat, which happened to be in the trunk of his car, and headed for Central and Tecumseh.

"It was chaotic," said Ducharme, now a detective in the Windsor police fraud squad. "Everyone was working their hearts out trying to get people out and offer them help."

Most of the injured were already out when Ducharme arrived, but he pitched in with the rescue and recovery. He and his partner, the late Bill Borre, were among the last to leave, having been ordered to stand watch until the last of the bodies were removed.

"The eeriest thing was that after all the bodies had been removed there were purses, wallets and ID strewn all over the ice surface," he recalled.

When he got home that night Ducharme left his boots outside on his porch to be rinsed clean by the rain. He didn't want his wife to see the blood.

Grace McLaren went to Met Hospital to wait and comfort her friends. The horror of that night will be with her the rest of her life.

"I have to leave church if they start to say the 23rd Psalm," she said. "I heard it eight times that week."

Wilkinson still works at Chrysler, but he's never been back to the French Canadian Club. For a long time after the tragedy he would start from his sleep, with nightmares of being trapped beneath a collapsing wall. He used to drive past the workplace of the victim he'd held, imagining that somehow the man had survived and was inside alive.

"I never talked to his family about it," Wilkinson said. "I wouldn't have known what to say. There were no last words to his wife or anything like that. He just wanted help so badly . . . I think he knew what was happening."

A coroner's inquest was held later that spring, but found no one to blame for the disaster. Although the curling club was 12 years old and had not been subject to regular inspections, the jury found no fault in its design or maintenance. The twister had been so localized the French Canadian Club across the street, now Club

Alouette, was undamaged. Instruments at the Windsor Airport never measured any wind gusts of more than 80 km/h and an Environment Canada meteorologist told the inquest his examination of the curling club showed no evidence of the "rotary wind effect" that would accompany a tornado.

But the inquest jury ruled the disaster had been caused by a tornado, and few who saw the damage or the twisted steel girders at several other buildings near Devonshire Mall damaged in the storm doubted a local twister had touched down.

Estimates at the time indicated the tornado was a moderate twister with a vortex windspeed of about 240 km/h. It was the most destructive natural disaster in Windsor since 17 died in a June 1946 tornado.

The determined members of the Windsor Curling Club rebuilt their rink, but high property taxes and declining membership did what the tornado could not. The club closed in 1990 and now houses Central Fitness.

Grace and Allister McLaren remained members of the club despite the horror they survived. They were curling in the Blue Broom Bonspiel on the first anniversary of the '74 tornado when by spooky coincidence, another powerful storm struck. At 8:10 p.m., a year, almost to the minute, after the tragedy, the lights at the Windsor Curling Club went out.

"We left the ice," she said. "A lot of us who had been there did. Some of the other curlers gave us a hard time about it.

"They hadn't been there that night."

Harrowing as that night was, and just when you probably think there cannot be a more horrific event tied to a curling club, we must pause and recall the doomed White Star liner *Titanic*.

At the eastern end of the country, the Mayflower Curling Club in Halifax became the toast of the Canadian curling world in 2004 as the home to both the men's and women's national champions. Allen Cameron of the *Curling News* declared that the two champions had "collectively ripped the heart of Canadian curling right out of the west and planted it firmly in Atlantic Canada." As columnist Chris Cochrane wrote in the Halifax *Chronicle-Herald* in the wake of Mark Dacey's dramatic 10–9 win over Alberta's perennial Brier champ Randy Ferbey, denying his quest for a fourth consecutive men's national title, the upset "not only snapped the long Nova Scotia losing streak at nationals and ended Ferbey's reign, they joined the [Colleen] Jones team in elevating Nova Scotia to true national curling powerhouse status." Commenting on the end of the Brier drought that has plagued Nova Scotia since 1951, Cochrane concluded, "The turnaround is complete." If it was historic, it was also a happier story than the original Mayflower club's brush with history in 1912.

Originally located at 2660 Agricola Street, later the site of an army-surplus store, the old Mayflower was pressed into service as a venue for storing and viewing the dead from the luxury liner *Titanic* after it struck an iceberg and sank on its maiden transatlantic voyage. With too few lifeboats mandated for a ship carrying roughly two thousand passengers and crew, nearly two-thirds perished in the frigid North Atlantic. In the aftermath of that tragedy, a small host of coroners and morticians set to work preserving, displaying, and identifying the rows and rows of bodies. Of the 328 bodies recovered, 209 were brought to Halifax by four Canadian ships chartered by the White Star line. More than one hundred were simply buried at sea. The experience led to a more efficient method for identifying human remains that would prove invaluable five years later when two thousand Haligonians died in the 1917 Halifax Explosion.

Author Alan Ruffman, who is credited with writing the most authoritative account of the role Halifax played in the *Titanic* disaster, chronicled the rest of this sad legacy in his 1996 article "Halifax and the Titanic Victims" for *Journal of the British Titanic Society*:

> Once victims were returned to Halifax, a temporary morgue was set up in the Mayflower Curling Rink near the northwest corner of Agricola and McCully Streets. From there, identified bodies were shipped out to families or interred in Halifax according to families' wishes. The Halifax Deputy Registrar of Deaths, John Henry Barnstead, supervised the handling of victims, with all personal effects kept in small canvas bags, numbered to match the body number assigned at sea. Careful records of the artefacts were kept and can be inspected today at the Public Archives of Nova Scotia. J. H. Barnstead's son, Arthur S., was to be appointed head of the Mortuary Committee five-and-a-half years later after the devastating Explosion in Halifax Harbour when Halifax and Dartmouth had 10 times as many victims to deal with.

In the end, 150 *Titanic* victims were buried in Halifax cemeteries between May 3 and June 12, 1912. Nearly one-third remained unidentified. The Mayflower's grim role was unique among curling clubs around the world—until terrorists exploded Pan Am Flight 103 in the air over Lockerbie, Scotland, four days before Christmas 1988, killing 259 aboard the 747 jetliner and on the ground. The local curling club—later home to Britain's 2006

Olympic skip David Murdoch—was converted into a temporary morgue.

While tragedy often claims dozens, hundreds, or even thousands of people, the loss of one curler devastated the residents of Cranbook, British Columbia, in May 2006. Robert Necombe, forty-nine, had coached high-performance curlers there and in Calgary. He died alongside paramedics Kim Weitzel and Shawn Currier in a vain attempt to rescue Doug Erickson, who had succumbed to toxic gas at a decommissioned mine.

In every tragedy, even those involving their comrades, paramedics, police, and firefighters are first on the scene. Odds are good that some of them curl. The police and firefighters have their own national curling associations; both are renowned for their curling fundraising activities for charity. Curling is as traditional as the police raising money for the Special Olympics and the firefighters passing their boots to collect coins to combat multiple sclerosis. Both groups gather by the thousands to mark the passing of fallen comrades. On the day that thousands of police gathered to bid farewell to RCMP Constable Dennis Strongquill, gunned down in the line of duty, a handful played host to Scottish police curlers on a trans-Canada goodwill tour.

IN THE HACK

THE FUN HOUSE

I am sitting in the Royal Canadian Mounted Police Curling Club in Ottawa, watching my son, John, and assorted police officers and civilians curl for a good time and to raise funds for the Special Olympics—the preferred police charity. Aside from some two-handed belly flops back before he started attending school, this Cops for Curling bonspiel marks John's first real attempt to toss and sweep rocks. Admitting my bias, I think he does well, if initially a little uncertain on how to hold the broom while shooting. Bottom line, he and everyone on the ice are having a good time. And they're helping a worthy cause.

Both of my children have now curled. Daughter Jodi enjoyed the experience in high school gym class, tossing stones at the same club where wheelchair curler Richard Fraser has played and coached for so many years. However, she spent more time playing competitive fastball and hockey as well as high school volleyball—the sport she plays each summer on an Ottawa beach to raise money for charity. Both Jodi and John have recently discovered golf.

As I watch my son curl and laugh, I flash back two years to an earlier visit to the same club when touring Scottish coppers were playing their Mountie hosts on the Ottawa stop of their Canadian goodwill tour. Growing up in the "wee toon o' Fergus" did nothing to prepare me for that encounter and the rolling Rs in their brogue. Retired Chief Constable Bill Moodie, insisting that his current role was "ambassador," presented me with a miniature "Fife Constabulary" billy club—but no powers of enforcement—while explaining, in some detail, the curling connection to such Scottish locales as "Clackmananshire" and the "Trossachs." I was introduced to Detective Inspector Gordon Gilchrist, whose father, Jimmy, started the Scottish police tours in 1974. I pointed out to the detective that he was now the same age his father was in 1974. His colleagues roared with laughter—and in that instant I transformed "Wee Gordie" into "Old Gordie."

What I remember most of that encounter is that both Scots greeted me by asking, "Did you know our wheelchair curlers just won the world championship?" I am proud to say that I did.

THE EIGHTH END

IS THERE A DOCTOR
IN THE HOUSE?

*J*im Miller was police chief in Woodstock, Ontario, when an F3 tornado touched down on August 7, 1979, leaving two dead and $7 million in damage in its wake. The carnage reminded him of scenes from his war days.

Three years later, the tragedy was more personal as his long-time friend Ray Tebo, a member of the Oxford County Ontario Provincial Police, died of cancer. Tebo had been incredibly well liked and respected by his city and OPP colleagues, and they wanted a way to remember him. They decided a curling fundraiser for cancer research was perfect. Miller has been organizing the event since 1983, raising many thousands of dollars along the way.

The Ray Tebo Memorial Bonspiel typically draws police, as well as judges and Crown attorneys, from across the province. You don't have to be a cop or justice employee to participate, but each of the sixteen rinks is required to have at least one officer—male or female. In their own way, the curlers are seeking justice, raising money to battle the killer that stole their fallen comrade.

The police connection to curling dates to the North West Mounted Police and their Great March West. There are tantalizing snippets of information and old photographs that clearly show that some early Mounties curled.

Perhaps that traditional connection is why, at the 2005 Edmonton Brier, the curlers and their audience were so deeply affected by the drama playing out in the city that weekend. On March 3, four Mounties were tragically murdered at nearby Mayerthorpe, and a massive memorial service was planned for March 10 in Edmonton, during the Brier. An estimated thirteen thousand police officers from across Canada, North America, and beyond headed for Edmonton to show their solidarity and respect for their fallen brothers, Peter Schiemann, Anthony Gordon, Brock Myrol, and Leo Johnston. With most city hotels filled by the curlers and their legions of fans, accommodations had to be found for the visiting officers. Edmonton Police and the RCMP put out an alert for billets in private homes and quickly received more offers than they needed. A minute's silence was held at the opening ceremony of the Brier and an honour guard stood before a crowd that would swell to 281,985 over the next week—the largest crowd ever to attend a national curling championship. The Brier curlers wore blue ribbons in memory of the slain Mounties.

The Mountie tradition continues to this day, most notably at the RCMP Curling Club in Ottawa, but has spread to other forces across the land, with teams from each province competing to win the coveted national curling championship. With its stated objective "to promote the game of curling in Canada and to encourage fraternal relationships amongst police forces in Canada," the Canadian Police Curling Association (CPCA) traces its history to 1955. Created by the Canadian Association of Chiefs of Police to encourage "fellowship and liaison among Canadian police officers" as well as to promote the game, the first National Police Bonspiel was organized and held at the Granite Curling Club in Winnipeg on March 12, 1956. That one-day, four-event bonspiel involved sixteen squads—one representing each of the provinces (as we still do today) plus four teams representing four of the major police forces in Canada: the RCMP, the OPP, the CPR Police, and the CNR Police.

In March 1972, Rothmans sponsored the first truly Canadian Police Curling Championship at the Thistle Curling Club in Hamilton, Ontario. Labatt Breweries replaced Rothmans until 1990; however, despite the loss of its major corporate sponsor, the CPCA has consistently raised funds for worthy causes. In 1996, the CPCA adopted the Special Olympics as its charity of choice, donating many tens of thousands of dollars since to that program and various other charities from coast to coast. But the Special Olympics remain, well, special.

Firefighters knew long before September 11 the perils of their job and took comfort from the knowledge of what they could do and what they had done. Some curl—often for good causes. The best-known member of the Canadian Firefighters Curling Association (CFCA) is probably Brier and world champion Ed "The Wrench" Werenich, who has also won the coveted Fire Hydrant trophy a few times over the years. Vancouver firefighter Aubrey Neff organized a Vancouver Fire Department League and the British Columbia Firefighters Curling Association. In 1958, he wrote to firefighters in every major city in Canada, proposing a Dominion Firefighters Curling Championship. His dream eventually became the CFCA, which holds the only competition that gathers firefighters from every province and territory in Canada to vie for a national championship. Every province and territory has now hosted this event. Neff died in Vancouver at age seventy-four in 1997, but as the CFCA website notes, "One man's dream remains a reality for all who continue to champion his cause."

Fundraising and supporting good causes are not limited to emergency responders. The Sandra Schmirler Foundation may be the most instantly recognizable name—possibly worldwide—in Good Samaritan curling, but a host of fundraising and celebrity bonspiels across Canada have curlers lining up for the chance to curl alongside elite curlers, rubbing shoulders for a good time and a good cause. Curlers from across Canada and beyond have brought big hearts and big bucks to the house, playing to raise money for a host of worthy causes. Charity bonspiels often raise funds for research into heart disease, cancer, spinal cord injuries, and multiple sclerosis; they support children's hospitals and contribute to arthritis treatments and the purchase of Braille and audio books for the blind. Perhaps the best attended are the "celebrity spiels," where elite curlers lend their names and give their time to curl with their own teams, but just as often, it seems, to give club curlers a chance to curl with the legends of the sport.

The granddaddy charity event is most certainly the Heart to Heart Bonspiel, an annual tournament founded twenty-three years ago by three-time Brier champ Rick Lang and held in Thunder Bay. Over the years, that popular event, played at the Port Arthur Curling Club, has raised more than $800,000 for the Heart and Stroke Foundation. But recently it's experienced dwindling turnouts as well-intentioned organizers for a host of other causes cram more and more events into the final weeks of the curling season. In April 2004, the venerated Heart to Heart nearly stopped beating. According to a story written by journalist Reuben Villagracia in the local *Chronicle-Journal*, the celebrity bonspiel came "within hours" of being cancelled as organizers raced to fill holes in the all-star lineup and scrambled to ice seventy-two teams. They pulled it off, the event was saved, and cold cash was raised for a good cause.

That was the good news. Even if the $25,468 raised for the Heart and Stroke Foundation was down from the $28,900 raised the previous year, Colleen Syrja, an executive with the organizing committee, was able to find the silver lining, commenting, "Down a little bit, but not a lot, which I'm happy to see." Fellow organizer Jim Glena was a tad less optimistic, commenting to the *National Post*, "We're down from 32 to 24 teams. It seems that the curling season is getting longer and longer for the competitive teams. Interest seems to be waning in our area for the curlers who enter the spiel." As journalist Adam Daifallah observed, charity events seem to have slid into a rough patch, at least partly because the lion's share of events are crammed into the last few weeks of the season.

Still, there was enough interest and support in 2004 to hold an event that raised $1,500 for the children of North Bay curler Scott Patterson, who had been killed in a car crash that February. That cheque was accepted on behalf of the family by celebrity skip John McClelland, Patterson's Granite Club teammate.

The Heart to Heart was the inspiration for a fundraising tournament at the Avonlea Curling Club in Toronto. Paul Savage recalls that after attending the Thunder Bay celebrity bonspiel for several years, he and teammate Neil Harrison saw the potential for something similar succeeding in southern Ontario. They weren't the only two. As early as 1998, several Avonlea curlers—including Ed Werenich, John Brockest, Gene Glaze, and others—were discussing how to give back to the community through a charity bonspiel. By the time the first fundraiser was played, in 1990, the "lunch table group" had expanded to include Alison Goring and Susan Brower as well as Savage and Harrison. Over the next sixteen years, it has raised well over $1.6 million for children with special needs, and to help fund a variety of programs at local centres for everything from research and development into prosthetics to special needs programs that allow kids to "focus on their abilities rather than their limitations."

The Avonlea had sixteen sheets, which meant it could accommodate sixty-four teams. Settling on the name "Kurl for Kids," organizers selected the Easter weekend to host their first event, figuring a long weekend would be best to have so many teams play. They organized a committee and started contacting celebrity skips. The task of finding sixty-four big-name curlers proved less daunting than they feared. They sold out that first year and raised more than $80,000 for the Hugh MacMillan Children's Foundation. Over the next decade, they raised more than $1 million for different children's charities.

By 2004, Kurl for Kids was recognized by the *National Post* as "likely the most prominent among the many charitable fundraising bonspiels and events the world of curling runs every year." The event has raised close to $1.3 million for a variety of causes since its inception, ranging from Toronto's Variety Village to the Sandra Schmirler Foundation, the 2007 charitable recipient. And except for watching the Masters Golf Tournament on TV, Daifallah wrote that there aren't many Easter weekend rituals for curlers aside from annual celebrity fundraisers like Kurl for Kids, which he deemed to be likely the most prominent.

Sadly, as has happened in Thunder Bay, the number of teams, and therefore the amount of money raised, has declined over the years. The drop in funds raised has been matched, according to some recent criticisms, by the quality of the ice, and the suitable playing surface has been reduced to only a few of the original sixteen sheets. There have been other problems, most notably Avonlea closing its doors in the summer of 2006. (The charity bonspiel found a new home at Toronto's Tam Heather Country Club.)

But the pioneering efforts in Toronto and Thunder Bay are just the tip of the iceberg. In September 1991, just three months after being named executive director of the Manitoba Division of the Canadian Arthritis Society, Dan Bernaerdt received a call from Gregg Hanson, then the chair of the provincial division (later the president and CEO of Wawanesa Life Assurance Co.), asking him to set up a meeting with TSN curling analyst and curling legend Ray Turnbull. When they met, Turnbull told them the story about the Heart to Heart Tournament in Thunder Bay and suggested that a celebrity bonspiel was something the Arthritis Society should consider implementing in Manitoba.

As luck would have it, Bernaerdt had noticed, while reviewing the society's files soon after being hired, that Ken Watson, whom many consider to have been Manitoba's most legendary curler, had left his entire estate to the Arthritis Society on his passing (Watson's wife had suffered from very severe arthritis). The celebrity bonspiel was initially named the Ken Watson Memorial Bluebird Celebrity Bonspiel, aptly paying tribute to the legendary curler while incorporating the bluebird from the society's logo. This title was shortened to the Bluebird Celebrity Bonspiel, and the trophy for the more competitive "A Side" event was named the Ken Watson Memorial Trophy.

Over the past thirteen years, anywhere from twenty-four to thirty-two teams have competed in the bonspiel, each one skipped by an elite celebrity curler. A minimum of four out-of-town skips are brought in each year. The others, all from Manitoba, must have been at least a provincial champion. Many are Canadian, and some are world, champions. Manitoba skips have included Turnbull, Don Duguid, Terry Braunstein, Barry Fry, Jeff Stoughton, Kerry Burtnyk, Vic Peters, Connie Laliberte, Kathy Gauthier, Karen Fallis, Kathy Overton-Clapham, and Jennifer Jones. Out-of-province celebrities have included Guy Hemmings, Pierre Charette, Kathy King (Borst), Kelley Law, Paul Savage, Marilyn Bodogh, Heather Nedohin...and the list goes on.

Curlers pay a $60 registration fee, which guarantees them a minimum of three six-end games, a roast beef dinner on the Friday evening—the icebreaker banquet—a buffet dinner and dance on the Saturday evening, and prizes for everyone. Pledges are raised for arthritis research, and the top fundraisers—those who raise more than $1,000—get to choose their skips. Their names are placed in a hat (three hats, actually, based on the position that each curler prefers to play) and drawn to select the teams on a first-come, first-served basis. It is, in Bernaerdt's words, "a fun event" that gives the once-a-week club curler the opportunity to curl with and against provincial, Canadian, and world champions. The whole weekend is a great time of friendship and camaraderie—and helping out a worthy cause. These events comprise the essence and spirit of curling, perhaps more than anything else—good people doing good things in the friendly spirit of competition and cooperation. After a one-year hiatus in 2004 to allow the Arthritis Society to change the event's format for the first time, organizers of the new-and-improved Bluebird Celebrity Bonspiel vowed to return "better than ever" in 2005. Alas, neither the best efforts nor intentions proved sufficient. With so many worthy causes seeking participation from curlers, the Bluebird is no more and only time will tell if this noble effort for a worthy cause will be revived.

The scene repeats across Canada as clubs step to the fore, anxious to add "good cause" to the good times already associated with curling. The Spinal Tap Mixed Bonspiel, held in Thornhill, Ontario, raises funds for, and public awareness of, spinal cord injuries and research into finding ways to restore limbs to life, all part of the Canadian Spinal Research Organization's "Shoot for a Cure" campaign. On March 3, 2001, three-time provincial finalist Chrissy Cadorin skipped her team—dad Peter Cadorin, mom Sandy Cadorin, and Scott Jenkins—to a perfect eight-ender, duplicating Paul Flemming's perfect end in the Kurl for Kids at Avonlea on April 10, 1998, with teammates Paul Linetsky, Bill Chapman, and Eleanor Payment.

There are other bonspiels for other causes. The Rideau Curling Club in Ottawa and the Shawville Curling Club across the river in Quebec raise funds for the University of Ottawa Heart

Institute—a local medical shrine that is so popular with the local population and businesses that its own twelve-hour telethon raises millions of dollars. On the West Coast, the Vancouver Curling Club hosted its eighth annual Charity Skins Bonspiel from March 4 to 7, 2004, to raise money for the Canadian National Institute for the Blind.

Modelled on the TSN Skins game, the popular club spiel is touted as "an even playing field for curlers of all levels—allowing everyone to compete for dollars and raise money for a good cause." The cause, in this case, is to also provide a level playing field for blind and vision-impaired students and working-age adults who are in constant danger of falling behind their sighted peers because so few books are translated into Braille or transferred to audio. The money raised at the Vancouver club goes toward the CNIB initiative "That All May Read..."—a seven-year, $33-million program to re-engineer book production and convert the library collections to a "digital environment," which is currently estimated to be only 3 per cent of all books and materials. As the CNIB's first nationwide campaign for talking books since the conversion from vinyl records to cassettes in 1975, the initiative hopes to bridge the "information divide" by nearly doubling library collections from 61,000 to 118,000 titles.

Breast cancer research is probably in the top three beneficiaries from celebrity curling bonspiels, along with kids and hearts. The Calgary Winter Club draws a small army of celebrity curlers to Curl for a Cure for breast cancer. In 2003, the lineup included Kevin Martin, Kelley Law, Cathy King, Marilyn Bodogh, Paul Gowsell, Guy Hemmings, Cheryl Bernard, Ray Turnbull, and Shannon Kleibrink among the elite curlers tossing rocks for the Alberta/NWT Chapter of the Canadian Breast Cancer Foundation. It's an impressive array from a club that fancies itself a "House of Champions," home over the years to such world-class curlers as Ed Lukowich,

John Ferguson, Neil Houston, Brent Syme, Paul Gowsell, and Kelly Stearne. There were twenty-two local squads entered in the 2003 event, each raising a minimum of $2,000 in pledges for the foundation. A celebrity curler joined each team as a fifth player as they played four games, winners to be determined by total points scored.

In an article for the *Calgary Sun*, sportswriter Al Ruckaber put the event in context, noting that its purpose was more significant than its results. That sentiment is underscored by Bernard, one of the curling elite (a three-time Alberta women's champion and the founder of the celebrity bonspiel), who told the *Sun*, "The whole intent is to raise money and awareness for the foundation. The rest of it is just for fun for the rinks entered."

"The response has just been great," Bernard said, confirming that every one of the teams had exceeded the $2,000 goal for pledges—some by significant amounts of up to $10,000 or even more. What organizers had hoped would be an opportunity to raise between $40,000 and $50,000 for the foundation actually rose closer to $60,000. That, said Bernard, laid the groundwork for future efforts.

But even that was only part of the story. Ruckaber paid special attention in his article to an inspiring quartet that had named itself "Team Survivor." All four women on the team—Flo Markin, Norma Jean Jensen, Sam Butterwick, and Linnea Whetley—had beaten the potentially lethal disease that remains the most common form of cancer to afflict Canadian women. They were the reasons, literally the living proof, this celebrity spiel and so many others like it are so necessary and so popular. It was, admittedly, the elite players who were signing the autographs, but it was Team Survivor who delivered the larger message shared by every curler and fan there who dropped something into the donation box—cancer can be beaten! Why not have a good time doing it?

Three years later, Bernard's Curl for Cancer is a staggering success. Calgary's economic boom has resulted in corporate team entries, many from Alberta's "black gold" oil industry, bringing in more funds than ever before. The 2006 event, featuring thirty-two teams, raised a stunning $350,000 for a four-year total of $880,000—more than the Heart to Heart's twenty-five years combined. The 2007 event pushed the grand total above one million dollars! Even the Calgary Stampeders CFL football club iced a team, four mammoth humans adorned with heavy metal T-shirts, mullet wigs, and ripped blue jeans, adding some good-natured mayhem to the annual mirth. Sadly, Bernard lost her own father to cancer in 2005, and one of the original members of Team Survivor—Sam Butterwick—also succumbed that year. However, a determined Team Survivor stubbornly grabbed their brushes and matching uniforms—and a new teammate—for their 2006 appearance.

Whatever complications may crop up, ranging from bad ice to blizzards, these charity celebrity bonspiels seem to succeed by keeping their formats breathtakingly simple. While varying portions of the entry fees are earmarked for worthy causes, those who pony up enough can buy the chance to play with an elite curler of their choosing from the national or international stage. Sportswriter Daifallah, who has curled in the event, termed that opportunity a "major incentive" and wrote that he was lucky enough to pick two world champions—"the flamboyant Marilyn Bodogh and the loudest yeller in the sport's history, Russ Howard."

But even the Kurl for Kids event struggled. The number of teams plummeted to half the original sixty-four squads that had filled two full draws at the mammoth sixteen-sheet Avonlea facility. In 2004, the charity bonspiel moved to east-end Toronto's Tam Heather Country Club, the home of 1998 Olympian Mike Harris. The biggest name that year belonged to the lovable

Quebec skip Guy Hemmings, who, despite being a "highly recognizable, amusing and popular curler," had not, Daifallah noted, won a Brier.

"Over the last several years we've had a bit of difficulty getting teams," organizer and retired police officer Fred Willison told the *National Post*. "You begin to wonder sometimes if the bonspiel has reached its shelf-life. People are busy. Easter is a family time."

Daifallah credited Willison with co-founding and running the spiel, but noted that 2004 would be Fred's last year. He was leaving town and leaving it up to others to take over and carry on. He praises folks like Willison and Jim Glena as the "unsung heroes" of curling, noting that these events are mammoth undertakings pulled together by volunteer committees who begin working on the next year's event almost the day after the current event concludes.

"For the most part, the factors causing these spiels' troubles are beyond their control," he wrote. "The main problem: There's just too much going on."

Gerry Peckham, manager of high performance for the CCA, who founded a now-defunct charity spiel in Prince George, British Columbia, agreed: "The curling calendar is becoming increasingly busy and the available weekends that do not conflict with any other curling initiative are very difficult to come by."

For instance, La Releve East, a training camp for young elite curlers sponsored by Sport Canada, took place in Guelph, Ontario, the weekend after the men's teams had played a full week in St. John's for the final Grand Slam of the season, the PharmAssist Players' Championship. Provincial mixed championships were scheduled for the following week.

"A week here and a week there, and you're gone for the whole month, haven't seen your family and are out of holiday time at work," the article continued. "And when there are so many different charity spiels, it's tough to commit to more than one."

Daifallah cited several examples to underscore the end-of-season congestion that forces curlers to choose which events they will attend and which they must miss. Heather Nedohin, wife of Dave, who throws skip rock for Randy Ferbey's Alberta team, runs a charity spiel in Edmonton, and Cheryl Bernard, the Calgary runner-up in the 1996 Scott Tournament of Hearts, started an event in 2003—Curl for a Cure—while her father was dying of brain cancer. Her efforts raised $143,000 in the first year. These two worthy causes, both in Alberta, may end up competing for name curlers.

You don't have to be original to succeed. The Canadian Spinal Research Organization modelled its new "Shoot for a Cure Curling" campaign on the successful hockey initiative "Shoot for a Cure." The organization helps operate bonspiels for the charity and to support wheelchair curling. The first one-day event raised $23,000.

And, of course, there's the Sandra Schmirler Foundation, which raises the bar while raising money for families with seriously ill children. The Schmirler Foundation's events, advertised with some incredibly poignant moments crammed into just a few seconds of television commercial air time, range from a live telethon on the eve of the Scott Tournament of Hearts to club bonspiels like the 2003 Hand in Hand women's tournament held at the Cornwall Curling Club. The Prince Edward Island Curling Association and sponsorship from Scott Paper covered the curlers' expenses. Divided into competitive and semi-competitive divisions, the event had a $100 entry fee per team that was donated to the Sandra Schmirler Foundation. Admission for spectators was free; the competition was priceless.

The Meaghan Hughes squad, which curled out of the Charlottetown and Cornwall clubs, won the competitive section, defeating the Suzanne Gaudet team from the Silver Fox Curling and Yacht Club by a score of 9–8. Leading 7–2 after six ends, Hughes seemed to have a lock on the win, but Gaudet rebounded for three in the seventh end. The seesaw battle continued as Hughes scored a deuce in end eight, while Gaudet notched two in the ninth and stole another in the tenth. The game was even closer than it sounds. Gaudet had enough rocks in the house to win the game in the final end, forcing Hughes to draw to the four-foot between two guards to seal the win with teammates Sinead Dolan, Michala Robinson, and Erika Nabuurs. Donna Butler defeated Myrna Sanderson 11–1 in the competitive section consolation final. Both rinks were from the host Cornwall Curling Club.

Round-robin play had wrapped up on the Saturday evening, with two squads from the host club finishing first with perfect 4–0 records in their respective pools in the competitive section. But the semifinal and final games scheduled for the next day were delayed a week by a snowstorm. That probably just added to the anticipation—and eventual gratification—of the hometown fans as Gaudet and Hughes emerged for their dramatic final showdown by edging their opponents by one-rock margins: Gaudet 10–9 over Cornwall club's Donna Butler, and Hughes requiring an extra end to get past Myrna Sanderson, also from the host club, 9–8.

But the overriding result for all involved was the more than $1,400 the event raised for the Sandra Schmirler Foundation. Ironically, there are just so many glad hearts and good causes that the few celebrity curlers are spread too thin. Daifallah concludes that there are dozens of charity bonspiels now—all for worthy causes—that it would be impossible to list them all. But that, he insists, doesn't mean the curlers are not willing to help out at a good cause. They just can't be everywhere at once. He concluded:

"Nobody can accuse curlers of not doing their fair share for charity, even if some events are experiencing some rough times."

It's the same south of the border, where the Eau Claire Curling Club in Wisconsin hosts the National Kidney Foundation Bonspiel in aid of the state chapter. And next door in Minnesota, the Duluth Curling Club hosts the wildly popular House of Hearts celebrity bonspiel to raise funds for the American Heart Association, conceived by husband and wife Tim and Amy Wright, who were frequent celebrity skips in Thunder Bay's Heart to Heart Bonspiel. Although both are former U.S. national curling champions, they considered that event to be the annual highlight of their seasons. At about the turn of the millennium, they hit upon the idea of holding something similar at their home curling club in Duluth. Tim credits Amy with getting the ball rolling, assembling an "awesome" committee, including media man Jeff Laundergan and printer Steve Payette to spread the word. Using their connections with world-class curlers, they were able to assemble an amazing roster in just three years. The popularity of the event can perhaps best be measured by the sheer rise in competitors. Acknowledging that it was a bit of a struggle to get their club members to participate that first year, they have nevertheless soared from fourteen squads in their debut bonspiel to twenty-eight in 2003—with a waiting list to participate!

The third annual House of Hearts, played March 18 to 21, 2004, had a roster of twelve world champions, several Canadian and American national champions, and seven state and provincial champions—including two-time world champion Al Hackner, two-time world junior champ John Morris, and the reigning U.S. and world champ, Debbie McCormick. There were more listed as pending to lure curlers to pay their $75 registration fee and bring pledged donations to the AHA. Norwegian Olympic gold medallist Pat Trulsen was there, but cancellations just days prior to the event by Randy Ferbey (on the heels of losing the final game of the Brier to Mark Dacey), and Ed Werenich (with a job conflict), left the organizers scrambling. Paul Savage, the Olympic alternate and Hall of Famer was contacted but modestly declined, unconvinced he was still a strong drawing card. But those who did show up raised an impressive $43,588 in 2006, for a five-year total of nearly $130,000.

Founded in 1891, the original Duluth Curling Club played in a tent, supported by two retaining walls—until the tent blew away in a blizzard. Another building was then converted for curling until a proper structure was erected on the waterfront in 1897. The current building is its fourth, and can be expanded to provide up to thirteen curling sheets for major events, making it the largest curling venue in America prior to the 2002 Salt Lake Winter Olympics. The club's website notes that it has hosted two world championships, the U.S. Olympic Trials, and numerous national events. Two Duluth Curling Club members—state champions in 1926 and 1947—have been inducted into the U.S. Curling Hall of Fame for their service to the sport. Several other club foursomes have also contested—and won—state and national championships, a few going on to the Olympics and world championships.

Second in membership only to the curling club in St. Paul, Minnesota, the Duluth club is a natural forum for such an ambitious fundraiser, which raised more than $30,000 for the Northland Chapter of the American Heart Association in its first two years. Open to curlers of any skill level, the event's limited space is allocated on a first-come, first-served basis. Like many charity bonspiels, curlers register as individuals, not as squads, in this uniquely formatted twenty-seven-team bonspiel. Each squad boasts a celebrity curler or skip with a variety of U.S., Canadian, and world curling experience and success. The top five fundraisers get their choice of celebrity skip and position. The rest are drawn from a hat by the celebrity skips at the opening banquet to form their teams. Weekend event passes are sold at the door with all proceeds from the $5 ticket sales going to benefit the American Heart Association. Money is also raised throughout the weekend through curlers' entry fees and pledges, a live celebrity auction, door prizes, gate admissions, and program sales. AHA area director Judith Grytdahl was duly appreciative in 2003, saying, "This is a wonderful fundraising opportunity for the American Heart Association. The money raised in this event will be used for cardiovascular disease research, and to provide credible information for effective prevention and treatment of heart disease and stroke."

Curlers aren't doing themselves any harm by getting out on the ice and walking, sweeping, tossing, and laughing. Then there are the psychological benefits of social interaction, particularly for elderly curlers who share good times with others who, like themselves, might otherwise have no place to go, no one to see. As Doug Titus, the icemaker at the Navan Curling Club in Eastern Ontario commented, "They're better sitting here watching through the glass than cooped up at home alone, watching television." His sentiment is echoed south of the border by Dr. Jan Dawson, a family practice physician at Duluth Clinic-Hibbing and himself a curler, who cites a curler still active in his nineties as the example of what the game can mean to seniors, saying, "I can't think of any other ninety-plus-year-olds that do that. It's wonderful to think that there are activities [seniors] can do, and curling is a sport you can do from childhood to late adulthood." Dawson, who began curling in grade school with his friend and colleague Dr. Charles Decker, emphasized the importance, from a mental health perspective, of the social element of the sport that gets people out of the house. He stresses that keeping active is essential to a person's mental and physical well-being, and that curling is a way of accomplishing that.

"It's very important, in my opinion," he said. Curling, walking, biking, or any activity is important physically from a cardiac standpoint and for the enjoyment of life and well-being. Taking part in the sport also provides curlers with an outlet for competitiveness. As for the ninety-something curler who is held up as the example of what curling can mean to a senior, his only lament is that it's getting harder to hit the broom.

There is other evidence of the physical and psychological benefits of curling closer to home. Canadian Press reporter Donna Spencer wrote that sixty-year-old Gloria Campbell made her debut as the "oldest rookie" in the history of the Scott Tournament of Hearts, shooting second rock for Anne Dunn's Ontario squad at the 2003 tournament in Kitchener, Ontario. Not bad for a woman who, had despaired of ever having a shot at a Scott title when Dunn's team lost at the provincial finals many years earlier. In Kitchener, all of her teammates were in their fifties: Dunn was fifty-five, third Lindy Marchuk was fifty-three, and lead Fran Todd was fifty-seven. At the other end of the age scale, Prince Edward Island second Robyn MacPhee was making her Scott debut at nineteen. Team Dunn had entered the Scott playdowns only as a warm-up for their provincial senior playdowns. However, they won it all, beating Anne Merklinger in the semifinal and another Ottawa squad skipped by Darcie Simpson, in the final.

Campbell told Spencer her gang was not going to let their ages defeat them, then adding, "I'm sure the teams from other provinces looked at us and thought 'My God, how old are these people?' Especially me being the eldest." The heavy sweeping didn't seem to bother her, and she attributed her longevity to her "good curling genes"—her father, George Moss, ran masters marathons at seventy-three. But whether it was her genes or her dedication, Campbell didn't overlook the importance of mental toughness, concluding, "I think a lot of sports is psychological. You certainly do have to execute, but mentally if you don't have the right outlook, you've probably defeated yourself before you start the game."

In 2006, Dunn, Marchuk, and Campbell won their fourth national seniors championship, and their second world seniors crown—a new event on the global curling calendar. Their beat goes on.

The physical benefits for those who step onto the ice are undeniable. Studies have shown that in just fifteen seconds of sweeping, elite curlers can double their heart rates, which is comparable to what happens to Olympic-calibre sprinters in a two-hundred-metre race. Requiring the stamina of a sprinter and the strength to throw a forty-two-pound rock along the ice with takeout speeds of up to fifteen kilometres per hour—with sweepers often getting their workout just trying to keep up—curling is a sport that blends athleticism with finesse, precision, and strategy. Curling also allows you to become as good as you can be, sometimes with a bit of help.

The innovation of the throwing stick has prolonged curling for seniors. It's no longer rare to find curlers in their eighties and even nineties, but some purists still have a problem accepting the stick that allows curlers to play long after their knees are shot and it's impossible to crouch in the hack. In 2003, Winnipeg curler Garry Parker, who has a bad knee, filed a human rights complaint challenging a new rule prohibiting the use of the curling stick in provincial and national competitions. Canadian and world curling associations argue that the sticks, popular with elderly and disabled curlers, give users an unfair advantage. Parker, who under the ban can't compete in the senior provincial playdowns, says the rule discriminates against disabled curlers. This is similar to the situation when American golf officials tried to ban the use of golf carts until Casey Martin's victorious Supreme Court challenge.

For those who are concerned about participating, or simply can't participate, in a strenuous, high-impact sport, curling has been described as "a sport for any age and level of ability or competitiveness." CCA statistics suggest that more then 90 per cent of curlers are strictly recreational participants "who are neither willing [n]or expected to perform as elite curlers." While curling is not a high-impact sport, conventional wisdom suggests it is a good idea to do a few stretches to prevent muscle pulls before stepping onto the ice.

The Potomac Curling Club in Washington, D.C., refers to curling as Canada's number one sport and D.C.'s newest Olympic sport. Its website also describes the game as a balance between finesse and stamina. Equating its exercise value to that of a brisk game of table tennis, the site notes that in an average two-hour game, curlers, certainly those playing in the front end, walk two miles up and down the ice. Add vigorous sweeping to the equation and you've got a strenuous cardiovascular workout. Since the climate is controlled on the ice, it concludes, curling is a great way to stay active and feel good all winter long.

There has been a whole new approach to curling that trains young curlers to not just become technically pure performers but also adopt and maintain a healthy lifestyle. The days of an elite curler being threatened with banishment from the Olympic Trials for obesity or the inability to perform a single sit-up are gone. Today, athletes would be more likely to expect a shipment of mineral water than the fifty cases of Labatt's Blue Ed Werenich received years ago, at the brewer's expense, to cheer him in his quest for the world title. The days of hungover curlers stepping gingerly onto the ice for an early-morning game may still—may always—persist among some club curlers, but the elites are focused on health and nutrition. There are people out there who give the same attention to diet that Shorty Jenkins gives to ice.

Kelly Anne Erdman, a registered dietician who authored *Eat to Perform* for the Canadian Sport Centre in Calgary, offers a detailed regimen for curlers to benefit from maximum nutrition on the day of a tournament. The goal of pre-game nutrition, she writes, is to prevent hunger and low blood glucose while ensuring maximum mental readiness. That requires the curler to consume balanced meals with a small amount of protein to slow the digestive rate. Carbohydrate-enriched foods can be eaten an hour or two before the game. Recommended foods include bagels, fruit, unsweetened juice, peanut butter, and scrambled eggs. And fluids. Lots of fluids. During the game, to prevent low blood glucose and dehydration, and to ensure maximum mental readiness, curlers should consume carbohydrates whenever possible, especially midway through the game. And, again, fluids. Lots of fluids. Curlers should, however, avoid highly sweetened beverages and foods like soda pop, candy, and chocolate bars, which may provide only "a quick spike of energy followed by a low-energy crash." Recommended foods include Fig Newtons, unsweetened juice, bananas or other fruits, granola or cereal bars, dried fruit bars, muffins or bagels, and sport drinks or sports bars.

The regimen doesn't end when the last stone is cast. Between games, curlers should refuel before the next match by rehydrating and elevating blood glucose levels. They should try a sub, soup and a sandwich, stew and a bun, or vegetarian pizza. And juice. If all this sounds like sacrilege to the minds and bodies of veteran curlers, Erdman reminds athletes that while it is up to them to do what they want and eat what they want, this regimen simply affords good nutrition "designed to allow you to do what you have trained so hard to do."

At the 2002 Winter Olympic Games in Salt Lake City, Rhona Martin's team won the women's curling gold medal for Great Britain after a breathtaking final. The importance of diet and nutrition trailed close behind. The U.K. National Sports Medicine Institute considers curling an endurance sport that also requires mental agility to set strategy. Curling requires its athletes to be on the ice for up to three hours per game, often playing three games a day during competitions, further complicated by breaks measured in minutes or hours, and for these reasons studies have found it to be extremely demanding mentally as well as physically. Training hard to maintain "high levels of flexibility and cardiovascular fitness" may not be enough, and the dietician becomes part of an extensive team of physiologists, sports psychologists, team coaches, and physiotherapists who take a holistic approach.

As Calgary's Erdman concluded, no diet or nutrition can make an average athlete great, but "poor nutrition can make a great athlete average!"

There is still an old guard of elite curlers who take perverse pride in their ability to win a Brier and a world championship and earn an Olympic berth on a less healthy diet, like two-time U.S. Olympic curler Myles Brundidge, who lists "meatloaf and cheeseburgers" among his passions in life. Others insist that two-time world champion Ed Werenich destroyed his game by shedding flab and getting fit, under orders from the CCA, because it reportedly threw off his delivery in the process. American sports columnists in the *New York Times* touched on those topics at Nagano, underscoring the differences between curlers and more traditional full-medal athletes, citing Werenich who, having narrowly missed qualifying for the 1998 Games at the Olympic Trials, lamented that the sight of him on the podium, fifty and overweight, might cause even him to laugh. As for the women curlers, the *Times* reported that Sandra Schmirler won her third

Canadian title when she was six months pregnant, then later added a new dimension to the Olympic Trials by essentially calling a timeout to breastfeed her nine-month-old baby. It's unclear what the American scribes thought of her winning an Olympic gold medal a short time later.

This new emphasis on health and fitness, along with the presence of a rulebook, elevates curling beyond a game to a true sport. That could go far in appealing to Americans, who offer a vast potential market for the roaring game. Interest is growing. The media reported in March 2006 that the World Curling Federation expected a $12 million share of marketing and television ratings from Turin—up from $4 million in Nagano and $8.3 million in Salt Lake City. Much of those revenues were earmarked for worldwide television production. The Asian market is looking promising; curling ratings peaked at 12 million in Japan. And the Americans, who perhaps got their first glimpse of the game in 2002 at the Salt Lake City Olympics, are a lot more interested since winning their first Olympic curling medal at Turin. The roaring game remains fodder for their late-night talk shows—but they're starting to laugh with us, not at us.

IN THE HACK

HOLDING FOR THE GOVERNOR

*I*am on hold for the governor of California. Actually, I am talking to Darryl, the aide to Governor Arnold Schwarzenegger who will determine if I get past "hello." We have established that it is frigid in North Gower and balmy in Sacramento but Darryl seems to be stumbling over my wish to interview the governor for a curling book, unaware that "The Governator," and his father before him, was an Austrian champion of that country's version of curling. I do not try to pronounce *eisschiessen*, as "curling" seems sufficiently problematic.

"You want to interview the governor?"

"Yes, please."

"About curling?"

"Yes, please."

"The ice game?"

"Well, ice sport, actually...but yes, please."

"Where they toss those heavy things down the ice?"

"Yes, please."

"The governor?"

"Yes, I would like to ask Governor Schwarzenegger, who has cited the importance of his curling youth to at least one Senate committee, whose curling background has been mentioned at least in passing by the mainstream American media, if he preferred the draw to the takeout game, if he still curls, and if he has, or has any intention, or if he's been asked by the American Curling Association or the U.S. Olympic committee to help promote the sport."

I pause for breath. Has Darryl not seen the 1997 feature film *Batman and Robin*? Does he not realize that anyone, even a diabolical villain, named Mr. Freeze has to know something about curling? I talk faster.

"I won't take much of the governor's time," I add, trying not to sound desperate.

"As you can appreciate, the governor gets many, many requests for interviews."

"Eh?"

Finally convinced that I am simply a Canadian on a mission, Darryl feeds me the secret media-request email address, noting that the governor just granted an interview with an American motorcycle magazine, so who knows, my odds might not be that bad.

I thank Darryl and then ask how many interview requests are there ahead of mine.

"Four hundred."

Sigh.

I email my request. I get an immediate response, thanking me for my interest in interviewing the governor but adding that he cannot possibly comply with every request. I am unsure what this means. I'm guessing my request has been "Terminated." A pity. I know the name of the American president rumoured to have been born in Canada, violating the clause in the U.S. Constitution that currently prevents the governor from becoming president because he was born outside the United States. I believe his being mentioned in a curling book could have delivered him the Electoral College votes from Minnesota and Wisconsin. Maybe more, given the rising American interest in the roaring game.

Ah, governor, what might have been.

I take some comfort in learning that the United States Olympic Curling Association has fared no better in accessing Schwarzenegger. Rick Patzke of USA Curling tried to contact him as early as 1997, before he was governor. The closest he got was to be turned down twice by his personal agent.

But curling has never been easy in America, or predestined. In fact, it arrived by shipwreck.

THE NINTH END

TEE LINE, HOG LINE, BOTTOM LINE

*C*losing schools in Newfoundland and Labrador to allow students a chance to watch Brad Gushue curl for Olympic gold at Turin hearkens back to the mass audiences for the final game of the 1972 Soviet hockey summit and to the empty city streets across the land as all of Canada seemed to cluster at their TVs to watch Canadian millionaires beat American millionaires for Olympic hockey gold at Salt Lake City thirty years later. If the crowds greeting the returning American bronze-medal curlers from Turin seem modest in comparison, don't underestimate the win's potential impact on network broadcasting. New clubs have already sprung up in the United States, as far south as Austin, Texas, and if the Americans are legitimate contenders for an Olympic medal, the American media are interested in sharing it with the world. And that's a good thing for the roaring game.

The Americans are making the same strides in curling that they did in women's hockey: playing catch-up, but catching up. If that's at least partly due to the early instruction and support they received from Canadians like Ed Lukowich and Rob Meakin, they'll soon have their own talent—and money—coming out of the shadows. Admittedly, interest is soaring in Asia—notably in Japan and South Korea, with China close behind—but the next great expansion of the roaring game, thanks largely to television coverage and the Olympic Games, will most likely be into the

United States. Hilton Hotels came aboard to sponsor USA Curling in 2006, the same year that the Associated Press reported on the thirteen tons of granite curling rocks—"coveted supplies"—sailing from Britain to fill the shortage in new curling clubs springing up across America as a result of the splash the sport made at the 2006 Olympics. With a loan from the World Curling Federation, clubs in Minnesota, Arizona, Tennessee, Michigan, Colorado, Indianapolis, Wyoming, California, New York, and Nebraska lined up to shell out up to $7,600 for each sheet of curling rocks. Across America, all eyes were trained on the broom—and the 2010 Vancouver Olympics.

It was no accident that the question of the sport's popularity among the Americans was raised by an International Olympic Committee executive prior its becoming a full-medal sport. There are millions and millions of dollars at stake for organizers, sponsors, and broadcasters every time a major sporting event is staged and televised to millions of viewers and consumers. No athletic event rivals the Olympics for sustained international coverage. Interestingly, curling was barely covered by CBS during the Nagano Games in 1998. When the rights for Salt Lake City went to NBC, it not only aired many hours of curling coverage but also promoted the sport prior to the 2002 Winter Olympics. People tuned in—and stayed tuned. There are some who would argue that it was about time, considering the sport had come to America before baseball.

The saga of curling in America begins with a shipwreck that for a second time denied the Windy City the claim to be the first curling centre in the United States (Adam Fergusson had visited the future site of Chicago in 1831 and turned back, saying it was too swampy for settlement). In 1832, a group of Scots intent on settling in the area that is today Chicago were shipwrecked on Lake St. Clair. Straggling ashore at Michigan, they looked around, liked what they saw, and stayed put. If they had curling stones, those went down with the ship. Like the early Scots in Fergus, the Scots in Michigan carved their first curling rocks from hardwood trees. At the first deep freeze, they started tossing their hickory stanes. Curling had come to America.

The stranded Scottish farmers organized the first curling club in the United States at Orchard Lake, near Detroit. They curled on Lake St. Clair, whence they had come. The club was officially founded at the home of Dr. Robert Burns. The bard would have been proud. But like the rift between Fergus and the Royal Kingston, Milwaukee, Wisconsin, lays claim to being the "oldest continuously operating" curling club in America. That club was founded about a decade later.

Other clubs sprang up in Boston (1839) and Chicago (finally, in 1854), separated by Madison, Wisconsin (1846), which has taken a page from the Fergus Curling Club to declare *itself* the "oldest continuously operating" curling club in the United States (and where some men reportedly improvised by using their wives' irons to curl). In 1867, Canada became a dominion, about the same time twelve American clubs united to form the Grand National Curling Club. The sport continued to spread westward, and by 1880 fourteen clubs had formed the North-western Curling Association. Since then, curling has spread to twenty-six states, thriving in the north with pockets of dedicated curlers in the south and west, stretching from Florida to Alaska. And the number is growing. While most clubs are rural or located in small towns, the St. Paul club in Minnesota once boasted more than seven hundred members.

The first U.S. curling championship in 1957 drew ten state champions to Chicago, which had finally become a major curling centre. The United States Curling Association became the national governing body for the sport in 1976 by uniting the United States

Men's Curling Association (USCA) (established in 1958) and the Women's Curling Association (USWCA) formed in 1947). There are about twenty thousand registered curlers in the United States, with probably as many once-a-year social curlers, playing in 133 clubs at 107 rinks and 20 hockey/curling rinks. Once involved, the Americans proved to be good curlers. In 1965, Bud Somerville's squad became the first non-Canadian team to win a world championship, and won it again in 1974. The skip, from Superior, Wisconsin, was the first inductee into the USCA's Hall of Fame. In 1992, he skipped his team to a bronze medal at the Albertville Olympics, where curling was a demonstration sport.

Some early curling history in America has been harder to unearth—or perhaps remember. In the October 2001 edition of the Scottish-American History Club newsletter, James McBain, the son of Hughston M. McBain, who was primarily responsible for curling in Chicago, chronicled this early mystery about how curling came to New York City:

> In 1904, during excavation for a subway where the Municipal Building now stands in New York, a perfectly preserved curling stone was found seventy feet beneath the street level. Mystified construction workers, once they were convinced that the stone was an implement in an old Scottish game and not an Indian relic, resorted to an old survey map and discovered that early in the nineteenth century a pond existed on the site. Further investigation proved that the pond was where the New York Caledonian Curling Club was wont to hold its bonspiels...and that the club paid a city politician twenty dollars a year for the use of it. The same politician also sold the pond's ice to an iceman for another twenty dollars, which proved something of a hazard to the sport.

Although this series of events may have had little or no archaeological value, it at least established curling as one of the earliest known organized sports in New York, predating football, baseball, and even golf. What has happened to curling since some luckless player lost his stone through the municipally juggled ice on that lower Manhattan pond is an interesting and only little-known story.

In the same edition, Hughston M. McBain noted in his article "The Roaring Game" that curling spread rapidly from Quebec out to the Western provinces and from Boston and New York to the wilds of Michigan, concluding, "For well over a hundred years, it was the most popular of all American winter sports."

Why do so few Americans know anything about the sport? To say that curling has an image problem in the United States is to suggest that it is sufficiently familiar to have an image. Timothy D. Jacques, in one of his "Curling 101" articles on Allsports.com, takes the U.S. media—particularly CBS—to task for what he calls sloppy coverage at the Nagano Winter Olympics. Claiming that curling in America suffers from a "Dr. Jekyll and Mr. Hyde" complex, he notes that outside the "ice-belt" Great Lakes Region and New England, "curling is almost unheard of due to a lack of facilities and ... the ignorance of the mainstream media."

There were numerous inquiries across America about starting new curling clubs after the 1998 Nagano Olympics that Jacques argues came despite, not because of, TV coverage, which he found to be lamentable:

The lack of knowledge by the media was brilliantly demonstrated by CBS at the 1998 Winter Olympics. CBS's sloppy research revealed only 500 curlers in the

United States (there are actually about 15,000 to 17,000) and that there were only a handful of clubs (there are over 120). Add on a few stereotyped misnomers and CBS came to the brilliant conclusion in early 1997 not to cover the sport. The only mention of curling came from a few information segments on *48 Hours* that were so biased and lopsided, it was more comedy than journalism.

Jacques accused CBS of frequently interrupting matches with their loud commentary—which was never used. When outside events were disrupted by heavy snowfalls during the first week, he said, CBS opted to show figure skating practices and fluff pieces rather than other events.

"The only fair coverage came from TNT (albeit short at times) who hired famous curler Ray Turnbull to do their commentary," Jacques continued. "With the exception of the Canadian Broadcasting Corporation, TNT showed more curling segments (game play, commentary, background stories) than any other media outlet." TNT, it should be noted, is a specialty cable channel not available to all viewers. Acknowledging that the print media were generally more positive toward curling, he didn't find their coverage particularly objective or well informed. Finally, he reported, while CBS's network coverage was poor, oddly enough its Internet coverage was half-decent.

Jacques found things much improved four years later during the Salt Lake City Winter Games; NBC shone compared to CBS's "bungling and shoddy coverage," airing more than fifty hours on MSNBC and CNBC. Jacques also found other media to be more positive and aggressive in seeking sources for curling coverage, citing ESPN, FOX Sports, the *New York Times*, and, to no one's surprise, the BBC, which got to report the U.K. women's gold-medal performance—that nation's first Winter Olympic gold since figure skaters Torvill and Dean's 1984 win.

The clincher, for Jacques, were the "unbelievable" audience ratings, as 600,000 to 800,000 Americans tuned in to watch round-robin games and more than one million watched the play-offs and the medal games. Those ratings, he noted, were "higher than all of the shows MSNBC and CNBC televises during its own prime-time slots." Thanks largely to the media interest, many of the matches in suburban Ogden were sold out months in advance and scalpers were doing a brisk business, with tickets selling for as much as $200. The payoff for American curlers came within weeks as new members and the curious crowded local rinks and new clubs started popping up across the land—three in Tennessee, two each in California and Florida, and others in Oklahoma, Oregon, Pennsylvania, Texas, and Utah.

Another key factor in curling's increased visibility at the Salt Lake Winter Games was the advance promotion given to the sport by NBC. Looking northward, the US Curling Association produced, in collaboration with the World Curling Federation and the CBC, an Olympic curling primer, *Rock Stars: The World of Curling*. This was prior to the release of *Men with Brooms*, and CBC was vital in getting Leslie Nielsen and Paul Gross to co-host the program. World champion Colleen Jones and Olympic medallist George Karrys were also recruited as co-hosts. Karrys was a technical adviser on *Men with Brooms*, which was due for release during the Games. With that movie set for release, the project made sense to everyone, especially as the TV special was an excellent forum to advertise the movie. *Rock Stars* aired on the Outdoor Life Network in December 2001 and January 2002. CBC also aired the program in March.

The program revolved around two U.S. Olympic hopeful teams in staged games against two teams of all-star athletes from other sports, including many Olympians, from speed skating, biathlon, skeleton, synchronized swimming, skiing, and even a Women's National Basketball Association player.

"The concept was to show, rather than try to tell, that curling is harder than it looks, and can be a lot of fun," Karrys explained. Another key goal was to "prime" an unfamiliar U.S. market for the debut of curling as the newest Olympic sport. The program came off well, interspersing on-ice action with explanatory segments, famous curling shots from CBC's vast archives, sneak-preview scenes from the upcoming film, and one-liners from Gross and Nielsen. In addition, selected sources—from Sweden's Peja Lindholm and Germany's Andy Kapp to Edmonton's David and Heather Nedohin and junior curlers from Yellowknife—had submitted home video footage of themselves during the previous summer, which appeared as commercial intros and extros in the final product. The program came off very well.

The American media began to take note; writing in the *Deseret News*, Olympic specialist Julie Dockstader Heaps wondered if the 2002 Winter Olympics would do for curling what the World Cup had done for women's soccer several years earlier. Chronicling the origin and expansion of the sport in America, she noted that there were 15,000 curlers and 135 clubs in the United States, with more forming as a result of the Olympics' popularity. It didn't hurt that the Americans had a virtual family affair with their Olympic curlers.

Jay Weiner of the Minneapolis–St. Paul *Star Tribune* had introduced Mary Liapis and her curling family to his readers. Mary, seventy-three, was kin to three of the players on the American curling teams—son Mike and his daughters, Kari Erickson and Stacey Liapis. An estimated 125 fans, including the mayor and a state senator, had seen them off. The sisters had been curling competitively since 1988. Their dad, who had been introduced to the game by their mom, was their coach. All curled at the Bemidji Curling Club, which had produced twenty national championship teams since 1979. Curling with two friends, Kari and Stacey were state junior champs within a year and national junior champs a year after that. They won nine out of ten games at the U.S. Olympic Trials.

With that sort of drama and that type of material to promote Olympic curling in 2002, the ratings went through the roof. No one was more surprised than NBC. The network bosses and producers realized they'd stumbled onto possibly the best thing since Johnny Esau convinced CTV to start televising figure skating decades earlier, and they set out to take advantage of it. The network decided to air an hour on both the U.S. Nationals and the world championship in Winnipeg in 2003. The importance of that decision to the future of curling, at least in America, was hammered home by the CCA. Noting that many Americans had their first exposure to curling on MSNBC or CNBC during the 2002 Winter Games, the CCA reported that the widespread coverage had tripled those networks' average ratings whenever curling was aired. On March 13, 2003, the CCA issued an urgent media release, underscoring the importance of what NBC was about to do:

> In the hectic minutes following the women's gold medal curling game at the 2002 Olympics last February in Salt Lake City, an NBC executive who had been surprised by the interest in curling on his network made a comment to a World Curling Federation executive, who instantly developed his own look of surprise. That remark? "Call me."
>
> From that simple conversation comes this weekend's historic broadcast of the 2003 USA Curling National Championships on NBC. This one-hour program will be

the first of its kind on a national U.S. network. No matter what the weather is in your part of the country, you need to be watching this program, and you need to get all your friends to watch, and their friends, and so on.

The immediate future of televised curling in the United States could very well hinge on the outcome of this show, and a subsequent program about the 2003 Ford World Curling Championships which will be broadcast on NBC.

The Americans were equally effusive. Veteran TV producer Jim Carr described curling as "a fascinating sport that combines strategy with skill and precision," while executive producer Bob Hughes promised viewers that "once you watch it, you're totally hooked." The numbers once again bore out their optimism. As reported in *The Globe and Mail*, the 2003 U.S. Nationals drew a 1.4 rating (about 1.5 million U.S. households) for NBC, while the world championships, held in Winnipeg, drew a 1.2 share— good enough for eighth place among the top ten network sportscasts for that week. To underscore what that meant, consider that ABC had earned a 1.2 rating last year for its first National Hockey League telecast of the season. Reporter William Houston went on to note that during 2003, in the wake of the Salt Lake Olympics, USA Curling's membership had increased 10 per cent and a dozen new clubs had sprung up in such exotic locales as Scottsdale, in sun-baked Arizona, and Knoxville, Tennessee. Based on those ratings, *The Globe and Mail* confirmed that NBC Sports would again use Canadian broadcasters Don Chevrier, Don Duguid, and Elfi Schlegel to call the 2004 tape-delayed U.S. curling championships.

Such advances on American network TV are impressive, particularly when you stop to realize that in 2002, the only other top-ten reference to curling was by late-night television host David Letterman, who on February 18, 2002, suggested ways to make the game "more exciting":

10. How about calling it anything but "curling"?
9. Instead of weird lookin' Norwegian dudes in sweaters— babes in lingerie
8. Only allow French judges
7. Sweep the stone toward the hog line and then...okay, I don't know crap about curling
6. Is it too much to ask for one curler to bite another curler?
5. Throw in one of them miniature-golf windmills
4. Instead of a granite stone, use the frozen head of Walt Disney
3. 40 per cent of final score comes from the swimsuit competition
2. You don't think curling is exciting? What are you, insane?
1. First place gets gold medal, the rest are sent to Camp X-Ray

Two nights later, Jay Leno gave Tonya Harding, Russian figure skaters, and Clinton interns a break to take his own shot at curling: "It's not that airport security guard's fault he fell asleep. He was watching Olympic curling."

Curlers have endured verbal jabs for years and weren't perturbed. Print reporters and columnists were more scathing and more amusing; they just didn't have the audience of the television show hosts. On the same day that Letterman took his potshots, and at least alerted a few million Americans to the fact that curling was in the Olympic Games, *Miami Herald* humour columnist Dave Barry picked up where he had left off at Nagano, writing, "Terror swept aside: the real story of curling."

OGDEN, Utah—This is the site of the Olympic curling competition, which has approximately 15 security personnel for every spectator. The tight security is necessary because curling is a prime target of terrorists. "If we can stop them from curling, then we will have won," is a phrase often heard at terrorist gatherings.

Ironically, curling is almost unknown in many parts of the United States. But if you go anywhere in Europe or Asia, you will find that it is almost unknown there, too. The only places where it is known are Bemidji, Minn. (pop. 11,884) and Canada (pop. 10,315). But it is huge in those places, because it is one of the very few sports that combine the excitement of a heavy piece of granite sliding slowly across the ice with the excitement of chunky broom-wielding people in bowling attire sweeping furiously in the stone's path, like janitors on speed.

As Gerry Geurts wrote at Curlingzone.com, by the end of the Salt Lake City Winter Games, curling had been mocked and stereotyped by everyone from Leno to cartoon character Homer Simpson. And more and more people tuned in. Yet the American media still wrestled with the issue of whether curling was a game or a sport. While that debate was often tongue-in-cheek, often focusing on the usual issues of the age, physical condition, and even dietary habits of the curlers, there was also a general consensus that it was hard to cheer for a sport you don't understand. Conversely, there were reports of fans cheering wildly for anything — even hauling out the equipment to measure shot rock — who probably also didn't know anything about the game.

Unfortunately, some of the best lines and keenest insights have been delivered off-camera by a Hollywood superstar who could do a great deal to promote the game he claimed to love in testimony to a U.S. Senate subcommittee holding hearings on "21st Century Learning." Arnold Schwarzenegger left no doubt of the role the sport had played in his childhood:

> I was lucky growing up. I had two parents who kept me on the straight and narrow 24 hours a day. Every day when I came home, my mother was there to greet me at the door. She sat with me, helping me with my homework, making me read out loud until I got every word just right.
>
> Only after my homework was finished could I go outside where my dad or a coach would take over my instruction and take me skiing [or] sledding or work on my ice-curling technique or soccer kick or whatever sport was in season.
>
> The bottom line is that there was someone there for me 24 hours a day, coaching me, teaching me, mentoring me, telling me they loved me, telling me that I could achieve anything I set my mind to, that if I worked hard enough I could turn any dream into reality. It was this foundation that built my self confidence and enabled me to achieve so much in my life.
>
> When I came to America in 1968, I had empty pockets but I was full of dreams, desires and determination. I believed I could accomplish anything I set my mind to— a belief that has strengthened with time.

With that type of endorsement, and the sport's television history, it should have been an easy sell to the Americans. After all, pioneer station WGN had broadcast the first U.S. men's curling championship tournament from Chicago Stadium on March 8,

1957. And while television ratings are equally important in Canada, we also enjoy the additional benchmark of attendance to gauge success. Many curling supporters believe that curling is experiencing a boost in popularity, in terms of both players and spectators. Yet, while attendance figures have generally increased since major national championships were moved into NHL-sized arenas, new attendance records are far from assured.

The 2004 Brier marked the fifth time that Saskatoon has played host—the other years were 1946, 1965, 1989, and 2000—joining Toronto, Calgary, and Halifax as the only cities to have hosted the event at least five times since the championship began in 1927 in Toronto. The last two times the Brier was staged in Saskatoon attendance records were reached. In 1989, 151,538 fans surpassed the 106,394 who attended the Brandon Brier in 1982. In 2000, Saskatoon drew 248,793—eclipsing Edmonton's record of 242,887, set just a year earlier. Calgary ranked second, drawing 245,296 in 2002. All those figures dropped a notch when Edmonton raised the bar again in 2005—setting a new Brier record with an audience of 281,985. But the numbers faltered in Hamilton in 2007.

The Steel City had drawn 88,894 fans the last time it had hosted the Brier, in 1991. Expanding the playing sheets to six from four for the only time in Brier history eliminated morning draws and reduced play to fourteen from twenty-one draws. Hosting the national championship at the spacious Copps Coliseum eighty years after the first Brier had been played in Toronto, a short drive up the Queen Elizabeth Way, augured well for the organizers. Alas, despite all good efforts, the curlers were soon complaining about small crowds and bad ice. Early draws attracted less than four thousand fans to an arena that could seat 16,500. Organizers had hoped total attendance would surpass 100,000. When the CCA announced the number of tickets that had been sold, optimistic estimates soared to 120,000 then 150,000. They were still tabulating as I write this.

The numbers got a small boost when Prime Minister Stephen Harper and his security entourage swept into the building on less than twenty-four hours' notice. Harper does not curl, but is considered a Friend of Curling for attending Briers over the years prior to grabbing the reins of power in Canada. But if he was familiar with the game and its traditions, curling, or at least Brier fans, was a new experience for at least one of his Mountie body-guards, who lamented to the press: "They told us to watch out for odd people when he got here. The first guy I saw was wearing a gopher on his head. Where do you start?"

And this was rinkside, far from the sociable party-hearty Brier Patch imbibers.

The curlers, already dismayed by the small crowds, were soon cursing the ice and, by extension, icemaker Dave Merklinger, who dramatically defended his ice and his staff. He had them scrape the ice, then show the debris, ranging from a human hair to broom bristles, to the complaining curlers. He could monitor and control the ice texture and temperature through the computerized sensors embedded in the ice and his personal attention to peb-bling the ice, but he had no say in what the curlers wore or used on the ice. Nor could he stop the Mounties from letting the full effect of global warming breeze into the rink when they opened the huge lower-level doors for the prime minister's limo.

Merklinger later summed up his feelings to a reporter, insisting that the ice in his late-night rye and coke wasn't as good as what he'd made at Copps Coliseum. No one complained about Merklinger's ice at the ensuing tournament in Edmonton. Total attendance for the 2007 World Championship in that city was 184,973 including 10,082 for the final game between Canada and Germany, won by Glenn Howard. These figures beat the old record set in Winnipeg in 2003. If Edmonton lands the 2009 Olympic curling trials, as many presume it will, the city has a chance to raise total fan attendance to one million for major curling events over the past decade, when added to the 1999 Brier (242,887) and the 2005 Brier, which set an all-time world curling attendance (281,985). That's 708,842 for three events, needing another 291,158 at the Olympic trials to cap one million at four events over a decade.

Ironically, what was deemed disappointing attendance for the men's curling would be considered a huge success for the women's championship. At the 2004 Scott Tournament of Hearts in Red Deer, more than 107,000 seats were sold, ensuring Red Deer a spot in the history books as second in overall attendance figures for the Canadian women's curling championship, edging London, Ontario (105,065 in 2006), and far surpassing St. John's (72,799 in 2005), Kitchener (67,209 in 2003), and Brandon (88,022 in 2002). Red Deer finished second only to Regina at 154,688 in 1997. But that year was also the first Olympic Trials for full-medal status, and those numbers were huge too.

Those first Olympic Trials proved to be hugely popular with viewers, Con Griwkowsky reported in the *Edmonton Sun*. Television numbers released by the CBC showed a total audience of 1.7 million to see Mike Harris advance past Kevin Martin to earn the right to go to Nagano, while an incredible 2.7 million watched Canada's sweetheart, Sandra Schmirler, beat Shannon Kleibrink. The men's figures were reportedly lower than for the Brier final, and Schmirler's numbers were just off the 2.8 million who watched the Scott Tournament of Hearts final. It's no surprise to anyone who ever watched "Schmirler the Curler" that her numbers were so high. She has been credited by curling broadcasters with elevating the image of the game with her incredible curling, her easy smile, and a pleasantness that seemed never to crack no matter how sorely tested. But since her untimely passing in March 2000, at the age of thirty-six, the curling hierarchy has taken steps to separate the men's and women's world championships, which several elite women curlers, including Colleen Jones and Joan McCusker, have denounced as a step certain to hurt their game and their crowds, which will in turn make it harder to find sponsors for the women's championship. Sponsors get more viewers for the men's.

Sponsorship has proved to be stable, if comparatively rotational, in men's curling. There was a worrisome gap between Nokia's bowing out and Tim Hortons' stepping up to sponsor the Brier, beginning in 2005. The CCA had stated publicly that it would consider sponsoring the event if no corporate saviour stepped forward. While actual numbers remain guarded, there has been broad speculation in the media that sponsoring the Brier required a $1 million investment by Nokia, the previous corporate sponsor. While some may fret that number is big enough to scare off potential sponsors, others argue that it is a sound investment for having your company's name and corporate logo beamed into homes across Canada, and beyond, for a solid week of elite competition. By contrast, Scott Paper (now known as Kruger Products) has stuck with the women's national championship since 1981, only recently changing the name to the Scotties Tournament of Hearts. The company proudly claims that this has become the longest uninterrupted sponsorship of an amateur sport in Canada.

But for all that, there are rising concerns that women's elite curling is heading for trouble, if it's not already there. Media accounts document, and the CCA has confirmed, a disturbing trend across the country of women curlers who are opting not to pursue the brass ring of national or international triumph. In 2005, a year when 177 Ontario men's teams registered to contest the path to the Brier, only 52 women's squads pursued the Scott, down from 60 in the previous years; several of Ontario's sixteen zones did not field an entrant. No one can say if it's the cost, the commitment, or just a matter of family or career before curling glory, but splitting the world championships in terms of gender seemed a strange decision at a bad time to many observers. Women have a long and storied curling history in Canada, dating to their defeat of the first touring team of Scots in 1903. Vera Pezer won the first Battle of the Sexes in 1972, upsetting Oreset "The Big O" Meleschuk decades before Ed Werenich ignored Marilyn Bodogh's pregame cartwheels-in-a-kilt distraction to wrench back male bragging rights. Sandra Schmirler won at every level of competition and, in the end, simply won our hearts. Still, women's curling has fared better on the world stage when paired with the men's.

Colleen Jones, perhaps the most recognizable woman curler worldwide, was first and loudest off the mark in expressing her frustration—and doubtless speaking for many others—by lamenting to the media, in April 2004, "I think the women are going to have to curl naked in order to get people out there. I'm not kidding. You're going to have to hope for an Anna Kournikova to come along to really jazz it up."

While that didn't happen, Jones hit closer to home than she'd imagined. Women's curling drew more voyeurs, if not viewers, than ever before—and the notice of *Playboy*—when the "Naked Calendar" appeared a year later. The headline writers had a ball. The calendar project was conceived by Spanish photographer Ana Arce, who had skipped the Andorran women's team for three seasons and was one of the models. Arce confirmed that she was out to change the image of the sport—while raising some money for the teams of her models, from Denmark, Italy, Spain, England, Poland, Germany, and, yes, Canada. Arce admitted to the media that Canadians were tougher to recruit than Europeans. Thus did women curlers join the ranks of their sisters in women's rugby, water polo, and cross-country ski teams—and they shared some US $50,000 for their trouble. A 2007 calendar followed that initial blockbuster.

Having annoyed the women curlers, the CCA dropped the second shoe and was accused of putting the boots to all curlers and their fans regardless of gender, age, or playing ability by negotiating a new broadcasting deal with the CBC that would move many major games to its Country Canada channel, not available on basic cable. The money was apparently good, but curlers and their public were outraged as their beloved matches were switched to a channel some thought had fewer Canadian subscribers than Al Jazeera. With CBC assuming exclusive ownership, TSN was unceremoniously hoofed from the sport after twenty years. Following a hellish season of vitriolic complaints from curling's manic TV fans, the 2005 contract was adjusted to allow TSN to return, and curling vanished from Country Canada. But in 2006, the CCA snubbed the CBC—the founder of Canadian and world curling TV coverage dating back to the 1950s—and awarded, without tender, an exclusive new contract to TSN, running from 2008 to 2014, effectively giving the boot to the public broadcaster.

The return to increased television coverage was expected to satisfy all but the most rabid fans. For them, twenty-first-century technology offered a small host of online venues: *The Curling Show*'s ten-minute weekly podcast interviews with "the people who shape the game"; the *Curling News*'s popular weblog delivering curling stories and off-season games beamed live to your computer screen.

Ironically, the best thing for Canadian women's curling might be for the Americans to finally make it to the top of the Olympic podium. We will find out in Vancouver and Whistler in 2010.

IN THE HACK

OLYMPIAN REVELATIONS

I learn over brunch at the Chateau Montebello that Richard W. "Dick" Pound is the type of guy who will literally give you the coat off his back—if you're Mike Harris and you're skipping the Canadian Olympic curling team at the first Winter Games where it's a full-medal sport, and you want to march in the Opening or Closing Ceremonies or mount the podium to receive your medal, and if the men's and women's hockey teams have stolen all the extra-large uniforms.

It was probably the smoothest problem-solving gesture in the history of the Olympic movement, just one more facet to the man who likely comes as close to a Renaissance man as possible these days. Pound is a scholar and a past Olympian swimmer, a veteran member of the International Olympic Committee, and chair of the World Anti-Doping Agency, which helps safeguard international competition against drug-enhanced performances. He is also the chancellor of McGill University and a partner in the Montreal office of the prestigious Stikeman-Elliott law firm. In his spare time, he authors books—five and counting as I write this.

Pound has graciously invited me to meet him at the Chateau and has taken time from his weekend retreat with Stikeman-Elliott colleagues to chat about curling's road to the Olympics. Even the initial small talk is revealing. I learn, for example, that some of his formative years were spent in Elora, Ontario, about five miles downstream from my hometown, Fergus. Its curling club was founded in 1839—which ties in. When he excuses himself, it's to go curling. It turns out the Chateau has its own sheets for guests and for rent. Pound is considered "the ringer" by the young lawyers, who look uncertain as they get their instruction from staff prior to walking onto the ice. Grappling with the laws of physics and mathematical probabilities, while concentrating on retaining their balance, the rink quickly fills with the roar of the rocks, shouted encouragements, and laughter.

It's infectious, even if it is a far cry from the Olympic podium.

THE TENTH END
THE OLYMPICS

$\mathcal{N}$ewfoundlanders hold two things sacred—Beaumont-Hamel and the Brad Gushue curling squad. Jack McDuff, whose boots were bronzed and displayed for bringing the first Brier to the Rock, follows close behind.

Beaumont-Hamel and the Turin Olympics are ninety years and worlds apart. The former is commemorated every July 1 in tribute to the soldiers of the Newfoundland Regiment who walked out of their trenches and into the valley of death known as no man's land on the first day of the First Battle of the Somme in 1916. Ordered to advance at a walk into a withering German machine-gun crossfire, the regiment was virtually destroyed within forty minutes. Of the 752 men who moved out at 9:15 a.m., 658—including all 26 officers from the elite families of St. John's—were dead, wounded, or missing: a 91 per cent casualty rate, the second-highest of the worst day in the history of the British army.

Interestingly, the *Nor'Wester* newspaper highlighted the Gushue team's visit to Indian River Academy in Springdale alongside the planned departure of Indian River High student Rebecca Rice, who had been invited to attend the ninetieth commemoration of Beaumont-Hamel on a youth pilgrimage to the battlefield. Gushue, aged twenty-five when his team won men's curling gold at Turin, would have been an old man in those trenches. His accomplishment is far happier and, in its way, apparently, just as revered. Tributes to the fallen continue in Newfoundland nearly a century after that ill-fated attack wiped out a generation in a matter of minutes, most recently two commemorative poppies being painted near centre ice of the Broomfield hockey arena by the Royal Canadian Legion Happy Valley/Goose Bay Branch. While that is not quite the same as a curling club, curling is played in every Legion provincial and territorial command, and regular and senior curling rate national status as Dominion sports.

Coach Toby McDonald had been a member of McDuff's 1976 Brier championship team. McDuff himself had been mentored by Sam Richardson, a member of the legendary Saskatchewan family that dominated Canadian curling for years, winning four Briers and Scotch Cups—then symbolic of world excellence—in five years. The curling torch had been passed from generation to generation to generation by curlers spread nearly right across the country. Gushue capped it all with his six count in the sixth end to lock the gold medal against the Finns.

Since returning from Turin with Canada's first gold medal in men's Olympic curling, Gushue and his squad have been honoured and feted around the Rock. Starting with the two thousand people who crowded St. John's International Airport to welcome the conquering curlers home, the team that "rocked the Rock" has been wined, dined, and feted by everyone from members of their local club to Premier Danny Williams. Team members have been awarded honorary doctorate of laws degrees from Memorial University (named to commemorate the men of Beaumont-Hamel and where Gushue earned his bachelor's degree in business administration), declared role models by the premier, and attended the official opening of a portion of the Team Gushue Highway—accompanied by junior curlers from the St. John's and Baly Hally clubs. (Newfoundland also won the Canadian and world juniors, and Corner Brook's Bas Buckle and his foursome won the senior men's world title. Gushue's home St. John's Curling Club also boasts the 2001 world junior men's Karcher champs—Gushue and others—and the 2005 Canadian mixed titlists—and, of course, Brier Bear.)

The team toured schools, which had closed to watch their gold-medal performance, and exchanged high-fives with the exuberant kids. The media reported invitations to attend the Junos, to drop a puck at a Montreal Canadiens NHL game, and even to play bingo in Eston, Saskatchewan. Lead Jamie Korab was actually able to make that last commitment but joked to the media he couldn't go back after winning $80. It was a pretty heady time as the young Newfoundland curlers, and veteran Russ Howard from New Brunswick, were thronged by jubilant fans who either saw themselves as potential gold medallists or were at least convinced that this was a sport they could play.

The Gushue team's collective medal count surpassed the province's previous total Olympic medal count: Andrew Crosby's gold medal for rowing at the 1992 Barcelona Summer Games and a silver medal for hockey to Dwayne Norris from the 1994 Lillehammer Winter Games. Canadian curlers have not missed the Olympic podium since curling was made a full-medal sport at the 1998 Nagano Winter Games, and their six medals—two gold, two silver, and two bronze—lead all other nations. But the Canadians have not dominated as expected—a sign that there are good curlers everywhere and a reminder that, in the roaring game, anything can happen on any given day.

While the Americans were ecstatic with their first bronze medal for men's curling, and the women are expected to push onto the podium, possibly as early as 2010 at Vancouver, there has always been an expectation among Canadians that they should almost always win curling gold. But then we used to say the same thing about hockey, and our only predictable success at the Olympics these days is in women's hockey. While the American women won gold, defeating the Canadians at Nagano in 1998, the Canadian men's and women's teams both won at Salt Lake in 2002. The women did it the hard way, playing short-handed for much of the game.

But the Canadian curlers were shut out of the gold at Salt Lake, the men taking silver and the women bronze. The men won silver at Nagano, while Sandra Schmirler's team took the first Olympic curling gold. Everyone knows that. But just how it came to pass that curling became a full-medal sport in Japan four years earlier than expected is less well known. To understand that, you need to talk to someone who was there. Someone like Dick Pound.

Better known for his Olympic involvement over the decades, as the one-time potential head of the International Olympic Committee and currently the head of the World Anti-Doping Agency, Pound is also a pretty decent curler—and an Olympic athlete in his own right. He threw his first schoolboy rock in Three Rivers, Quebec, in 1956, primarily to see what the sport was like. Born in St. Catharines, Ontario, he moved around quite a bit growing up as his father followed engineering jobs across central Canada, first to Toronto, where his younger brother was born, then to Elora, just five miles from Fergus, where his youngest brother, Robert, was born. From there, it was on to Quebec, migrating from La Tuque to Montreal via Three Rivers, with an intervening jaunt to the Pacific coast.

Pound was about six when his family moved to Ocean Falls, British Columbia, a village of about three thousand people— roughly four hundred of them kids—and a short hop by seaplane from the rock bearing Alexander Mackenzie's centuries-old graf-fiti. With little avenue for hockey or skiing, passions for kids his age back East, Pound dove into swimming. Turns out he was very good at it. In fact, there were a lot of good swimmers in Ocean

Falls. That was due, at least in part, to coach George Gates, who had followed Mackenzie's footsteps from his native Scotland to the rain forest and 230 annual inches of precipitation in Ocean Falls. The results were impressive: in every Olympiad from 1948 to 1976, at least one member of the Canadian Olympic swimming team called that village home. Pound began swimming the fifty-yard freestyle soon after moving to Ocean Falls; at age eighteen, he took his Olympic plunge at the 1960 Games in Rome, a year after his international debut at the Pan Am Games in Chicago. Placing sixth in the hundred-yard freestyle in Rome, his 4 × 400m medley relay team came within a long flutter stroke of a bronze medal, finishing fourth. In 1962, at age twenty, he won the 110-yard freestyle at the Perth Commonwealth Games.

Rome was a paradise for a young Olympian, filling Pound's expansive mind with a deeper sense of history. It was his first trip to Europe, and he marvelled at the ruins of the Coliseum and the Forum, walked along the Tiber River in the footsteps of the Caesars where, in a most un-curling-like fashion, they plotted and murdered to gain or retain power. The experience confirmed his penchant for history and he remains a history buff to this day, an interest that has factored in the books he has written about his law firm, a retired prominent judge, Canadian facts and dates, the Olympics, and even a motivational primer based on an ambitious array of high-impact quotations.

The son of a Queen's graduate—they called it a bachelor of applied science rather than an engineering degree back then— who had enlisted in the Royal Canadian Air Force during the Second World War, Pound recalls that his father had been a bit old for active duty, then flashes his infectious grin as he explains that his dad had charitably conceded he would probably contribute more to the war effort by designing combat aircraft than flying and crashing them.

Curling entered his life with Martin Dufresne, a banker with the Canadian Bank of Commerce (as CIBC was then known) who organized schoolboy curling at Three Rivers High School— the only English-speaking secondary school in the city. Curling seemed a natural outlet for Pound. He enjoyed both the challenge and camaraderie, had a roaring good time playing the roaring game, and continued to curl when his family moved to Montreal. Enrolling in Mount Royal High School, he continued to curl schoolboy, joking that he eventually began throwing "unreliable" third rocks for his school team at the Mount Royal Curling Club across the street. Curling in the men's evening league at his father's club, the Montreal Thistle, where he played lead and later threw second stones, Pound recalls that his major contribution was "energetic sweeping" for which his "patient" skips forgave whatever bewildering strategy he seemed to attach to his shooting. He did, however, possess the hand-eye coordination and fine motor skills to shoot his way into the finals of the club's billiards tournament.

By the 1960s, Pound's focus had switched to post-secondary education. Earning a bachelor of commerce degree in 1962 at McGill—a school he enjoyed so much he went on to chair its board of governors before being named its chancellor—he went on to add a BA at Sir George Williams. He followed that by becoming a chartered accountant in 1964; he completed law school with a degree in civil law in 1967 and was called to the bar a year later. Today, he's a partner at Stikeman-Elliott, the niche tax-law boutique that grew into a renowned firm with worldwide operations.

That rapid series of academic accomplishments gave new impetus to Pound's career aspirations, along with a new sense of priority. He had passed on the chance to compete at the 1964 Summer Games in Tokyo, but hanging up his swimming trunks

did not mean abandoning the Olympic movement entirely. Pound
had worked hard for everything he got out of life. He was evolving into a modern Renaissance man, a wholesome blend of
academia and athletics with a no-nonsense approach that prevented him from suffering fools gladly but was tempered by a rare
sense of commitment and compassion. The essence of his philosophy is that you give back to others as payback for what others
have given to you. It's part of a value system no doubt ingrained
by his parents and coaches like Dufresne and Gates. He started by
coaching *collège classique* students in Montreal, the francophone
equivalent of junior college, then rose to the position of treasurer
of the Quebec section of the Canadian Amateur Swimming
Association before progressing to the Canadian Olympic
Association, now the Canadian Olympic Committee, serving as
secretary, then becoming president in less than a decade. In April
1978, a year and a half after the Montreal Olympics, he was "co-
opted" to join the International Olympic Committee.

The first to admit he doesn't play political games well, Pound
has had mixed fortunes at the IOC. His crusade to provide results
and widespread benefits for as many people as possible has not
only tweaked the sensitivities of some of his international colleagues, but also engendered a respect for consistency and
integrity. Pound doesn't mince words, so no one ever need wonder where he stands on any issue or where they rank in his esteem.
He acts when others posture and has figuratively put more than
one nose out of joint. It was inevitable that Pound would continue working behind the scenes for the Olympic movement, to
help pass on to others some of the opportunities he had enjoyed
and to encourage others who were working hard to achieve excellence in their fields as he had. His virtue lies in his focus on doing
everything he can to sustain and expand the Olympic dream and
its ideals, while embracing all possible deserving sports and

athletes who share those ideals and want to share the dream. When Canadian and international curling officials came knocking, Pound did everything he could to open the door.

The roaring game made its Olympic debut as a demonstration sport at the first modern Winter Games in Chamonix, France, in 1924. Play was restricted to men's teams that year. Britain won the gold medal, Sweden took the silver, and France won bronze. All games were eighteen ends. In 1932, Lake Placid included curling as a demonstration sport for women. Eight men's teams—four from Canada and four from the host United States—competed in a round robin. Canada won the gold and the United States won silver. All games were sixteen ends. Curling disappeared from the Garmisch-Partenkirchen Winter Games hosted by Nazi Germany in 1936, replaced by *eisschiessen* ("ice shooting"), the game portrayed by the Belgian and Dutch masters whose art instigated the Continental claim to inventing curling and a sport much more familiar to the Bavarians and Austrians. The national champion for the latter was Arnold Schwarzenegger's father, Gustaf. The Games disappeared after that for the duration of the Second World War. Peace returned in 1945 and the Olympic dream was revived in 1948. Curling was soon back on the agenda.

The first Canadian push for full-medal status was made at the 43rd Session of the IOC in Rome in the spring of 1949. On April 26 of that year, Canadian IOC member Sidney Dawes proposed that curling be added to the program of the Winter Games. There seems to have been no formal response, and no further mention of it can be found in the minutes. Pound suggests this may have been due to Canada causing its share of problems in ice hockey back then, as the ongoing professional–amateur bickering played out for years...and years...and years.

From 1920 to 1948, Canada had dominated international and Olympic hockey, winning an impressive twelve gold and two silver medals. It may well have been that the last thing Europe wanted or needed was a return to Canadian hockey dominance when the Games resumed after the Second World War. But if the IOC was worried that approving curling as a full-medal sport would automatically make Canada the dominant power in another winter sport, they might have relaxed: Canada's international hockey domination would soon come to an end. The enduring feud with the Soviets over what constituted an "amateur" player would not start until 1952, and, prior to that, there were indications that the Canadian house was falling into disorder as arguments raged among the professional and semi-pro leagues and amateur players over who should represent Canada on the world stage. The debate led to no resolution, and several well-intentioned ventures—most notably Father David Bauer's efforts to recruit and train a true squad of amateurs—marked a gold-medal drought that plagued Canada from 1952, in Oslo, until the 2002 Salt Lake City Winter Games. There were a couple of boycotts along the way, with Canada refusing to ice a team in 1972 and 1976 over what Pound has dubbed the "shamateur" issue, but Canada returned to the fold in the 1980s, and the drought continued. Canada came close to a gold medal in 1994 but lost it in an overtime shootout against Sweden and had to settle for silver. Nagano marked the first time that the NHL effectively altered its schedule to allow all professional players a chance to represent their country at the Olympics. The Canadians failed to win a medal, but amid all the hockey hoopla in the run-up to the Games, including the introduction of women's hockey as a full-medal sport, few paid much attention to curling.

After the stalled attempt to consider admitting curling at the 1949 meeting in Rome, the next effort to make the game a full-medal Olympic sport took place behind the scenes at the final Scotch Cup in 1967. Delegates from seven curling nations, including Canada, had created the International Curling Federation in their bid for approval from the International Olympic Committee for full-medal status—a dream unfulfilled for another three decades. But there was hope. After all, curling had been admitted as a demonstration sport as early as the first modern Winter Olympics—before the event even bore that august name—and Canadian teams had done well, if not always good enough to win the gold medal. The curling crusade got a boost at the 1988 Winter Olympics when Calgary reintroduced the game as a demonstration sport. Fans flocked to the rink, lining up to buy 21,000 tickets to watch the return of the roaring game. The six-day bonspiel sold out long before the last ticket was sold for the historically popular skiing events. This time, there were venues for both men and women. The Norwegians won the men's gold medal, Switzerland took silver, and Canada settled for bronze. The women fared better, winning the gold medal. Sweden won silver, Norway the bronze.

Curling resurfaced as a demonstration sport in Albertville in 1992. The best Canada could do was a bronze medal for the women's team, behind Germany's gold-medal performance and Norway's silver. In men's action, Switzerland won gold, Norway took second, and the United States won the bronze. That same year, serious discussion began for admitting curling as a full-medal sport. Convening in Barcelona, the IOC Executive Board was advised against rushing to include curling or women's ice hockey for the 1994 Games in Lillehammer, Norway. There was hope, however, that both could be included at the 1998 Olympics in Nagano. The debate over the inclusion of curling turned "lively" but, in the end, most delegates favoured adding the sport.

The only question was whether to target the 1998 Games in Japan or the 2002 Games in Salt Lake City. The latter would allow more time for curling to develop as an Olympic sport. It seems that no one was aware it had made its Olympic debut in 1924 (the IOC ruled in 2006 that curling was an official, full-medal event that year and not a demonstration sport as commonly believed), or that curling organizers from seven countries had been lobbying to get in for a quarter-century. In any event, those in attendance at the Executive Board were quite favourable toward including curling but balked at making a decision until the IOC Co-ordination Commission had visited all possible sites. In the end, IOC Sports Director Gilbert Felli of Switzerland supported the inclusion of both curling and women's hockey in principle, but the date for their debuts as full-medal sports was left unresolved, pending further consultations with other branches of the IOC and the Nagano Organizing Committee (NAOC).

There was staunch support voiced for including the roaring game, and the NAOC had confirmed it wanted the IOC to approve curling for 1998—but not yet. The timing was critical, and the decision was secondary to political concerns unrelated to the Olympics playing out behind the scenes. On the eve of domestic elections, Japanese citizens were seeking redress through the courts to recover an estimated $7 million paid out of tax dollars to lobby the IOC to bring the 1998 Olympiad to Japan. It was not the time to announce the expansion of the Games by introducing new sports that might require an additional venue—possibly at additional cost.

But none of that prevented serious discussion around the table by the IOC Executive Board members. The Swedish member, Gunnar Ericsson, wondered aloud why the roaring game had disappeared from the Olympic program after the 1924 Games in Chamonix. While no one seems to have mentioned Lake Placid, Calgary, or even the recent Albertville, he pressed on, noting that the sport boasted two million active players worldwide, equally divided between men and women and proving that curling was demonstrably popular and ideal for a shared venue, as both sexes could play on the same regulation ice surface. The rules were "crystal clear." Not only was the sport inexpensive to play, but it exuded an enviable charisma. Perhaps most important, it already enjoyed good television coverage and ratings. Ericsson recommended curling be included at the 1998 Nagano Games. IOC President Juan Antonio Samaranch, who had done so much to make the earlier Olympiad in Seoul a resounding success by personally conciliating between the potentially explosive polarized agendas of North and South Korea, asked if another ice surface would have to be built to accommodate the curlers, but was assured that a good ice technician could convert hockey ice to curling ice within eight hours.

There were other concerns laid to rest. Curling was not, as some members seemed to think, an old man's sport played only for recreation. Physical conditioning and accuracy were required to play the game. Commenting on the balanced support from the IOC Winter Sub-Commission, Swiss member and IOC Vice-President Marc Hodler noted the surprisingly strong resistance from a delegate from a country in which curling was "very strong." While the reference remained deliberately vague, there seems little doubt he was referring to Canadian Ken Read—the first non-European Alpine ski champion in the earlier era of the "Crazy Canucks" and first Canadian to sit on the IOC's Athletes' Commission, from 1985 (four years after its inception) until 1998—who had been widely quoted in the media for suggesting that including curling would open the door to bowling, darts, and ballroom dancing. His concerns were dismissed at the time by an unnamed member who quipped, "Ken is not a supporter of many sports that don't require you to wear boards on your feet."

By contrast, Hodler expressed the view that curling was a new type of sport for the Winter Games and should be welcomed. It was a team sport but was not judged; results could be measured. And while the Association of International Olympic Winter Federations (AIOWF) was not keen to carve a seventh slice of the money pie for a new partner, there was no financial argument against including curling. That seemed to be enough to persuade Pal Schmitt, the Hungarian member, to support the introduction of curling for Nagano, provided that hockey and curling could share the same arena.

All seemed to be going well for curling, but none of these positive sentiments stopped the Russian member, Vitaly Smirnov, from reminding the IOC Executive Board that the Program Commission, which he chaired, had rejected curling on several grounds, primarily because it did not involve strenuous physical activity and also because his commission did not consider it a serious sport. He added his concern that curling could also require additional facilities. For all those reasons, he left no doubt that he was very much against the proposal to admit curling as a full-medal sport.

In contrast to those remarks—the first and only voice raised among the IOC executives against—Judge Keeba Mbaye of Senegal supported the sport's inclusion, swayed in great part by the warm recommendation from Hodler. Arguing that the "expenditure of physical energy" should not be the deciding factor, and noting that the same could be said about shooting events, Mbaye endorsed the proposal for Nagano, conditional on the ultimate agreement by the NAOC.

Pound jumped into the fray next, disagreeing with the sentiment that curling was not an energetic sport. Perhaps the only curler in the room, he knew from possibly blistered first-hand experience about energetic sweeping. Pound had been consulting "at the highest levels" with Canadian and international curling officials, including Roy Sinclair, head of the International Curling Federation, soon to be renamed the World Curling Federation. If the board members around the table that day had any reason to suspect Pound might have a bias toward what was generally viewed as a "Canadian" sport, they also knew his reputation for integrity. If curling was "Canadian" at that point, it was also demonstrably inclusive, open to men and women on equal terms. The sport was exciting, even dramatic at times. And television had made the game both comprehensible and wildly popular, with not only curlers but also a new core of fans who may never have tossed a rock, swept a stone, or even set foot inside a club-house. The game required strategy, stamina, and skill. It was a true sport and a legitimate contender for full Olympic status, per-haps combining the Olympic ideals of competition and camaraderie better and more easily than any other.

As the discussion played out that day, Pound was spared hav-ing to make all these points. With the exception of Smirnov, there seemed genuine and generous support for embracing curling. He did assure his colleagues that curling, played at the highest elite levels, was very physical and dismissed any concerns over needing additional facilities as a false issue, arguing that a city could build a new facility if it wanted to, but that it certainly wasn't neces-sary. Hockey ice could be converted to curling ice given the advanced ice-making techniques that had come into vogue, largely as the result of Shorty Jenkins's pioneering efforts.

After learning more about the skills required to play the game, and the rules governing it, IOC President Juan Antonio Samaranch asked if curling was popular in the United States. Pound assured him it was in the northern states where conditions were ideal for winter sports. That seemed to satisfy Samaranch, as he then suggested to the Executive Committee that it propose to the IOC Session that it include curling for 2002 and, provided that the Japanese organizers agreed, for 1998.

In the end, the Executive Committee agreed in that session to add curling, women's hockey, two men's and women's short-track speed-skating races, and freestyle skiing aerials, and to retain freestyle moguls as Winter Olympic programs, subject to the approval of the host committee. There seemed no doubt now that curlers would be reaching for the Olympic rings in Utah in 2002. It was now up to the Japanese to determine if it could begin four years earlier.

That December, the IOC Executive Board confirmed its intention to introduce men's and women's curling at the Nagano Olympiad, provided that conditions on facilities, necessary officials for competitions, accommodations, and other unspecified concerns were met. Negotiations would continue with the World Curling Federation and other organizations. In other words, it seemed a done deal, with only minor tweaking left to complete. The Japanese stance was less firm, with the NAOC agreeing only to discuss the conditions for holding men's and women's curling. The committee finally offered its conditional agreement to introduce the sport at its Olympiad, with one last "if." All conditions had to be met, which required virtual unanimous consent from the international delegates sitting around the table. The majority were European, but no one really seems to have anticipated a major stumbling block. Compared to the Summer Olympics, already congested with twenty-eight sports, the six competitions in the Winter Games had lots of room for expansion. It was far less complicated to add a winter sport than to embrace a new summer sport. Still, until every T was crossed and every I dotted, the consent of the NAOC remained conditional.

Finally, in June 1993, the final piece slid into the puzzle as the NAOC reported its plans for the xviii Olympic Winter Games to the IOC Executive Board. Director General Makoto Kobayashi confirmed that the committee had agreed to include women's ice hockey as an official discipline and curling as an official sport. Elite curlers had a new goal in life: Olympic gold.

The highly touted Canadians enjoyed mixed fortunes in Nagano—the women won gold, but the men did not. In hindsight, there may have been omens in Canada of what would play out in Japan. Mike Harris's Olympic woes began before he ever left Canada. Arriving in Calgary to select his official uniform, he found that it had been first-come, first-served. Last-come, last-pick proved to be an unhappy alternative for Harris and his team. Everything over a size 9 seemed to have been scooped by the men's and women's ice hockey teams—and the monsters who push the bobsled—leaving the curlers short several key pieces of wardrobe to be worn in the Opening Ceremonies and on the medal podium. Without even a new issue of ceremony boots, Harris took the outfitters at their word when they promised him that his uniform would catch up to him in Nagano. The full uniform never showed.

The day before they were to start practising, the Canadians had larger worries. With time on their hands and bored, they decided to try their hands, well, actually their feet, at snowboarding. There was a hill behind their quarters, what the Canadians considered maybe a good-sized tobogganing hill, small enough that the athletes rode an escalator, not a ski lift, to get to the top. Along the way, the curlers noticed the hill was not covered with powdered snow but with gleaming ice, solid as a curling stone and clearly nothing but dangerous. By this time, all their opponents had gathered in the Village windows to watch the show, and there were no thoughts of backing down.

"Once one guy goes, everybody has to go," said third Richard Hart.

"We had rented these snowboards and everything," recalls lead George Karrys.

It was messy. A routine of taking off and instantly crashing quickly became the norm, as the high-performance athletes simply got up, rode to the top of the hill, and tried again (and failed). All except Harris, who somehow managed to stop himself halfway down the hill without crashing, and remained still, clinging to the ice as his teammates repeatedly tumbled down around him. Then, out of nowhere, second Collin Mitchell hit a fast patch and raced all the way down the slope. Near the end, the board caught an edge and dumped Mitchell headfirst onto the icy packed snow at the bottom of the run. Back on the summit, his teammates howled with glee, doubling over with laughter—until they noticed he wasn't moving. Worse, there was no way to reach him without boarding down the path he took. In the end, Mitchell was rescued, he recovered, and he curled, and the squad covered their scrapes and bruises at a live news conference the following day.

Alternate, team coach, and father-figure Paul Savage met the foursome as they limped into the Village complex, fairly leaping with excitement that teams from other nations could not believe what they were seeing. After shouting warnings to the other athletes not to mess with the crazy Canadians, he whispered a warning to his teammates: "The [CCA] coaches want to kill you though, so watch out."

It was hard to understand, then, why Ken Read had ever worried about curlers bringing a wimp factor to the Olympics. The Harris team had clearly established themselves early as the Kamikaze Kanucks—bolder, more brazen, and much more bruised than Read's Crazy Canuck Alpine skiers of an earlier generation. No self-respecting curler on that team was going to strap boards on his feet to break his fall.

With Mitchell rescued, recovered, and able to curl, Savage had more free time to relax and have some fun. Before leaving for Nagano, he swore he was coerced, or at least duped, by the younger athletes—notably the entire Schmirler squad—into getting a tattoo to commemorate the historic event. Everyone was planning what design they would get, but the next day, when he asked them what they had got and where they had put it, everyone admitted they had backed out. Not Savage. Like many of the skiers and women hockey players, he had braved the needle and, at a later press conference in Japan, dared to bare where. As the press admired a maple leaf painted onto his forehead, Savage opted to show them the real deal. Turning his back on the assembled media, he dropped his pants and mooned them with his curling rock and Olympic rings, each ornately gracing a bare cheek. The first he knew of the media reaction was when he bumped into columnist Christie Blatchford the next day and she screamed, "Hey, Paul, I saw your ass on the front page of the *Toronto Sun*." The next confirmation came from his wife, Barbara, who suggested over the phone that he keep his pants on in future.

Suddenly, what would not have been a problem in a Summer Olympics, where only the weightlifters would normally command extra-large wardrobes, was a potential annoyance for the Canadian curlers. There was concern that Harris would have to skip the Opening Ceremonies, or parade distinctly clad from all the other Canadian athletes—likely unique among all athletes from all nations. His teammates were already wearing their matching sneakers in a show of solidarity because of his missing winter boots, but the winter jacket was another matter. Lead George Karrys recalls his skip lamenting his misfortune to Pound, who happened to be a close friend of Harris's mother's husband at the time. Pound, reasoning that friends do not let friends miss, or clash with, the dramatic Olympic Opening Ceremonies, and believing that an official jacket should more properly be worn by Canada's first potential curling medallist than by "an aging sports official," promptly lent his jacket to Harris.

There are, not surprisingly, some variations to the story, but the essential point is not in dispute—Harris lacked a team jacket at a crucial moment. Whatever happened at the Opening Ceremonies, Harris vividly recalls the aftermath of the gold-medal game. The Canadian men and women curled well in the Olympic round-robin series, seemingly coasting into the play-off round. In the semifinal, Harris overcame a rising fever to rout the Americans and advance to the gold-medal game against Switzerland. No thought seems to have been entertained about having Savage, a veteran high-pressure skip, step in to call the championship game. Harris seemed to have shrugged off the flu bug that had been raging through the athletes' village, but overnight, his temperature soared and misfortune followed. The fever spiked at 103 degrees just prior to the gold-medal game, throwing him off his game and relegating his squad to a silver medal.

Gracious, if unhappy, in defeat, the Canadians waited to mount the podium for the medal presentations. Harris still did not have his dress uniform, and the choice was either not to mount the podium—a potential incident that could be mistaken as poor sportsmanship, the antithesis of both curling and the Olympic movement—or have the entire squad accept their medals in their curling clothes. At least then they would look like a team. As Harris recalls the moment, "I'm bitter, I'm sick, I'm pissed off we lost. The whole experience didn't sit well." That is when he was handed a leather Roots Team Canada jacket. He knew at once it was not his pristine new uniform arriving in the nick of time, recalling, "It was used. Well used." But the moment was saved. The Canadians graciously accepted their silver medals, and Harris returned the coat. A few weeks later, Pound caught up with Harris at a family celebration and formally presented him with his official team jacket. Harris donated it for auction at a celebrity bonspiel to raise money for the Special Olympics.

But the true importance of the Japanese stepping up to launch curling as an official Winter Olympic sport can likely best be summed up in two words: Sandra Schmirler. If the men felt they had laid a golden egg in the final game, Team Schmirler curled to a truly Cinderella finale that made the skip a national treasure and Canada's sweetheart in the tradition of marathon swimmer Marilyn Bell, figure skater Barbara Anne Scott, and Hollywood starlet Mary Pickford. That would all have been lost had the Japanese not agreed to debut curling as a full-medal sport at Nagano. Their effort enshrined a Canadian sports icon whose competitive spirit was balanced by her humanity, inspiring all who met her or just watched from afar. Her legacy endures in the foundation that bears her name, headed since its inception following Schmirler's untimely death in 2000 by her keen rival and true friend Anne Merklinger. While she and Harris would return to a future Olympiad with the CBC, Schmirler would never have another chance to return to the podium. As the Japanese had sagely observed, timing can truly be everything. Without Japanese agreement to make curling a full-medal sport, there would have been no full-medal Schmirler the Curler's miracle on ice.

There is a final footnote to this story that underscores how much individual Canadians have done to promote the roaring game to other countries that have adopted and learned it well enough to give Canadians serious competition in the race for international championships, while improving international relations in a troubled world. Having, I hope, proven that the Scots invented curling, let us lay to rest Fast Eddie Lukowich's facetious

Norse claim. In fact, the Canadians took curling to Denmark—
ancestral home of the Vikings.

On the eve of Sandra Schmirler's historic gold-medal game
against Denmark's Helena Blach-Lavrsen at the 1998 Nagano
Winter Games, Doug Graham and his wife, Gerry, were surprised by a long-distance call at their Manotick home just
outside Ottawa. Recognizing the voice of a Danish friend, they
probably weren't totally surprised when she asked who they
were going to cheer for in the final curling game. They never
really answered. But if the Danes had triumphed that day, the
Grahams could have taken part of the credit—or the blame. This
Canadian couple is credited with helping to introduce curling to
Denmark. In a way, they had no choice if they wanted to continue playing the game that had become a big part of their lives.
The roaring game had long afforded them the opportunity to
meet new people, socialize with old friends, and spend time
together in a pursuit they both enjoyed.

Doug and Gerry never claimed to be innovators of the game,
but there's no doubt they were gracious curling ambassadors to
Denmark, diplomatically crediting Ib Asbjorn's efforts to introduce the sport to his native land after being introduced to it when
he lived a few years in Toronto. His good intentions and
admirable efforts went largely unrewarded; by the time the
Grahams arrived on the scene, he was apparently one of seven
Danish curlers—not quite enough for two teams. That rose to
nine in 1967, when Doug was transferred to Denmark by his
employer "for a year." He and Gerry arrived, unable to speak
Danish, read a newspaper, or enjoy a radio broadcast. Television
was so rudimentary as to be unwatchable, unless you were interested in prolonged pastoral scenes, often populated with grazing
cattle. Anticipating a long, cold, isolated winter, they contacted
the Canadian Embassy to locate the nearest curling club, driven

perhaps equally by their desire for social and cultural interaction as for the exercise. They were stunned to learn the Nordic land had no curling club.

Their disappointment was short-lived. Word spread quickly that two Canadians had arrived who were looking for a place to curl. Within days, Asbjorn invited them to join him and the six other enthusiasts. With that single introduction, Danish curling leaped to two full squads with a spare. If both Grahams curled, which seemed inevitable, probably as competing skips as the most—the only—experienced curlers, it meant relegating one of the pioneer Danes to the sidelines, but any need for substitute players was overshadowed by the fact that, for the first time, there could be two competitors on the ice at the same time. If, of course, they could find ice.

Any elation the Canadian curlers may have felt to find others interested in curling was as brief as their earlier disappointment at find no curling clubs. The Grahams grimaced when they recalled the ice in a local skating club, gouged by skate blades, flooded by a Zamboni, then haphazardly pebbled just enough to ensure the rocks would dive to one side or the other; the result was ice that was sometimes so heavy that there was no hope of getting a rock to the far end. The house was identified by pale green splotches that only the skip could see; the button was marked by a red pylon. None of that mattered to the Danes. They just wanted to curl. They promptly invited the Grahams to join them to play at an international bonspiel in Sweden. That sounded fine to the Canadians, except for one small problem—they had no idea how to get to Sweden, let alone find the curling club if and when they got there. No problem. The Danish curlers gave them directions to the nearest ferry and agreed to meet the Grahams at dockside at eight-thirty in the morning.

If the Canadians arrived with any optimism for their international debut, the short voyage to Sweden may have dampened that enthusiasm. Everyone knows that curlers love to party, but the Danes raised it to a new level. In the old days, it was not unheard of for Canadian skips to take a bottle onto the ice—certainly when the game was played outdoors, but the tradition apparently followed the early matches indoors, where whiskey could be stored in hollowed broom handles. However, even the most dedicated imbibers usually waited until the game was over or at least in progress. Not so the Danes. The Grahams marvelled at their ability to pack away a particularly potent brew, called *Gameldansk*, while still at sea. It may have had medicinal values, but it did little to enhance the players' accuracy. If the Danes were unabashedly there to party, the Swedes viewed their competitive sports very seriously. This mattered in a contest where the Danes' inebriation was further complicated by the need to conduct the bonspiel in three languages—Swedish, Danish, and English. But the outcome was clear enough.

"We were crushed," Gerry later recalled, neglecting to mention the score.

Although the scoreboard results were frustrating, there were larger accomplishments. Losing in Sweden had done nothing to sour the experience. In fact, the event proved so popular with the Danes that they decided to host their own international bonspiel and invited teams from Sweden, Norway, Germany, and Switzerland to compete at the Copenhagen Curling Club later that same season. All showed up and the event was proclaimed a roaring success by everyone.

This was back in 1967, and the novelty of a bonspiel—especially one that featured five Scandinavian and European teams—spawned the first remote telecast on Danish television, then in its infancy. The fact that the TV engineers had no remote equipment was no deterrence to ingenuity. By good fortune, the studio was across the street from the skating arena that was being used as the curling rink; the TV technicians simply laid lines to connect the buildings, plugged in their equipment, threw a switch, and started broadcasting. Anything that moved went on the air, whether on-ice curlers or a passing fan in the stands. If you were in the arena, you were on the air—live!

The Grahams weren't the only Canadians to distinguish themselves in Scandinavian curling that Centennial year. Canadian transplant Bob Woods skipped his Swedish championship team—Totte Åkerlund, Bengt af Kleen, and Ove Söderström from the Fjällgården Curling Club—to a silver medal at the Scotch Cup, in Perth, Scotland, against that country's native son, Chuck Hay. In fairness to the Danes, the Swedes had been playing the roaring game since another Scot, William Andrew MacFie, introduced it in 1852 and founded the first European curling club outside the United Kingdom, the Bohuslänska Curlingklubben, which continues to operate today.

Doug Graham was temporarily reassigned to England in 1968. By the time he returned to Denmark in 1971 there were about two hundred curlers on the ice in three arenas. Introduced to a Swedish woman at the end of another bonspiel, he smiled and extended his hand in curling friendship; she seethed and slapped his head, nearly spitting two words: "Canada! Hockey!"

He was initially stunned by her reception, until a friend translated the blow as payback for the blood trails left on the ice by Team Sweden a short while earlier when they had played Team Canada in the violent run-up to the 1972 Soviet hockey summit.

If the Grahams played a major role in bringing curling to Copenhagen, Doug was also the catalyst for getting Danish curlers on the ice in Canada. Air Canada was flying into the Danish capital and trying to develop a larger market there in the early 1970s. Doug had a friend who happened to be the Air Canada European manager and he proved receptive to the Canadian's suggestion that it would be good publicity for the airline if they flew a Danish team to the 1973 Silver Broom world championship in Regina. After all, Air Canada was sponsoring the event and flying in curlers from far and wide.

The Danes responded to the ensuing invitation to their national champions by sending a team composed of their top four skips. Doug, who had played third on the actual championship team, happily stepped aside for a Danish curler, personifying the chivalry of curling by foregoing his own shot at the world stage. Immediately upon their arrival in Regina, the Danish team was whisked away by CCA officials for several days of intensive training. "They worked the hell out of them," Doug recalled. It worked. After being blown away by the traditional curling powerhouses in their first five draws, the Danes rebounded to beat Norway in their sixth outing before losing a close game to Italy, then to Germany by only one rock. The Danes—and the Grahams—were pleased.

"We didn't disgrace ourselves," Doug says, beaming, years later.

The men returned home from Regina very enthusiastic about Canada and curling. The next year, playing closer to home in Berne, Switzerland, Denmark tied France and Germany for fifth, still out of the medals but ahead of veteran curling powers like Scotland and Norway. Italy trailed the pack with the same 1–8 record it had in Regina.

The men's program was evolving nicely. The Danes proved they deserved to be on the world stage. In 1979, Denmark iced its first women's team at the world championship, finishing just behind the middle of the pack. They fell to tenth place the next year, then rebounded to fifth a year later. Helena Blach (later

Blach-Lavrsen) skipped both those teams and returned with virtually the same squad to win it all in 1982—raising Danish
women's curling from worst to first in just three years. All those
early experiences flooded back with the phone call the Grahams
received from Denmark a quarter-century later to ask them who
they were rooting for in the looming gold-medal showdown at
Nagano between Canada's Schmirler and Denmark's Blach-
Lavrsen teams. They didn't answer then and haven't answered
since. It's enough to savour the memory of the role they played in
transplanting a sport they love to a country that adopted them.

Other significant ambassadors have spread the gospel of the
roaring game to the world. Ray Turnbull and other early Brier
and world champions went first, followed by Shorty Jenkins and
his disciples as they spread the gospel of good ice. In 2004, icemaker Ian MacAulay capped his duties at the European
championships with hops to Bulgaria and Cuba. Another Ottawa
icemaker, Kirk Smyth, got a call from the World Curling
Federation's Keith Wendorf asking him to go to Kazakhstan. His
mission was reportedly to introduce curling to a group of enthusiastic people, conduct an ice-making course, help teach umpire
and instructional courses, and organize a bonspiel. Wendorf gave
him a week to do it.

The challenge must have seemed daunting; travelling to a
central Asian country, described by Pavia as the ninth largest in
the world, with a population of almost seventeen million non-
curlers. Smyth's goal was to reach the estimated forty "diehard,
rookie curling fanatics" among the one million residents of
Almaty. The driving force was Victor Kim, seventy, the president of the Kazakhstan Curling Association, the director general
of the country's national Olympic committee, and head cheer-
leader to shepherd his country's bid to host a future Winter
Olympic Games.

The WCF had shipped rocks, brooms, and anything else needed to launch the sport. Anything that didn't arrive—like the rock handles that went missing en route—was handmade by the determined and resourceful Kazakhs. Only Kim had even seen curling before, but under Smyth's watch everything came together as hoped. To prevent language complications like those experienced by the Grahams at their first international bonspiel, Wendorf had recruited Alexander Kirkikov, the head of the Russian national team, to translate. Kirkikov has been involved with Russian curling since he won that association's first annual St. Petersburg Trophy in 1993. Known then as "the Canadian from Lahr," he had also skipped the German national team for years, reaching the world championship final game in 1983. Not bad for a transplanted Canuck who left home to tour Europe for a year—and stayed.

Wendorf is perhaps the most accomplished Canadian curling ambassador in the world, credited by curling authority and author Bob Weeks as having coached and instructed in more countries around the world than any other curler, including Japan, Norway, Denmark, Sweden, Austria, Germany, Russia, Hungary, the Czech Republic, and New Zealand, where his efforts were rewarded with a unique honour—the Wendorf Rock.

Wendorf grew up an army brat, travelling, like the Merklingers, from base to base across the country. He began curling while attending high school in Oromocto, New Brunswick, learning well and quickly; his team twice won the provincial championship for novice players with less than seven years' experience.

In 1972, with his arts degree in history and philosophy from the University of New Brunswick in Fredericton, Wendorf followed his father to Germany. The plan then, he told Saint John *Telegraph Journal* reporter David Young twenty-seven years later, was to stay for a year, then return home to get his law degree. Instead, the Rhine Valley became his home. Landing a job as the manager of the golf and curling club at the Canadian air force base in Lahr, he carved a new life and touched many others through his ability to teach and motivate, and with his on-ice skills.

In all his years of curling, Wendorf says the improved ice consistency has likely done the most to change the game. That, more than improved techniques or any other advancements, he told Young, has allowed skips to take more daring shots than they would have fifteen years ago. He added, with a smile, "It's not that they're better athletes."

That may change with the new generation of curlers who are more devoted to fitness, diet, and nutrition. The younger curlers' ambitions got a boost in 2002 when the World Curling Federation announced that curling would make its debut at the twenty-first Winter World University Games, to be held in Tarvisio, Italy, in January 2003. Ten men's and eight women's teams entered from Italy, Canada, Switzerland, the United States, Norway, Great Britain, Japan, Russia, the Czech Republic, Korea, and Germany. Wendorf helped mentor that opportunity in his capacity as WCF curling development officer and, later, as director of competitions for curling.

Over the years, Wendorf's impact on curling in Germany became well documented, but he is most honoured for his efforts on the far side of the world. While New Zealand had been curling for the past century, delivery of the rock in that country did not involve sliding out of the hack. That changed in 1992, when the WCF asked Wendorf to help develop curling in a land better known for sheep and rugby and, more recently, as the Middle Earth associated with the lords of those other rings. Kiwi coach Edwin Harley, who skipped the first national team a year before Wendorf arrived, credits Wendorf with teaching him everything he knows about curling. When his Canadian mentor returned to Germany after a month, he left Harley a pile of curling books. In gratitude, the New Zealand curlers named their national trophy the "Wendorf Rock."

There have been other titles and accomplishments among the ice men. Just as pioneer Shorty Jenkins is widely hailed as the "King of Swing" for the extent of curl on his ice, icemaker Ian MacAulay and others praise Kirk Smyth as the "King of the European Ice Men." Smyth, MacAulay, and Dane Jurgen Larsen made the ice for the 2004 European championships in Sofia, Bulgaria. Dave Merklinger joined Hans Wuthrich in Basel, Switzerland, in 2006. The 2007 Euros are slated for December in Fussen, Germany. Merklinger and Wuthrich, who have worked nearly a dozen major curling championships across Canada and around the world, have been paired to make and maintain the ice at the 2009 World Curling Championship. Merklinger, who has relocated to the Vernon Curling Club in British Columbia, will be the head ice technician there for the 2008 Ford World Women's Championship then he will assist Wuthrich at the 2010 Vancouver Olympics.

These are just a few of the notable men, and the occasional woman, who seek to spray the perfect pebble. Each views the game differently, thinks differently, than the average clubhouse curler. All are accomplished curlers and several have competed at the elite levels: MacAulay, like Merklinger, made it to the Brier; Jenkins came close and began researching how to make good ice after a disappointing experience at the Ontario finals many years ago. MacAulay is worthy of particular note because he and his team proved that a "small" club team can still make it to the big ice. Skip Bryan Cochrane and third Bill Gamble began curling together as kids at the Russell Curling Club in Eastern Ontario. MacAulay, playing second, had never curled before moving to Ottawa from Prince Edward Island. The rink clicked with the addition in 2001 of Toronto transplant John Steski, who demonstrated he could curl on swingy "Shorty Ice"—which everyone concedes is an impressive feat.

In 2003, playing out of the RCMP Curling Club, Team Cochrane competed at the Halifax Brier in front of reportedly the loudest fans in the championship's history. Their new home club had given them the opportunity to compete against better curlers more often, but MacAulay explained that he and his teammates still considered themselves to be a small-town rink, capable of beating anyone on any given day, but not yet able to beat elite teams consistently. Their proudest moment was their 8–5 come-from-behind victory over former world champion and police curler Peter Corner to make the trip to Halifax. Trailing 4–1 after three ends, they fought back, scored three in the sixth, and shook hands after eight. Cochrane, who was allowed to use a whistle to direct his sweepers to compensate for a medical condition that affected his voice, led his squad to an early 5–2 record at the Brier before crashing on the ice like the doomed *Titanic*. Why? MacAulay smiles and mutters, "The Brier Patch." Ah, yes, the overriding sociability of curling is alive and well nearly 250 years after the Fraser Highlanders melted cannonballs and cast the first stones in Canada.

This all bodes well for curling in Canada and around the world. There has been some duck-and-cover finger-pointing lately between the CCA and the World Curling Federation over broadcasting and dividing the men's and women's events. That could change now that Canadian Les Harrison has taken the international reins. He was an air-traffic controller, so he should be able to withstand the pressure. He was the CCA's choice to sit on the WCF. He was also the only candidate to replace outgoing Roy Sinclair of Scotland, who retired in 2006 after six years on the job. Harrison is perfectly positioned to tap the growing American interest and build on early successes that began with Japan's late rush to include curling at Nagano in 1998.

As the only Asian nation to have previously hosted a Winter Olympics (Sapporo in 1972), Japan may still have had little familiarity with curling and perhaps less reason to rush its status to full-medal membership. But accepting the added responsibility of providing an additional venue, admittedly some distance from Nagano, was apparently an acceptable risk—and one that paid huge dividends for the sport in general and for Canada in particular. Curling had hit "the bigs" as a full-medal sport, but it had been a long and winding road with more swings than a sheet of Shorty Jenkins ice.

None of that was evident at the Nagano Closing Ceremonies, and some international press may still have felt confused at what they had just witnessed. In the pre-Olympic hoopla, many seemed quite unsure what to make of the curlers in their midst. Especially the Americans. Left to his own devices, *Miami Herald* humorist Dave Barry did what he does best—mocked the event, writing for CNN:

> Curling is very popular in Canada, which stands to reason inasmuch as Canada itself is basically a giant sheet of ice with things sliding on it. In the United States, curling is popular mainly in the Curling Belt, which stretches all the way from Wisconsin to another part of Wisconsin. But the curlers are enthusiastic, down-to-earth people, and they'd love to have more of us try their sport, which is a lot of fun once you get the hang of it. Not that I came close.

Nagano was just a warm-up for Barry. He'd be back in full force for the 2002 Olympiad in Utah, an American setting that allowed every major media outlet and every stand-up comic to take their best shot at the roaring game. Curling's arrival as a full-medal sport at Nagano in 1998, one Olympiad and four years earlier than many had thought possible, perhaps even plausible, may have caught the media by surprise. They'd be ready for Utah in 2002. For those who believe that mockery is the sincerest form of flattery, Nagano was a damned flattering moment for curling. But the best was yet to come.

In 2002, as curling followed the Olympics to Salt Lake City, the late-night comics took aim at the roaring game. But nothing could match the irreverence of a Canadian movie that rocked the curling world with laughter—and just plain rocked the Canadian film industry. *Men with Brooms* was perfectly timed, massively promoted—and made millions at the box office. In the process, it changed Canadian moviemaking forever.

IN THE HACK

THE ICE MAN SIPPETH

I am on the phone to my mother one Sunday morning when my phone clicks, indicating another caller. They'll have to wait. I cannot, in good conscience, put my mom on hold. Turns out I have missed a call from Shorty Jenkins, whose message says that he is blitzing up Highway 416 on his way to tackle an ice problem at the Ottawa Navy Curling Club. He'll pop in on his way by to put a face to what has been so far a voice over the phone.

He arrives bearing gifts—binders of notes and technical data, some of which I can actually decipher—on the secrets to making good ice. This is a welcome gift, as I am a bit of a techno-dolt. As we chat, I, ever the gracious host, offer a coffee to the man immortalized by a national Tim Hortons ad for his unquenchable love of the bean. He asks for cream. I have milk. Shorty winces but says nothing. I see no point in mentioning that the milk is 1 per cent.

The coffee is ready. I offer him milk and spoon, suggesting he doctor it to suit himself. Shorty pours the milk, stirs, sips. There is no sigh of satisfaction. We chat, adjourning outside to the front porch. I notice he has left his coffee behind. I offer to retrieve it. He waves off the offer.

I have become curling trivia: Who makes coffee so bad Shorty Jenkins can't drink it?

That would be me.

I feel bad. I feel even worse about feeling so proud.
I am Man with Spoon.

EXTRA END

SILVER SCREEN, GOLDEN MEMORIES

*A*fter Olympic gold, the silver screen may have had the broadest single impact on curling in modern times. Certainly you cannot discount expanded and improved television coverage. The programming on the small screen featured some very creative and innovative productions in the run-up to the Turin Olympics, notably Annette Norberg's Swedish team swapping "hurry, hard" for heavy metal, chains, and leathers to belt out "Hearts on Fire" with punk rockers Hammerfall. The Japanese took a more traditional approach to produce a movie called *Simsons*, which follows four young women trying to qualify for the 2002 Olympics. Interestingly, two of the four actors were actually quality curlers who qualified to play at the Turin Olympics. But no other movie, no TV documentary or rock video, has hit curlers and the general viewing public with the cultural impact of the hit Canadian feature film, *Men with Brooms*.

When co-writer/director/star Paul Gross pitched his idea for a curling film to Robert Lantos, head of Serendipity Point Films, the Canadian movie mogul reportedly smiled: "You mean men with brooms?" It was apparently that simple. The game was afoot; the pipers cued. Still, there were indications that a curling movie, even a successful curling movie, might not create a new cinematic genre in Hollywood. Certainly the initial announcement that the film was going into development did not set hearts a-twitter in the L.A. Fantasy Kingdom.

"It was like I farted," Gross told audience after audience in interview after interview, when asked how Hollywood filmdom reacted to his big-screen concept. "They didn't know where to look."

Alas, the furrowed brows, wrinkled noses, and glazed eyes did not end there. It is one thing to pitch an idea, another to have the idea optioned, quite another to go into development, and a very, very different thing to squeak through "Development Hell" to actually get the movie made. Fiscal scrutiny can be an overriding factor. Hollywood (North or South) is not, in the end, truly very concerned about flatulence. If it were, a good number of the bombs dropped on unsuspecting audiences would never have been made, and, if the moguls had a conscience, certainly never released. True, Hollywood and the government-created funding agencies in Canada exist to make movies. In a pure and perfect world, they would exist to make good movies, but that seems so subjective. So they adopt the one objective measurement that truly seems to matter—profits. Well, that's sort of an inside joke. As virtually every screenwriter who has ever signed on for a cut of a film's profits to top his Writers Guild wages can tell you, even the blockbusters that take in hundreds of millions of dollars somehow never manage to turn a profit. In the world of showbiz, the "biz" will always dominate the "show," leaving creative souls to wail that the bean-counters are running the asylum and demand that it be returned to the control of the inmates—the writers and other artists.

With all that taken into account, pitching a "curling flick" to studios keen to make movies but obsessed with making money—and for those who want to keep making movies, that means making lots and lots and lots of money—was a bit daring. While the movie seems to have been billed primarily as a romantic comedy there was no getting around the curling elements in a film called *Men with Brooms*. Ultimately, it was a story of redemption for its hero, Chris Cutter, played by Gross. Perhaps best known as the Mountie in television's long-running *Due South*, where he managed to sneak in a few curling references to confound his American police partner—and no doubt a few million U.S. viewers—even Gross conceded that the film is "no more a curling movie than *The Full Monty* was about men stripping."

So, what was it about?

In essence, *Men with Brooms* is, according to its publicists, "a Canadian romantic, comedic drama that follows four estranged friends who must reunite to overcome the past and win a second chance at life, love and the pursuit of the perfectly thrown rock." The movie has, in the words of an online review, "a lot of premise." Entitled, "Rink-rat redemption," the synopsis reads thus:

> Gross plays Chris Cutter, a former curling ace who comes home to the fictional town of Long Bay 10 years after he mysteriously left. No one knows why he ditched his fiancée, Julie (Michelle Nolden), at the altar, or hurled his team's curling stones into Trout Lake after blowing a big tournament. But when Julie's father dies, he leaves a will decreeing that his ashes be placed in one of the sunken rocks—and that Cutter's team reunite. Julie, meanwhile, has become an embittered astronaut, and her sister Amy (Molly Parker) is an alcoholic (surely a step up from playing a necrophiliac in her earlier debut film) secretly in love with Cutter. His teammates each have their own frustrations. James (Peter Outerbridge) is a drug dealer on the run from a thug, Neil (James Allodi) is a mortician married to an ice queen, and Eddie (Jed Rees) is trying to get his wife pregnant with his listless sperm. Serving as their coach is Cutter's father,

Gordon (Leslie Nielsen), a magic-mushroom farmer
who's nursing a back injury—and a grudge against his
son for dishonouring the game by cheating.

The movie was described by one reviewer as "a screwball
sports comedy iced with a frisson of romance," while another
praised Gross for his "daredevil leap" from the small to the big
screen, and for "trying to break the art-house mould of our cin-
ema—with its pathological themes of incest, necrophilia and
car-crash sex—to create a populist romp for mainstream
Canada." Slating the movie's release to coincide with the 2002
Brier, the money men behind the project were counting on
curlers paying to see the movie. They spread their risk as best
they could, billing the film alternately as a curling movie (to
appeal to curlers) and as a romantic comedy and a buddy comedy to appeal to city audiences and those said to be in "the
hinterland of small-town, suburban and rural communities." In
other words, pretty much everyone.

In the end, it likely didn't matter that the most powerful eyes
were watching the financial bottom line more closely than the
storyline. Happily, the movie opened to huge box-office sales
and generally good, sometimes rave, reviews. Gross had hit the
button, scored a knockout blockbuster, and hit the jackpot. In its
crucial opening weekend, *Men with Brooms* grossed a staggering
$1,040,000 ($US625,000) to record the highest opening weekend of all time for a made-in-Canada English-language feature
film in national release. Opening in 207 theatres across
Canada—more than 30 in the Greater Toronto Area alone—it
was also the widest opening for a Canadian feature, averaging an
impressive $5,024 per screen. All this according to A.C.
Nielson's Entertainment Data Industries, which is as close to
gospel as you're going to find, this side of Revenue Canada. Not

bad for a movie that reportedly cost $7.5 million to make and another $1 or $2 million to promote (media estimates vary wildly). To put this into perspective, consider that the average budget the previous year (2001) for a Hollywood film was US $47.7 million, with an additional average marketing budget of $31 million, according to *Ottawa Citizen* film critic Jay Stone, who accompanied the cast on much of their promotional tour, which he estimated cost $1.1 million, mostly for travel by private jet from Vancouver to Halifax.

It certainly didn't hurt that the movie's release coincided with the Winter Olympics in Salt Lake City, where curling was a full-medal sport for the second time and was "suddenly not a game for old men any more but was suddenly a hot, sexy sport for the young and the beautiful as well as for old men," as Stone observed. But the effort to promote the film was as strong as the timing was good. Stone suggested that it may have all started when Lantos signed on with Alliance Atlantis, the most powerful entity in the Canadian film industry, which was able to get CBC to promote it "through good luck and good timing." CBC began running ads for *Men with Brooms* during the gold-medal hockey game. Never a bad thing in Canada. The soundtrack featured, among others, the Tragically Hip (avid curlers who had a cameo in the movie as Team Kingston), and there was an accompanying book and promotion by everyone from Roots to Chapters-Indigo and the Canadian Imperial Bank of Commerce. The movie seemed to be everywhere, even before it was released. When *Men with Brooms* finally did hit the theatres that first March weekend in 2002, the reviews were admittedly mixed, but often effusive on both sides of the border.

"Curling laffer breaks Canuck records," Brenden Kelly penned in *Variety*, noting that the "Canuck curling comedy" swept its way into the record books with the best opening weekend for an English-Canadian film. To underscore the "biz" in showbiz, he immediately went on to report that the Serendipity Point Films production grossed $1 million Canadian (or $625,000 U.S.) for distributor Alliance Atlantis Releasing. The only Canadian film to rival those opening dollars was the "French-lingo" hockey comedy *Les Boys III* (2001). The movie's success—ranked fourth behind three Hollywood blockbusters that opening weekend—prompted Jim Sherry, executive vice-president and general manager of Alliance Atlantis Motion Picture Distribution, to claim the movie was great for the struggling English-language Canadian film industry: "It proves you can compete straight-on with the Hollywood films."

Kelly predicted an even greater impact in his *Variety* article, noting, "The timing of the box-office success of *Men with Brooms* is particularly propitious for the Canadian industry because federal funder Telefilm Canada is just kick-starting a major push to make more commercial pics." The Canadians too were now serious about making money because this flick proved you could. Lantos, best known for producing great films for niche markets, proclaimed, "At long last the myth that Canadians have no enthusiasm for Canadian movies has been shattered. This means more to me than a Palme D'or in Cannes. I feel jubilant and vindicated."

Writing for the *Toronto Star*, Peter Howell observed that the movie was "as Canadian as a bilingual corn flakes box, with its mostly Canadian cast, director and writers—Gross wore all three toques—and a story that involved a curling championship, a rampaging herd of beaver and a kilted bagpiper playing 'O Canada.'" Howell too attributed the record-breaking opening box-office success to its unprecedented promotion: "The movie was heavily advertised on television, and cross-promoted with a companion paperback novel and all-Canuck rock album. Gross and fellow actors criss-crossed the country attending screenings and giving interviews, including a night spent in Ottawa entertaining Prime Minister Jean Chrétien."

Promotion included screening the movie at the Museum of Civilization on the Quebec side of the Ottawa River. Sheila Copps, then deputy prime minister and heritage minister, also attended and expressed her pleasure with the first English-language feature to be made under a new film policy that included money for promotion. It was, Stone wrote, "an innovation that everyone seemed to know about but no one ever did anything about until now." In Copps's view, the policy would allow filmmakers to make movies people want to see and start building a truly domestic star system.

The American movie moguls had to have noticed, even if they didn't fully grasp why the film was so successful. Can a sequel, possibly titled *Terminator: The Triple Takeout*, be far behind? It's only a matter of time until they realize Arnold Schwarzenegger can curl, and when Schwarzenegger tires of the California governor's mansion—and he can't be elected president without a rather significant amendment to the U.S. constitution—anything can happen, especially if the Americans grab a gold medal at the next Winter Olympics. The Canadians had no immediate plans for a sequel and Gross was soon working on other projects. He seems to have had no problem getting funding for those.

Men with Brooms was also proof that you don't have to be a good curler to make a good movie that involved curling. To offset the cast's inexperience, a few recognizable names and faces were brought on board, in front of the cameras and behind the scenes. Colleen Jones, who once credited Russell Crowe's heroics in *Gladiator* (and coach Ken Bagnell) with inspiring her to rebound to overcome a bad start at the Scott Tournament of Hearts in Sudbury, Ontario, was pleased when Gross took her advice on duct-tape sliders and his sliding delivery. Other recognizable names and faces included Olympians George Karrys, who curled second for Mike Harris at Nagano, and Paul Savage, the tattooed spare for that historic debut Olympic rink.

It was no accident that Karrys and Savage worked together on *Men with Brooms*. Karrys was first off the mark, having read about the plans for the film almost a year before production began. He promptly fired off a letter to writer/producer/star Gross at Whizbang Productions and soon found himself consulting on the script, training the actors, mapping an array of trick shots, calling for donated equipment, recruiting his fellow competitors as extras, and hassling clubs to recruit thousands of volunteer "spectators." The one thing he wouldn't do, claiming a conflict of interest with his marketing job at the Canadian Olympic Committee, was pitch curling sponsors for their involvement. So he turned to his former Nagano coach, Savage, whose company was in the curling business, producing and broadcasting made-for-television curling events. With Gross, Karrys, and Savage, things began to come together. Karrys persuaded Gross to visit the live broadcast of one of Savage's shows—the M&M Meat Shops $100,000 Skins Game—to observe how curling is produced for television. Gross was sufficiently impressed with what he saw and hired Savage to sell all the product-placement deals for the movie.

At a later planning meeting, Gross surprised Savage by asking him if he had ever acted, then offered him a speaking part in the movie. Savage enjoyed the experience, and says his brief cameo doesn't reflect his total time on the set. Arriving for his first day, he was a tad surprised to find he had a private dressing room in a trailer. He made the rounds through hair, makeup, and wardrobe. Ready for his close-up, he then sat around for twelve hours waiting to shoot his first scene, the opening ceremonies of the cinematic Golden Broom championship. Savage aced his line—"And I'm Paul Savage"—adjusting his glasses just so. Savage proved helpful in other ways, lending several of his most cherished curling pins to wardrobe. They adorned Leslie Nielsen's tam throughout the movie. He also joined ACTRA—membership is mandatory for anyone with a speaking role—but laments that he has yet to receive another movie offer.

It was a new experience for the former Brier champ and curling Olympian. And this time, the audience got to see Savage in a different profile from his tattooed Nagano persona. Nor was he the sole Olympian to get into the act. George Karrys wound up on screen as the third for the rivals pitted against Gross and his squad in the pivotal championship match. Others invited to participate—for no paycheque— took up Karrys' offer and can be seen, sometimes only fleetingly, in the background. Glenn Howard is there, along with his second-year third Richard Hart. Three-quarters of the Wayne Middaugh team are there as well, two of whom had grown up throwing thousands of practice stones on that Brampton Curling Club ice, renamed Long Bay Curling Club for the film. Middaugh spent hours on the ice with his maternal grandparents, who managed the Bramptom club, learning to curl with his cousin, Peter Partner, who went on to win an Ontario Police Curling championship with Wayne's dad, Bob, in 1991. Big Gerald Shymko had flown in from tiny Yorkton, Saskatchewan, as did Winnipeg legend Jeff Stoughton, whose 360-degree "Spinerama" delivery captivated Gross and made it into the final cut. There was even a Swiss, Thomas Lips, who crossed the ocean to participate; he proved to be related to Hansjurg Lips, who had won demonstration curling silver at Calgary's 1988 Olympiad.

You get a sense of what was involved through examining some of the discrepancies in the film's continuity—little things like an out-turn released down the centre ice that magically curls into the house as an in-turn in the next shot. That, of course, was an editing function that had nothing to do with technical advice and seems to have been a minor glitch compared to some of the other problems encountered, and overcome, in making the film.

Shooting was marred by a heat wave (30+ degrees Celsius), which, combined with the apparent weakness of the Brampton ice-making plant and the heat generated by the lighting rigs and crowds, turned the ice to slush. This, in turn, ruined the shooting schedule. Gross knew that he was likely walking into a miserable experience in the editing suites, and he reportedly felt "resigned" to continuity errors in the curling scenes. He was also aware that he could never satisfy curling purists with every shot, a possible reason Karrys, the technical adviser (officially "chief curling consultant"), never saw the inside of the editing suites when work was in progress.

It is standard procedure for moviemakers to play fast and loose with the details of a story and take other liberties "for dramatic purposes." In fairness, without some dramatic licence it is doubtful a movie would ever get made on schedule—if ever. There were frequent reminders to that effect throughout the filmmaking process, when changes were made and discrepancies overlooked to further the storyline or to appeal to a broader audience beyond curlers. Karrys would have been expected to point out mistakes and offer suggestions, but he would never have had the final word. He presumably never lost sight of the fact that while he had the curling expertise, the film belonged to others.

For those who have spotted the errors, most often curling related, Karrys suggests they're viewed by most curlers he's spoken to as a kind of in-joke. Certainly they were never intentional nor included to aggravate the curlers in the audience. As in most movies, the continuity errors are more amusing than destructive and, Karrys adds, for those intent on finding the errors, there are others to be found beyond the stone reversing turn and angle:

some rocks stop abruptly and players lose their footing. In that heat wave, the ice was wet, looked wet, and was slippery. No one knew the poor condition of the ice better than Shorty Jenkins, who was cast as—wait for it—an icemaker. Denied a speaking part, Shorty made his mark with every wave of his pebble hose. But then, unlike the others, this wasn't Shorty's theatrical debut.

Flash back to the 1999 world championship in Saint John, New Brunswick, where our intrepid ice man is constantly dashing from the ice to the distant Tim Hortons courtesy table where he loads, then reloads, then re-reloads with coffee. It is no secret in elite curling circles that Jenkins enjoys his coffee. Shorty himself concedes, "I need my coffee or I get bitchy." And if that happens, he has been known to share his unhappiness with others. The problem this day was twofold: distance and volume. The coffee was located some distance from Shorty's work site, and worse, there were only small cups. He would gulp them down as he trundled off, making yet another return trip inevitable. And thus did the parade commence from ice to urn and back and back again and...Eventually, his repeat visits caught the attention of an astute coffee-and-doughnut higher-up, who wondered aloud, "Who is this guy and what is he doing?" Both questions were addressed in short order and the businessman was inspired.

To shorten a saga of truly epic proportion, Shorty Jenkins, a.k.a. Lord of the Rings, the Ice Man, and the King of Swing, was retained to star in a Tim Hortons television advertisement. He seems to have believed it was "a local thing," when, in fact, the ad beamed coast to coast for what some say was, for a national TV ad, an extended lifespan. When he was briefed on the details, Shorty warned the producers that the ice they were counting on for the shoot would be, shall we say, "not good." Or, in his preferred ice-rating vernacular, it would be "dog-shit ice." He was, of course, correct. A film of water covered portions of the ice, concentrated in the house, complicating rock deliveries and all efforts to film the commercial. Not even the legendary Jenkins has figured out how to pebble water. For the half-hour it took the crew to set up each shot, Jenkins relaxed (or what passes for relaxing for the human dynamo) and presumably gulped his java. To shoot the thirty-second ad required twelve-hour days, but Jenkins enjoyed the experience, commenting, "I got a lot of coffee." He also got a lot of recognition as he shot the ad wearing his trademark pink Stetson. He wasn't sure how much he enjoyed some of the attention.

Alerted by a friend that the CBC was running a segment on him on its popular *Royal Canadian Air Farce*, Shorty and Johanna tuned in. The friend neglected to mention that the segment was a spoof, and so they were a little taken aback to hear, "My hat's pink, my curling shoes are pink, my cell phone's pink, my leather thong is pink." For roughly the next minute and a half, the "Stubby Johnson" character raced back and forth, from the curling ice to the coffee counter, gulping humungous double-doubles and pebbling ever faster from a camera angle that made it look like he was whizzing on the ice. Jenkins was a little miffed until friends explained that being an *Air Farce* target elevated him to the status of prime ministers and presidents.

In *Men with Brooms*, Shorty seemed to have no problem getting into character; his pebbling scene remains perhaps the best in Hollywood history—just as Gross can claim to have made the best curling movie in cinematic history. If there were unexpected problems, the unanticipated arrival of pros like Savage, Karrys, Jones, and Jenkins certainly helped ease the pain. The final boon was the dual role willingly embraced by Gord Downie and the Tragically Hip, who signed on to not only record part of the movie soundtrack but also take a turn on-camera and on the ice. Avid curlers, they play a Kingston, Ontario, team, which is about as big a cinematic stretch as Shorty playing an icemaker. The Hip, it has been reported, are so keen to curl that they work their performances and recording sessions around the curling season.

Bringing in the pros helped Gross get the movie made, but he was on his own when it came to dealing with the media on the promotional tour. He was reportedly dismayed as they lined up at each stop to ask the same old question: Why make a movie about curling? The best account comes from the *Citizen*'s Stone, who had a unique vantage point as he accompanied the cast halfway across Canada. In the beginning, he reported, Gross would trot out the same answer to the same question, explaining that he wanted to make a film around a sport that knit a community together. Hockey was too political and too expensive to shoot because you need special cameras for the slow-motion scenes; curling is already in slow motion. Gross would conclude by saying that "curling has an unspoiled naiveté" (in the best sense of that phrase) that gives the film the right tone of innocence. But some of the reporters wouldn't let it go. When one persisted, asking how the film would have been different if it had been about hockey, Gross finally quipped that then it wouldn't be about curling. In the end, he would fire back a rhetorical "Why a ham sandwich?" or "Why not curling?" or "God told me to," and enjoy watching the reporter's eyes glaze. When he asked Stone, "Why journalism?" the *Citizen* reviewer shot back, "Because curling was taken." Gross finally settled for replying, "Because it's brand new," then adding, "and I know that I have made the greatest curling film ever."

On those rare occasions when the reporters came up with original questions, it too often seemed they had not done their homework, which, Stone says, annoyed Gross. Asked by one TV reporter what he remembers best about living in Calgary, where he was born, but left at age two, Gross mugged, "Being toilet trained." By contrast, co-star Leslie Nielsen took it all in stride. Asked if he could now throw a stone, he chortled that he could throw an entire basketball game, then he would wait patiently for the right stupid question to set off his concealed homemade flatulence machine. Yet some reporters, reviewers, and columnists made an effort to learn what was really involved in making a film like *Men with Brooms* and then shared their findings with their readers and viewers.

In his *National Post* article, "Of Ice and Men," Paul Quarrington wrote about what may have seemed to some an inconsequential scene—the beavers tootling across the dark road that force our heroes to a tire-screeching halt. Unable to marshal sufficient beavers to block a road, the moviemakers added some computer-generated creatures for effect. The scene had originally been written for "huge croaking frogs"—but that idea was pre-empted when it was used in the film *Magnolia*. For the real beavers to take their marks on cue, there was both a beaver "technical expert" and a beaver "wrangler" on hand to ensure accuracy and, apparently, beaver safety. The film's closing credits proudly proclaim, "No beavers were injured during the making of this movie."

Gross was disappointed with the expertise on beaver toilet habits, telling Quarrington that he was advised by the man from Science North in Sudbury, Ontario, that beavers could defecate only when they were in the water. "This," Gross stressed, "is manifestly not true. There was s— all over the road." (This lesson in our native wildlife was apparently absorbed by the reporter's young daughter, who was with him when the information was shared and who has since, Quarrington wrote, announced at various school functions and dinner parties that it is not true that beavers can poop only when they're in the water.) The beavers did, in fact, play a vital role in the movie. Appearing in the opening scenes of the movie—a "tipping-point" moment that *Citizen* critic Stone tells us appears in all movies to indicate whether a given audience is going to "get" the film—the beavers were used to gauge crowd response early. Winnipeggers will be cheered to learn they "got it" better than anyone else.

Interestingly, David Kinahan's review in *Toronto Life* opens by suggesting that Lantos and Gross must have made "a deal with the devil" to get their film opened so "fresh on the heels of Canada's patriotic Olympic fever." Actually, that particular deal was struck decades earlier by W.O. Mitchell.

The only Canadian author recognizable by initials alone, whose *Who Has Seen the Wind* has sold over a half-million copies in Canada alone since its publication in 1947, Mitchell updates the Faustian tale of soul bartering in his satirical *The Black Bonspiel of Willie MacCrimmon*. Hailed as "a sweeping saga" and "a hell of a good curling book," the classic 1965 curling homage tells the satirical story of a curling skip who sells his soul for a chance to win the Brier. In the terms of this pact with the Devil, in exchange for winning the Brier Willie must agree to curl in hell in the "Celestial Brier" upon his death. Willie and his team take on the Devil's evil foursome in a life-and-death challenge match to save his soul.

The book was adapted as both a stage play and radio drama, and remains perhaps the best-known book among an eclectic list including *The Grim Pig*, *The Velocity of Honey*, and the more obvious *Hey! Is That Guy Dead or Is He the Skip* that make at least passing reference to some aspect of the roaring game. But the granddaddy of the curling backlist must surely be *Yon Toon o' Mine*. First published in 1924, the book did for Fergus, Ontario, what Stephen Leacock's Mariposa did for Orillia. The characters, supposedly fictional, must have been identifiable enough to make author J.B. Perry publish under the pen name Logan Weir. More than half the book involves the preparations for the annual curl-ing match between the Auld and Free Kirks, an upset win by the local shepherd, and the detailed account of the post-match cele-bration. It seems unquestionably an homage to William Weems, the Fergus shepherd who won the day, entranced the crowd with his mealtime oratory, and was mortally wounded walking home.

Men with Brooms confirmed a vast audience beyond curlers who are willing to experience a good story well told. How often Canada can or will go to the well is impossible to predict. And how many actors can survive making a curling movie? Co-star James Allodi had played hockey for most of his life and never been badly injured, but when the Canadian actor played the mortician married to an ice queen, he recalled the peril of the roaring game: "Three weeks into curling I've got bone chips in both my elbows. I still can't lean on a table. I've got curling injuries, believe it or not, just from falling on our arses on the ice." Gross had a differ-ent take. He learned to play and enjoy the game, commenting, "There is nothing quite as liberating as a well-balanced slide." It apparently helped that Colleen Jones duct-taped his shoes.

Co-star Molly Parker may have had the last word, a poignant unscripted line that speaks to the power and popularity of the roaring game: "I wouldn't call myself a curling fan, but I am totally fascinated by what it is. A few years ago, I got really hooked watching the Canadian women's team play in the Olympics. I thought what incredible women they were—Sandra Schmirler and her team—they had jobs, children, husbands, yet there they were in Japan winning the gold in really intense com-petition. It was an amazing thing to me."

That is about as good a summation as you're going to find.

IN THE HACK

THE HAMMER

I stare down at every curler's nightmare—eight rocks littering the house. None are ours. It is a Peter, Paul, and Mary moment— "If I Had a Hammer..." Well, I do have the hammer but little else. A cluttered house. A narrow port. Conventional wisdom suggests an overhand Hail Mary takeout. I opt for a draw. My Catholic schoolboy opponents admire my faith.

Until now, I have never understood how anyone can allow an opponent to keep eight rocks in the house in an era when every player can legally take them out. Missing certainly seems to be a factor. Still, I calculate my odds. Curling in Fergus gives me history, tradition, and small-town virtues; my city opponents from Guelph have only incredible skill. No contest.

From the hack, the distant narrow port is less visible. My strategy is to hit the broom and bounce off a lot of rocks. After all, isn't the beauty of curling that on any day, anything is possible? I crouch, clean my final stone and the debris from its path, lift high, push hard, and slide gracefully while muttering my customary curling mantra: "Please, please, please..."

The front end never quits working. My vice skip, Rick Anderson, slides out to add his broom. I watch, enthralled, as the rock rumbles, curls, bumps, caroms, peels, and glides to bite the button. I can't remember if we counted one or cut them down to a couple. It doesn't really matter. They won the game, but I made *the* shot! It is my Olympic moment, my Brier, and every other title I never won and never will, all morphed into that single incredible moment. And that's the beauty of curling. The reward can be in the effort as much as the result.

Of the thousands of rocks I've curled over the years—in schoolboy, men's, mixed, league, and bonspiels—that is the one shot I remember. The beauty of a front end digging in, the symmetry of the sweepers, the rising passion in Rick's voice as the planets aligned for that brief moment. On that sole occasion I was, however briefly, the equal of any elite athlete. We left the ice defeated, but better curlers—and likely better people—than we were trooping in.

The challenge, the competition, and the camaraderie all matter. But, in the end, I curled that day—and every other—not because I was good, but because I could. There are thousands just like me on ice sheets around the planet. And that, in the end, is why the roaring game is such a roaring success. The house is truly a home, open to all...and a pretty good foundation for life.

ACKNOWLEDGEMENTS

*I*t takes many people to transport an idea to the page and then onto the shelves. I wish to thank several people at Key Porter Books who played vital roles in producing *The Roaring Game*: publisher Jordan Fenn quickly embraced the concept and put me into the good hands of vice-president of sales and marketing Rob Howard and senior publicist Jennifer Fox. Art director Martin Gould and senior designer Marijke Friesen eased the book's passage from concept to final cover. Special thanks to associate editor Carol Harrison, who made the book better and made writing it fun. Her humour was as constant as her guidance; neither ever faltered. My thanks also go to Jennifer Gallant, Beth Bruder, and Jennifer Scott for their earlier caring help. Special thanks to *Windsor Star* editor Marty Beneteau for extending the professional courtesy to permit me to reproduce that paper's article commemorating the twenty-fifth anniversary of the deadly tornado.

To my many collaborators who helped make this book a reality, please understand that I can't thank you all publicly without missing someone. I can say without hesitation that this book could not have happened without your help. Thank you. A few stand out for more than sharing their stories. The Shorty Jenkins, Paul Savage, and Clan Merklinger sagas—especially Anne's—provided the human side to sports history, and their good humour set the tone early. George Karrys, an Olympian, a publisher (*The Curling News*), and also media man of the World Curling Federation, willingly shared his experiences, insights, and contacts. His encyclopedic knowledge and global contacts were priceless in helping me get it right. If errors remain, they are mine alone.

Special thanks to my agent, Hilary McMahon at Westwood Creative Artists, who was the first to see the need for a different kind of curling book and whose faith and passion never wavered as she convinced first me, then others, to see that too. Hilary has produced a family in less time than I produced this book and this creation would also have been impossible without her. My thanks to her surrogates during her leave—Gloria Goodman and Alison Hardacre—for their professional assistance and the personal good humour.

Finally, as always, I thank my family. To Millie, who opened Hotel Mom when I was on the road. To my children, John and Jodi, who learned early it is wiser to have mom (a nurse) than dad (a writer) co-sign a loan application. And to my wife, Irene, who lets me be a writer, rarely comments on my pension potential, and almost never asks, "Are you done yet?" but is always there to care and comfort when the screen and my mind are blank.

I thank you all. I hope you enjoy the result.